BROWN, NOT WHITE

NUMBER THREE
University of Houston Series in Mexican American Studies

Sponsored by the Center for Mexican American Studies

Tatcho Mindiola
Director and General Editor

BROWN, NOT WHITE

School Integration and the Chicano Movement in Houston

Guadalupe San Miguel, Jr.

TEXAS A&M UNIVERSITY PRESS • COLLEGE STATION

LIBRARY OF CONGRESS CATALOGING-IN-PUBLICATION DATA

San Miguel, Guadalupe, 1950–
    Brown, not white : school integration and the Chicano movement in Houston /
Guadalupe San Miguel, Jr.—1st ed.
        p.   cm. — (University of Houston series in Mexican American studies ; no. 3)
Includes bibliographical references and index.
    ISBN 1-58544-115-5 (cloth : alk. paper)
    1. Mexican Americans—Education—Texas—Houston—History—20th
century.   2. Mexican Americans—Texas—Houston—Social conditions—20th
century.   3. School integration—Texas—Houston—History—20th century.
4. Discrimination in education—Texas—Houston—History—20th century.
I. Title: School integration and the Chicano movement in Houston.   II. Title.
III. Series.
    LC2688.H8 S26 2001
    379.2′63′097641411—dc21   00-011204

CONTENTS

Illustrations

TABLES

PREFACE

In the early 1970s thousands of Mexican-origin students, parents, mothers, and community members participated in a variety of legal and political actions against the Houston public schools.[1] They boycotted the public schools; attended rallies or informational meetings at local parks, churches, community centers, and homes; picketed the school board offices or individual schools; conducted various negotiation sessions with local school officials; established "huelga" (strike) schools; and participated in several litigation efforts. These actions were sparked by the local school district's effort in 1970 to circumvent a desegregation court order by classifying Mexican American children as "white" and integrating them with African American children. Although more than 85 percent of the white children in the Houston Independent School District (HISD) were Anglos, they were not significantly affected by this part of the desegregation plan.

Mexican-origin activists opposed the school board's decision and demanded that local school officials recognize Mexican Americans as a minority group. This was a highly unusual demand, because for many years activist Mexican Americans in Houston and throughout the country had viewed themselves as part of the white or Caucasian race in order to obtain social justice and equal educational opportunity. Now that their "whiteness" was being used to circumvent desegregation, however, many of them rejected this racial identity and acquired a new one. They were "brown," not white, as one of the slogans developed during a 1970 boycott of the Houston public schools indicated.

The struggle for recognition, probably the most important action of the Mexican-origin activist community in the city during this period, lasted for two years.[2] It ended in September, 1972, when the courts and the schools finally recognized Mexican Americans as a distinct ethnic minority group. The struggle's ultimate success eventually forced school officials and the courts to include Mexican American interests in the formulation and implementation of school policies and in the development of educational programs.

Who led this struggle for recognition, and what types of strategies and goals were developed to combat the school board's misuse of the Mexican-origin community's white racial status? Who participated in this effort, and what type of support, if any, was given by the Anglo, liberal population and by African Americans? This study seeks answers to these important questions.

The struggle for legal recognition likewise occurred at the height of the Chicano movement, i.e., the explosion of political and social activism within the Mexican-origin population. What impact did the swirl of new social, cultural, and political ideals during this era have on this struggle in general and on the racial and political identity of these activists in particular?

This study explores the history of this particular struggle for recognition and its intersection with the Chicano movement and other larger social forces during the era of protest in the United States. More specifically, it documents the diverse responses of Mexican-origin activists to educational discrimination in the early 1970s and explores the role that the ideology and practice of "Chicanismo" had on Mexican-origin grassroots activism in Houston, Texas. Houston was selected as a site of study because of the size of the Mexican-origin population there and the richness of data available for such a project. Houston has the largest concentration of Mexican-descent persons of any Texas city. Moreover, it has the largest African American population in the South, with the exception of Atlanta— a characteristic that allowed me the opportunity to comment briefly on the role of the African American community in the struggle for recognition in particular and on black-brown relations in general. Houston also possesses perhaps the best local Mexican American archival collection in the United States.

The general thesis of this study is that in the early 1970s the diverse responses to educational discrimination by Mexican-origin activists reflected a shift in the community's identity from one based on the politics, culture, and social change strategies of the Mexican American Generation to one based primarily on those of the Chicano Generation. The shift in consciousness was reflected in the community's rejection of whiteness, gradual social change, and conventional methods of struggle, and in its acceptance of a nonwhite racial status and a new politics of struggle based on mass mobilization and protest.

Despite this shift in identity, this struggle was not primarily a search for identity but a quest against discrimination. Identity became important to this quest, but it was not a central motivating or guiding force.

This book is divided into several parts. The first three chapters focus on the historical background of the Mexican-origin community in Houston. Chapter 1 is a brief overview of that community's social and economic evolution from the early 1900s to the 1960s. Chapter 2 focuses on the public schooling of Mexican-origin children for the same period. Chapter 3 discusses the nature of Mexican American political involvement during the first six decades of the twentieth century and focuses on the community's shifting identity and its responses to discrimination.

The second part of the book focuses on the emergence of school activism during the latter part of the 1960s. Chapter 4 describes the variety of efforts made by old and new organizations to improve the quality of education for Mexican-origin children in Texas during the 1960s. Chapter 5 focuses on the increasing emphasis given to desegregation by the summer of 1970.

Part 3 contains six chapters that address the origins and development of the struggle for legal recognition in the schools from 1970 to 1972. These chapters discuss the conditions under which Chicano activism in the politics of desegregation emerged, explore the role various groups and individuals with different political perspectives played in the struggle, and generally focus on the dynamics and tensions involved in opposing the school district's discriminatory actions from 1970 to 1972. The conclusion explores the significance of the struggle for legal recognition and relates these findings to the broader Chicano movement.

PART I

Origins and Development, 1900–60

CHAPTER 1

Diversification and Differentiation in the History of the Mexican-Origin Community in Houston

This chapter will provide a brief history of the Mexican-origin community in Houston prior to the Chicano movement era of the 1960s. Mexicans originally arrived in Houston in the latter part of the nineteenth century, but they did not become a significant ethnic minority group until the twentieth century.

The historical experiences of Mexicans in Houston during this century were extremely diverse and both different from and similar to the urban experiences of Mexican-origin individuals in other parts of the United States.[1] The diversity of experiences is reflected in their social development, occupational structure, ethnic identity, and political behavior. This chapter describes, in broad strokes, social and occupational developments in the history of this group during the years from 1900 to 1960. Chapters 2 and 3 will focus on education and on political activism and identity, respectively.

TOWARD SOCIAL DIVERSIFICATION

The Mexican-origin community increased in size over time and became a significant ethnic minority group by the second decade of the twentieth century. Mexicans settled in compact residential neighborhoods separated from each other by a variety of obstacles and established distinct barrios that were differentially affected by mainstream and ethnic institutions.

Prior to 1880 there was no significant Mexican presence in Houston.[2] This changed by the latter part of the nineteenth century. Between 1880 and 1930 the Mexican-origin population increased from around seventy-five to fifteen thousand. During the next three decades it grew by an additional sixty thousand.[3] With the exception of one decade from 1930 to 1940, the history of the Mexican-origin population has been one of explosive growth. Despite this growth, these people continued to constitute a small minority of the total population group. Mexican-origin individuals constituted only 2 percent of the total population in 1910; 5 percent in 1930; and slightly over 10 percent in 1960.[4]

Immigration from Mexico accounted for most of the population increase, since during the first several decades of this century the Houston economy attracted the vast majority of them to the city. The railroads and urban development between 1890 and 1910, the opening of the ship channel, the discovery of oil in the early decades of the twentieth century, and post–World War II economic expansion created an increased need for cheap labor. This labor force was provided by Mexican immigrants who were pushed out of Mexico by social, economic, and political developments. Primary among these were land displacement policies caused by Porfirio Díaz's economic policies in the latter part of the nineteenth century, political conflicts associated with the Mexican Revolution, and religious conflict during the Cristero Rebellions of the 1920s. Thus, between 1880 and 1930 large numbers of landless peasants, political exiles, and religious exiles left Mexico in search of better opportunities. After 1940 poverty and dire economic conditions encouraged Mexicans to leave their country, and many of them immigrated to Houston.[5]

Mexican-origin individuals residing in rural communities throughout Texas also moved to the city.[6] They were part of a larger urbanization process that began in the early decades of the twentieth century and increased after World War II.[7]

Immigration was the result of a process of chain migration in which individual immigrants encouraged family members or friends to leave Mexico and then helped them resettle in Houston by finding them housing and jobs through immigrant networks. This process facilitated immigration and contributed to the strengthening of family and kinship networks in the barrios of Houston.[8] The examples of Petra Guillén and Mary Villa-gómez, both lifelong residents of Houston, are illustrative of this important process. Guillén's family was brought to the barrio in the 1910s by an uncle who had preceded them. Villagómez, on the other hand, came to Houston as part of an eleven-member extended family migration. Both of these families were encouraged to leave Mexico or other parts of Texas and settle in Houston by a host of relatives and extended family members.[9] Their journey to Houston thus was not as disrupting of family and cultural traditions as is commonly believed to be the case for many Mexican Americans.

Prior to 1910 Mexican-origin individuals settled in various parts of the city. As Arnoldo De León notes, there were no "ethnic enclaves" in Houston during these years.[10] After 1910 barrios began to appear, and the reasons for settling in these barrios were varied. Racist real estate and bank policies undoubtedly played a key role in the formation of barrios. Security, cultural cohesion, sense of community, proximity to work, and affordable housing also helped the neighborhood take shape.

The first Mexican-origin neighborhoods in the early part of the twentieth century were El Segundo barrio in the Second Ward and El Crisol in Denver Harbor. El Crisol was close to the Southern Pacific Railroad yards. Its name was derived from the Spanish term describing the pungent chemicals used to preserve railroad ties—creosote.[11] El Segundo barrio was located along Buffalo Bayou a few blocks from the center of town. As early as 1908 a significant number of Mexican-origin individuals began to settle there, and by the 1920s its population became predominantly Mexican American.[12]

Three additional barrios took shape during the second decade of the twentieth century—the Northside, the Heights, and Magnolia Park. This latter barrio, southeast of the Second Ward, was located along the ship channel and became a Mexican neighborhood by the middle of the second decade.[13] By 1930 Magnolia Park became the city's largest barrio.[14] The Heights was an area to the north of the downtown district that had a sizable Mexican-origin community by 1920. In the next two decades all of these barrios expanded as a result of the continuing influx of Mexican-origin individuals.[15]

During the post–World War II period the barrios expanded further. El Segundo barrio pushed southwest of Commerce Street and extended into the area known as the old Third Ward. Magnolia Park likewise grew and eventually merged with El Segundo barrio. The merged communities came to be recognized as part of the East End barrio.[16]

In the late 1940s Mexicans settled and formed new barrios in areas away from the pre–World War II communities. New ethnic communities were established in Port Houston, southwest Houston, the Hobby Airport area, and the Bellaire subdivision. Mexican families likewise settled in the suburbs. By 1960 barrios could be found in suburbs such as South Houston, Pasadena, and Galena Park.[17]

With the formation of the barrios came the establishment of ethnic organizations, businesses, cultural institutions, and newspapers that helped to meet the varied social, cultural, economic, and political needs of the community. Ethnic organizations provided mutual aid, defense of democratic rights, fraternal companionship, entertainment, and cultural reinforcement. The first Mexican-origin organization, a patriotic group called La Junta Patriótica, was founded in Houston in 1907. The following year a lodge, a chapter of the Woodmen of the World (Los Leñadores del Mundo, or Haceros), was founded. During the next several decades a host of mutual aid associations, political clubs, civic groups, and recreational organizations were established. Organizations such as Cruz Azul, Comisión Honorífico, and Club Cultural Recreativo "México Bello" became important sources of community pride and unity.

Most of these organizations during the early part of the century overwhelmingly stressed "lo mexicano" or, as will be illustrated in chapter 3, reflected a "Mexicanist" identity. This consciousness was part of immigrants' experiences and part of their adjustment to life in the United States. Two examples of community organizations with a Mexicanist orientation and aimed at maintaining lo mexicano in the United States were the Sociedad Mutualista Mexicana Benito Juarez and the Club Cultural Recreativo "México Bello." The former, established in 1919, was a mutual aid society that emphasized caring for its members and making life more tolerable for them in the United States. It carried the name of an indigenous Mexican hero and utilized Spanish to conduct business. Similar to others founded during this period, this organization was not aimed at assimilation. It did not, as historian Arnoldo De León notes, "display an incipient Americanization." Its stress instead was "on Mexican ideals and values."[18]

The second organization, Club Cultural Recreativo "México Bello," commonly known as simply México Bello, was one of many cultural and recreational clubs that stressed Mexican ideals and values. It was also the most prominent and successful of these types of organizations during the 1920s and 1930s. Founded in 1924, México Bello tried to fill a void arising from "nostalgia for their native country." The central goal of this group was to preserve and uphold Mexican traditions in the United States through the presentation of Mexican dramas, picnics, leisure activities, and dances. "Raza, Patria, e Idioma" (Race, Country, and Language) was its motto, and green, red, and white were its colors.[19]

The number of social organizations grew in the post–World War II period. Unlike immigrant-based groups of the pre-Depression years, the majority of these post-1930 organizations gave themselves English names, utilized English as the medium of communication, and geared their activities toward interacting with U.S. citizens or becoming part of the mainstream. The baseball team called the Mexican Eagles and social clubs such as the Merry Makers or the Rolling Steppers are examples of these new types of organizations. During the 1920s the Mexican Eagles played Anglo-American teams from across the city and won most of their games. The Rolling Steppers was a dance club begun by a group of young men who sponsored citywide dances on a regular basis. It was based out of the Rusk Settlement House.[20]

In the 1930s other organizations that reflected the new biculturation emerged. One of these was El Club Femenino Chapultepec. This organization, founded in 1931, was made up of young Mexican women from the several Houston barrios who were born or raised in the United States. Most of the club's members were high school graduates, spoke English, and worked in the Houston Anglo business community. Its purpose was to promote pride in Mexican culture and in American citizenship. While the organization participated in various traditional Mexican activities such as the fiestas patrias, it also participated in more mainstream activities. Members, for instance, sold government bonds during World War II, helped the community to distribute sugar stamps, and assisted in other activities to help the war effort. In the late 1930s it conducted a study on the status of the Mexican-origin community in Houston and indicted Anglo society for deplorably mistreating this population.[21] Another important organization reflective of the new biculturation in the 1930s was La Federación de Sociedades Mexicanas y Latino Americanas (FSMLA). FSMLA was a civic organization comprised of both Mexican immigrant and Mexican American individuals. Its goals were diverse and aimed at the following: to promote loyalty to the United States, to defend the political and cultural interests of Mexicans living in this country, and to struggle for better wages and end employment discrimination against Mexican workers. Although it was an important organization, it lasted only for several years.[22]

Table 1. Selective List of Ethnic Organizations in the Houston Barrios, 1908–50

Name	Date	Source
I. MUTUAL AID ORGANIZATIONS		
1. Campo Laurel No. 2333	1908	p. 32, 68
2. Agrupación Protectora Mexicana	1911	p. 13
3. La Sociedad Mexicana "Vigilancia"	1915	p. 14
4. Sociedad Mutualista Mexicana Benito Juárez	1919	p. 32
5. Comite Pro-Repatriación	1930	p. 47
6. El Campamento Navidad No. 3698	1932	p. 68
7. Sociedad Mutualista Obrera Mexicana	1930	p. 69
8. Sociedad Mutualista Obrera Mexicana Women's Auxiliary	1936	p. 69
9. Sociedad "Unión Fraternal"	1940	p. 69
10. El Campo Roble No. 6	1920	p. 32
II. SOCIAL/CIVIC ORGANIZATIONS		
1. Orden Hijos de América	1921	p. 81
2. LULAC, Council #60	1934	p. 82
3. Latin American Club	1935–39	p. 85
4. Ladies LULAC Council No. 14	1935	p. 84
5. Texas American Citizens	1938	p. 90
6. Latin Sons of Texas	1939	p. 90
7. Junior LULACERs	1948	p. 111
8. Pan American Political Council	1948	p. 112
9. Club Familias Unidas	1948	p. 112
10. Ladies LULAC Council #22	1948	p. 129

One of the most important organizations founded during the 1930s was the League of United Latin American Citizens, LULAC.[23] This organization best represented the emerging Mexican Americanist identity in Houston. It articulated the new ideas about being Mexican in the United States and sought to integrate the population into this country's mainstream institutions. It was loyal to U.S. ideals and sought to eliminate racial prejudice against Mexican nationals and Mexican Americans. LULAC also struggled for legal equality, equal educational opportunities, and adequate political representation. Furthermore, it supported the biculturation of the Mexican-origin population. It sought to mold a syncretic culture based on the fusion of two cultural heritages and two distinct world-

Table 1. (*continued*)

Name	Date	Source
11. Pan American Club	1940	p. 90
12. Cooperative Club of Latin American Citizens	1940	p. 90
III. CULTURAL/RECREATIVE		
1. Club Cultural Recreativo "México Bello"	1924	pp. 33, 67
2. Club Deportivo Azteca	1920s	p. 34
3. Club Recreativo Internacional	1935	p. 67
4. Club Recreativo Anáhuac	late 1930s	p. 67
5. Club Recreativo Xochimilco	late 1930s	p. 67
6. Club Terpsicord	late 1930s	p. 67
7. El Círculo Cultural Mexicano	1930	p. 68
8. Los Amigos Glee Club	1930s	p. 68
9. El Club Orquidea	1930s	p. 70
10. Club Masculino Faro	1930s	p. 70
11. Club Femenino Dalia	1930s	p. 70
12. Sociedad Latino Americano	1930s	p. 70
13. Club Pan Americano of YWCA	1930s	p. 70
14. Club Moderno y Recreativo	1930s	p. 70
15. Club Femenino Chapultepec	1931	p. 70
16. La Federación de Sociedades Mexicanas y Latino Americos	1938	p. 72
17. Club Recreativo Tenochtitlán	1935	p. 86

Source: De León, *Ethnicity in the Sunbelt.*

views—the Mexican and the American. LULAC's intent was to incorporate the American identity into the existing Mexican one. "Mexicans," notes De León, "would adopt Americanism albeit they would retain their parents' cultural life.[24]

Further evidence of a Mexican presence in Houston was seen in patriotic celebrations. Two of the most popular were El Diez y Seis de Septiembre (September 16) and El Cinco de Mayo (May 5). The first celebrates the day in 1810 in which Father Miguel Hidalgo issued his cry for independence from Spain. The second commemorates the defeat of French intervention forces by the Mexican general Ignacio Zaragosa at Puebla in 1862.[25] As early as 1907 the Mexican-origin community commemorated the Mexican national holiday of El Diez y Seis de Septiembre. With several exceptions, this became an annual event that was celebrated every year, even during the Great Depression.[26] In the 1930s community groups also began to celebrate El Cinco de Mayo.[27]

In addition to social organizations and Mexican celebrations, community members also established a variety of businesses, cultural institutions, and newspapers. All of these played important roles in establishing a Mexican presence in Houston. Beginning in the 1920s a few businesses geared toward meeting the needs of the Mexican-origin community—e.g., *tienditas* (small stores), barbershops, restaurants, and cantinas—were established in the downtown area. Other barrios soon had their own budding business districts. During the 1930s and 1940s the Magnolia Park barrio had the most Mexican businesses in the area.[28]

The first newspaper founded in the Mexican community in the early 1920s was *La Gaceta Mexicana.*[29] By the end of that decade at least five newspapers reportedly served the colonia.[30] The most prominent of these was the semiweekly *El Tecolote,* edited by Rodolfo Ávia de la Vega.[31] Most of these newspapers had short histories due to lack of resources.

Cultural institutions such as theaters and musical groups were also established in the Mexican barrios. Commercial theaters showed a variety of Mexican and American films and showcased a large number of Mexican theatrical performers and artists. The first one in existence was El Teatro Azteca, founded in 1920. In the late 1930s El Nuevo Palacio Theater competed with El Teatro Azteca for clients. In the Magnolia Park barrio, community members established El Teatro Juarez in the mid-1940s.[32] La Sociedad Benito Juarez, which served the working class more than any other group, built a hall in 1928 to accommodate its activities that included dances, cultural performances, and fiestas patrias proceedings. EL Club México Bello produced Spanish-language plays in 1924 and utilized amateur actors from the community. Occasionally a group such as the Orquesta Típica of Miguel Lerdo de Tejada performed in Houston. His musical group played popular Mexican music.[33]

These organizations, newspapers, and cultural institutions not only met the varied needs of those it served, but they also counteracted the assimilative influences of the mainstream institutions and promoted either Mexicanization or selective acculturation. They maintained the spirit of lo mexicano in the community and encouraged the development of a dual identity that was neither American nor Mexican but a synthesis of both. These institutions thus became important instruments of change and continuity in the Mexican community.

Not all the institutions in the barrios were established by Mexicans. Anglos founded a variety of them. These individuals established churches, schools, and social welfare agencies, in many cases as a result of the Mexican community's desires or initiatives.

The establishment of mainstream institutions in the barrios began as early as 1912 with the founding of Our Lady of Guadalupe Church in El Segundo barrio. This church was founded as a result of the Mexican-origin community's desires to maintain its spiritual faith in an alien environment. Unwanted by established Anglo churches, Mexican immigrants maintained their faith through a variety of community and home activities. Some gathered in homes to pray the Rosary or to reenact Catholic rituals such as the *pastorelas* (a Christmas nativity play) or the *via crusis* (Way of the Cross ritual that commemorates the crucifixion of Christ during Easter). Many families likewise worshipped at their personal *altarcitos* (home altars) because of the lack of a church during the early years of the 1900s.[34]

These initiatives as well as the growth of the Mexican-origin population convinced the Catholic church leaders in the Galveston Diocese to establish a church for them in 1912. A dozen years later another Catholic church in Magnolia—Immaculate Heart of Mary—began to serve the Mexican population.[35] In the mid-1930s Our Lady of Sorrows Church was established in the Denver Harbor area.[36] This church was founded after several families from the barrios of El Crisol and Las Lechusas approached the oblate fathers at Our Lady of Guadalupe and petitioned them to send a priest to help them with their spiritual needs.[37] The nearest parish to these barrios was Our Lady of Guadalupe, but it was about two miles away. Lack of transportation forced many believers of the faith to walk this distance, and those unwilling to do so did not attend church services. The meeting between the oblate fathers and Mexican families eventually led to the establishment of Our Lady of Sorrows Church in that area.[38]

Not all of these churches were Catholic. A significant number of them were established by Presbyterians or Baptists. In the early 1920s, for instance, at least five Protestant churches were established in several barrios.[39] The number of Protestant churches continued to grow in the 1930s with the addition of three more.[40] By 1940 there were more Protestant churches in the barrios than Catholic ones; at least ten were serving the Mexican-origin population.

The number of Catholic and Protestant churches or the services they provided for Mexican-origin children and adults increased during the period after World War II. The Catholic Church, for example, expanded its parochial schools for Mexican children and sponsored a variety of cultural and religious activities aimed at strengthening the Catholic faith.[41]

Public schools also were established in the barrios, usually at the request of the community or in response to their desires. The earliest school to serve Mexican-origin children was Rusk Elementary. This school, located in El Segundo barrio, originally was an Anglo school, but by 1910 it served a predominantly Mexican student population. A separate school for Mexican children, named Lorenzo De Zavala, was constructed in the Magnolia Park barrio in the summer of 1920.[42] In the 1920s at least three, and possibly four, additional schools were established for Mexican children in several barrios: Hawthorne Elementary, Dow Elementary, Elysian Street School, Jones Elementary, and Lubbock School.[43] By 1940 almost thirty-six hundred Mexican-origin children were enrolled in these schools.[44]

Although local officials provided Mexican-origin children with access to public education during the first four decades of the twentieth century, it was limited to the elementary grades. Few Mexican-origin students attended secondary schools because of poverty, a history of failure in the lower grades, and/or exclusion from the higher grades. Mexican secondary school enrollment, for the most part, was a post–World War II phenomenon. The increasing enrollment can be observed through high school annuals. For instance, at Jefferson Davis High School, located in the Northside, few, if any children attended prior to the 1940s. By 1945, however, there were 13 Mexican-origin children attending. Six years later this number increased to 216. At John H. Reagan High, located in the Heights, Mexican children did not begin to attend this school until the late 1940s. In 1951 a few Mexican students began to enroll at Reagan. By 1956 approximately 65 out of 1,800 were Mexican students. At Milby High, located in Magnolia Park, Mexican students began to enroll in the late 1930s and showed a gradual increase over time. Between 1939 and 1942 a handful of students attended Milby.[45] This number increased to 18 by 1948 and to 49 by 1960.[46] The increasing presence of Mexican-origin children in the secondary grades testifies to their desire for education and self-improvement. But failure by local officials to increase greater access to educational opportunities at these levels ensured the continued subordinate status of this population group at midcentury.

Despite the presence of a rich communal life, barrios were still plagued by a multitude of problems. They generally were characterized by high rates of substandard homes, unemployment, poverty, crime, illiteracy, and ill health. Observers described them as "among the worst to be seen in any major city." In El Segundo barrio, for instance, some of the residents lived without privacy and proper sanitary conditions in homes that had been converted into boardinghouse arrangements or in makeshift homes erected along the banks of the Buffalo Bayou. In Magnolia Park barrio the streets were dusty and unpaved and Mexican-origin individuals lived in crowded substandard dwelling units that lacked furniture or indoor bathrooms.[47]

By the late 1930s social conditions in the barrios appeared to have worsened. A 1939 study conducted by the Works Progress Administration and sponsored by the Houston Housing Authority (HHA) indicates the deplorable condition of the barrios. The report showed that while Mexicans comprised about 5 percent of the total population, over 11 percent of them were living in dwellings classed as substandard, i.e., houses that lacked running water, proper ventilation and space, inside toilets, baths, and electricity. Barrio residents also earned less than six hundred dollars per year. The HHA proposed slum clearance and the development of new housing projects. Little, however, was done.[48]

A 1944 report found similar living conditions in the barrios in the vicinity of Canal and Navigation Streets in the East End barrio. Not only were there poor living conditions and deplorable health conditions, there were also "no recreation facilities, no playgrounds, no parks, no Boy's Clubs, nothing." Only rampant juvenile delinquency could be found in this barrio.[49]

Several studies showed that conditions continued to be appalling during the late 1940s and into the 1950s.[50] A 1958 report noted little improvement in the barrios. Diseases such as tuberculosis lingered there, and health services were grossly inadequate.[51] Although a low-cost housing development for Mexican-origin individuals was constructed in the early 1950s—the Susan V. Clayton Homes—it failed to significantly impact more than a few hundred people.[52]

Less dramatic than the social conditions in the barrio but more significant in the long run was the pattern of institutional discrimination that emerged during these years. Because of their immigrant or relatively powerless status as well as their racial and cultural characteristics, Mexican-origin individuals were treated as a subordinate group and discriminated against by public officials, religious authorities, and private agencies and individuals. This treatment was quite apparent during the 1930s when public officials, for instance, denied government assistance to Mexican-origin individuals in search of jobs by arguing that job relief applied only to "white Americans." Local relief agencies in the city refused to provide assistance to Mexican and African Americans when they ran out of funds in 1932. Local officials rounded up and jailed by the hundreds those Mexican individuals who did not carry proper documents. The federal government assisted local officials and deported many Mexican-origin people during the Depression years.[53]

Discrimination was quite common in public schools and in the churches. Public school and church officials, for instance, excluded or discouraged Mexican participation in these institutions and limited the children's entry to them or failed to meet their needs adequately. In most cases these religious and educational institutions were controlled and administered by Anglos. Those in charge did not hire Mexican-origin individuals as teachers or administrators until after 1960, thus ensuring their exclusion from the structures of governance or administration. Likewise, no Mexican-origin individuals were selected as priests or pastors for most of the churches in the barrios.

Those in charge did not respect or utilize the Spanish language in their daily operations. The Parent Teacher Association meetings as well as parochial school instruction, for instance, were all conducted in English. Similarly, no genuine effort was made to communicate with the parents of Spanish-speaking children in their own language. The primary purpose of these institutions was to Americanize or to teach the dominant culture to Mexican children. At times these institutions went beyond Americanization and sought to stamp out the children's linguistic and cultural heritage.[54]

Mexican-origin organizations usually and vigorously protested these varied forms of institutional discrimination and mistreatment. Their responses to institutional discrimination and mistreatment will be discussed in chapter 3.

Despite the presence of discrimination, a few individuals managed to take advantage of the learning opportunities afforded by the churches, schools, and other institutions. They advanced through the grades or assumed some minor leadership positions in these institutions. For them these institutions were instruments of opportunity. But for the most part churches, schools, and other institutions were instruments of subordination and assimilation, not tools of opportunity or biculturalism.[55]

The Mexican-origin community thus not only increased in size over time but became a significant ethnic minority group in the twentieth century. It also became more socially diverse as a result of different waves of immigration, settlement in distinct barrios, varying degrees of acculturation, and dissimilar treatment by mainstream institutions.

OCCUPATIONAL AND SOCIAL CLASS DIFFERENTIATION

The occupational and social-class structure of the Mexican-origin community became moderately differentiated over the years.[56] In the early twentieth century the social class structure was relatively stable. The vast majority of the Mexican-origin population was part of the working class and employed primarily in unskilled manual labor jobs. A small but influential number of these individuals, probably less than 5 percent, were members of the fledging middle class and employed in white-collar jobs. Most of these individuals were employed in the professions or were owners of small business establishments engaged in trade or commerce. The Mexican businesses were located in the old downtown business district between 1900 and 1930 or in new commercial areas in the various barrios after the Depression.[57]

Despite the lack of class differentiation in the early decades of the twentieth century, Mexicans were employed in a large number of occupations. At the turn of the century Mexicans worked as bookkeepers, railroad workers, tailors, clerks, carriage drivers, barbers, iron molders, and common laborers.[58] During the first decade of the twentieth century, some held jobs as tradesmen or as laborers in the railroad yards. Others were recruited to work in agricultural jobs in outlying areas. Still others, especially those who were underemployed, resorted to peddling, selling tamales, and operating chili stands on Houston's back streets. A few individuals had small businesses that served the Mexican community.[59]

Between 1910 and 1930 Mexican-origin individuals continued to be employed in a variety of jobs. In the early 1910s they worked as common laborers in the sewage business and in the railroad yards.[60] During the 1920s Mexican men found jobs as cooks, busboys, dishwashers, and waiters in Houston hotels, restaurants, and cafés; as bakers and butchers in small businesses; and as custodians, store clerks, and salespeople in retail, trade, and service industries. Others worked in large-scale industry jobs in construction or in the compresses as well as in smaller businesses such as cleaning plants, bakeries, and piecework manufacturing. A few women found jobs outside the home in small-scale, piecework manufacturing industries near their places of residence.[61]

Mexican-origin individuals during the 1910s and 1920s also held white-collar jobs. In addition to businessmen, some were entertainers, teachers, doctors, artists, and photographers. Among some of the medical doctors in the community by the late 1920s were Jesús Lozano, Ángel Leyva, A. G. González, and Luís Venzor. At least two individuals, P. L. Niño and Francisco Chairez, earned degrees as engineers from Rice Institute in 1928. Although relatively small, there was a vigorous middle class in the barrios of Houston.[62]

In the period after World War II the process of class and occupational differentiation increased. Social classes became more diverse as a result of the expansion of the middle class and of skilled employment within the working class. Male and female employment in middle-class or white-collar jobs increased significantly from 1930 to 1960. Male employment in white-collar work increased from 6.5 percent in 1930 to 19 percent in 1960. The increase for women was higher, going from 9.7 percent to 42 percent.[63]

The size of the working class likewise decreased during these years. In 1930 approximately 76.2 percent of men and 84 percent of women were employed in skilled or unskilled labor, the two broad categories comprising the working class. By 1960 the proportion of men and women employed in working-class occupations decreased. For males it was a moderate decrease of approximately 4 percent, whereas for females it was significant; only 42 percent of all employed females were working in skilled or unskilled work by 1960.

The working-class population within the Mexican-origin community became more skilled over time. This is especially true among males. The proportion of males employed in skilled employment increased from 13.9 percent in 1930 to 44.1 percent in 1960, whereas those employed in unskilled work decreased from 62.3 percent to 28.1 percent.[64] Unlike males, females experienced a general decrease in the proportion of those employed in both skilled and unskilled labor. The former decreased from 30.6 percent in 1930 to 21.8 percent in 1960. The figures for unskilled labor were 53.4 percent and 19.9 percent, respectively. Increased educational opportunities as well as structural changes in the labor market account for the increasing differentiation of the occupational and social class structure in the barrios.[65]

Despite the increasing class differentiation, the vast majority of the Mexican-origin population continued to be found in low-paying jobs. They were employed in the railroads and in city jobs such as sewage, ditch digging, construction, and other unskilled manual labor categories.

The concentration of Mexicans in low-paying working-class jobs meant that there was much suffering. The population continued to have higher rates of poverty and fewer opportunities than the general population. They also continued to be victims of discrimination by employers and private industries. As late as 1958 a series of articles on the Mexican-origin community indicated the extent of discrimination against this population in the area of employment and real estate. In that year the Mexican population was estimated to be over fifty thousand. Despite these numbers, it only comprised 5 percent of the total population of one million. This group, according to an investigative reporter named Marie Dauplaise, experienced subtle and overt discrimination. For the most part, Mexican-origin individuals were not hired in important positions. Although there were exceptions, she noted, the unwritten policy among the vast majority of the large corporations was not to hire people of Mexican origin with dark complexions and "a Spanish accent." These individuals could find white-collar or middle-class employment in retail stores, finance companies, or import-export firms, but even then they earned less than Anglos doing the same work.[66]

Real estate agents were reluctant to sell homes to Mexican-origin individuals in the "better" subdivisions of the southwestern and northern sides of town. However, homes in areas already designated as barrios by the real estate industry were affordable for these individuals.[67] This evidence indicates that while some Mexicans were making progress most were being denied equal opportunities. They were confined to nondynamic sectors of the economy and provided only with minimal employment opportunities.

CONCLUSION

In the twentieth century, then, the Mexican-origin community grew in absolute and relative terms, but it was still a relatively small part of the total population. Members of this population settled in various parts of the city and established a variety of institutions and organizations to meet their diverse needs. Although relatively small, this population became increasingly heterogeneous over time as a result of different settlement patterns, varying degrees of acculturation and immigration, and diverse forms of institutional treatment.

The community's occupational and social class structure also became more differentiated over time. Those employed in professional, white-collar, and skilled occupations gradually increased over time, especially after World War II. The majority, however, continued to be employed in a diverse number of unskilled and low-paying jobs. The majority of the Mexican-origin population also resided in barrios or segregated residential neighborhoods characterized by a high degree of poverty and institutional discrimination.

An important element in the social, political, and cultural development of the Mexican-origin population in the United States was education. Increased access to private and public forms of education not only contributed to the heterogeneity of this group but also strengthened its ethnic identity as a bilingual and bicultural population. The following chapter focuses on the extent and character of educational opportunities provided for Mexican-origin children during the twentieth century.

CHAPTER 2

PROVIDING FOR THE SCHOOLING
OF MEXICAN CHILDREN

During the twentieth century Mexican children in Houston received instruction from different types of educational institutions, including Catholic schools, private secular instruction, and public education.[1] Although diverse forms of schooling existed, by the late 1920s public education became the dominant means of formal instruction in the community as local authorities established an increasing number of segregated "Mexican" schools throughout the barrios.

Despite their location in the barrios, the schools were alien to the community and did not serve its specific needs. School board members, administrators, and teaching staff, for the most part, were non-Mexican, did not speak Spanish, and were indifferent or, at times, hostile to these children. Most educators viewed Mexican children as racially or culturally inferior. They also demeaned and denigrated their linguistic and cultural heritage. Generally speaking, school authorities took positions that clashed with the community's academic and cultural interests.

The community, for example, desired educational facilities for all children, but local officials denied Mexican children full access to the existing resources or failed to establish sufficient schools for them. The Mexican community also supported additive Americanization, i.e., the learning of American ways and the preservation of Mexican traditions. School officials, however, advocated subtractive Americanization—that is, they supported the learning of American cultural forms and the "subtraction" of the Spanish language and Mexican cultural heritage from the schools. Through these actions public school officials sought to legitimize and affirm the dominance of Anglo-only cultural and religious values.

The Mexican-origin community, likewise, sought to use the schools as instruments of upward mobility, structural integration, and civic involvement. But local school officials had other purposes in mind for them and sought to use the schools for reproductive ends. For public officials, the schools became instruments of social control aimed at reproducing the existing social class structure and the dominant-subordinate relations found between Anglos and Mexicans in the larger society. This dynamic interaction between two cultural groups occupying varying positions in the society and with quite distinct views and needs is reflected in the history of Mexican-origin education in Houston during the twentieth century.

ORIGINS OF PUBLIC EDUCATION
FOR MEXICAN CHILDREN, 1900–30

Public schooling for Mexican children in Houston originated during the first three decades of the twentieth century. Because of class bias, racial prejudice, inadequate resources, and their subordinate status in the larger society the nature of the education provided for this group of children was substandard and inadequate to meet their diverse needs. Mexican-origin individuals obtained increased but inequitable access to segregated and unequal schools. They also received an inferior quality education and a subtractive curriculum. The ultimate result was the establishment of a historic pattern of uneven academic performance characterized by a tradition of poor school achievement and minimal school success. Because of discrimination and high withdrawal rates from the public schools in the early decades of the twentieth century, segregation was confined to the elementary grades. Politics, prejudice, and population shifts were key in the establishment of segregated facilities during these years.[2]

Public school officials in Houston began to provide segregated schooling for Mexican-origin children in the early part of the twentieth century.[3] The earliest evidence of schooling for Mexican children is in 1900. In this year a handful of Mexican children enrolled in the old Rusk Elementary School located in the heart of El Segundo barrio.[4] This school originally was constructed to serve white children residing in the community, but once Mexican children began enrolling, the groups were segregated. Segregation initially began in the drinking-fountain area and in the cafeteria but soon spread throughout the school. As Anglo families found alternative schools for their children, local officials did little to discourage white flight and soon began to neglect the school's physical needs. By the latter part of the decade the deteriorating school building became a segregated school for Mexican children.[5]

The number of Mexican schools increased over time largely as a result of the growing presence of Mexican children in the various barrios. In 1920, for instance, public school officials in the Magnolia Park barrio built Lorenzo de Zavala Elementary largely in response to the growing number of Mexican children in the two predominantly white elementary schools in that community. At least one hundred Mexican children were attending Magnolia Elementary and Central Parks Elementary in this residential area. Most of these children, regardless of their citizenship status, spoke Spanish, had parents who worked in unskilled or semiskilled labor, and resided in overcrowded and substandard housing. Anglo parents expressed concerns over their presence in the schools and asked the school board to take appropriate action. The school was unable to deal effectively with these children since none of the teachers spoke Spanish. In order to accommodate parental concerns and overcome instructional difficulties the local school board members decided to build a two-room school made of white stucco for the Mexican children.[6] They named the school after a Mexican patriot of the Texas revolution and ad interim vice president of the Texas Republic in 1836—Lorenzo de Zavala.[7]

Unaware of the reason for the establishment of the De Zavala school and anxious to provide their children with learning opportunities, the majority of the Mexican population heartily supported this school. Soon after its establishment most of the approximately 100 Spanish-speaking children in the barrio enrolled in De Zavala. In the mid-1920s enrollment jumped to several hundred. Much of this increase was due to immigration and higher birth rates among Mexican-origin women. In order to accommodate the expanding student body, local officials in the latter part of the decade added more classroom and playground space to the school. By 1927 there were 576 children enrolled in De Zavala.[8]

Local school officials also accommodated the increasing number of Mexican children present in other parts of the city. They either established separate rooms in Anglo schools or built separate school facilities. Occasionally they designated existing schools for them. Mexican children in the Northside barrio, for instance, attended the old Elysian Street School or Anson Jones Elementary School. Mexican children residing in the Fifth

Ward attended Dow Elementary. Those in the Sixth Ward enrolled in Hawthorne Elementary.[9]

The Mexican school phenomenon was not limited to Houston. Data from other parts of Texas and the Southwest, although incomplete, show that local officials constructed or established segregated facilities for Mexican children whenever there were significant numbers of them in the school district. Parental fears of racial intermingling and Anglo prejudice as well as linguistic and educational concerns were given as reasons for establishing these schools.[10] In Corpus Christi, for instance, public officials built a school for Mexican children as early as 1896. Other smaller communities such as Seguin and Kingsville began to establish separate and unequal schools for Mexican children in the early decades of the twentieth century. The number of Mexican schools increased significantly during the 1920s. By the beginning of the Depression in 1930 over forty independent school districts had established separate school facilities for Mexican children.[11] The growth of separate and unequal schools for Mexican children occurred in most areas of the Southwest and the Midwest.[12]

In addition to establishing segregated schools, local officials also developed a variety of administrative practices that served exclusionary and discriminatory purposes. Some of the most common practices included the failure by local officials to hire Mexican Americans as administrators, teachers, and counselors or the efforts to eliminate the use of Spanish in the schools and to neglect the needs of the schools in the barrios.

Generally speaking, local officials could ignore or dismiss the Mexican community's needs because of the lack of Mexican Americans in school decision-making positions such as the local school board. Their absence was related to a variety of factors, including the relatively small size of the Mexican voting-age population, the large number of noncitizens, the high rates of poverty, and discriminatory voting requirements. These same factors also discouraged the community from electing individuals from the barrios who could represent them on the board.[13]

The lack of Mexican American school board members and of members sensitive to this community led to the failure to recruit and hire Mexican American administrators or teachers. During the first three decades of the twentieth century only two Mexican-origin individuals were hired as public school teachers: Mrs. E. M. Tafolla and J. J. Mercado. Both of them became teachers of Spanish in the secondary grades of the Houston public schools during the 1910s and 1920s.[14] No Mexican Americans, however, were hired as administrators in the schools during this time period. Teachers and administrators, as one scholar noted, were usually "outsiders," i.e., Anglos, who preferred to be in non-Mexican schools.[15]

The pattern of institutional discrimination was also reflected in administrative efforts to eliminate the use of Spanish in the schools and in the school board's neglect of the Mexican facilities. The first evidence of neglect was in 1924 when local district officials failed to appoint a school attendance officer to the Segundo barrio area where Rusk Elementary was located. By the 1920s Rusk was a predominantly Mexican school, although many additional Mexican-origin children were not enrolled. A local civic club urged the local school trustees to employ an attendance officer to encourage their enrollment. The school district refused this offer, and as a result a "tremendously high non-attendance rate" was recorded at the school.[16]

Local administrators and staff also sought to suppress the Spanish-language abilities of Mexican children. Several administrators at Rusk and De Zavala, for instance, developed "No-Spanish-speaking rules" in the 1920s. These rules discouraged the use of Spanish on school grounds and encouraged the use of English only. Those caught speaking Spanish were punished or expelled. These rules provided a negative and humiliating experience for those students attending the elementary grades during these years.[17] They also contributed to high dropout rates in general.

The prohibition of Spanish in the schools was in keeping with the state and national efforts to eliminate cultural diversity in American life that emerged in the latter part of the nineteenth century. The subtraction of Spanish from the emerging public schools, in other words, was not an isolated development; it was a general phenomenon that affected all non-English languages.[18] The campaign to remove Spanish from the public schools in the Southwest was merely the regional expression of a national campaign.

The subtraction of Spanish from public education in Texas was accomplished through the enactment of progressively stronger English-only policies over the decades.[19] These policies not only prescribed English as the medium of instruction in the schools, but they also discouraged, inhibited, or prohibited the use of Spanish and other languages. In some cases language designation was accompanied by discriminatory legislation and practices against those who spoke the minority language.[20]

Efforts to eliminate the use of Spanish in the public schools increased after World War I. This campaign eventually led to the formulation, enactment, and eventual implementation of an English-only language law for the schools. This language law, passed in 1918 by the Texas legislature, prohibited the use of Spanish and all non-English languages for instructional purposes and mandated the sole use of English in the public school curriculum. The English-only bill was different in several respects from earlier versions enacted in the nineteenth and early twentieth centuries. First, it applied not only to teachers but to principals, superintendents, board members, and all other public school personnel. Second, in order to ensure its implementation, the state legislature made it a criminal offense to teach in a language other than English.[21] In 1923 this policy was expanded to include all the private schools in the state.[22] The development of "No-Spanish" rules in the Houston public schools attended by Mexican-origin children was the logical outcome of the "subtractive" statewide policy mandating English only in education.

Not limited to administrative practices, discrimination was also found in the curriculum. The curriculum provided for Mexican-origin children during the early decades of the twentieth century was culturally subtractive—that is, it devalued the children's Mexican cultural heritage and sought to remove or "subtract" it from the content of the schools.[23] The subtraction of the Mexican cultural heritage from the state's public school curriculum occurred between 1850 and 1890. Public school officials were able to remove courses containing Mexican history and culture from the schools because of the small size of the Mexican population, its increasing social subordination, and the dominating influence of Anglo leaders.[24]

The curriculum in the Houston public schools reflected these historical influences and was subtractive by the time Mexican-origin children began to enroll in the early twentieth century. Houston's curricular policy, in general, was based on an idealized notion of the American national cultural identity that evaluated the religious, cultural, and community heritage of Mexican-origin people and rejected it from the schools. More specifically, this identity was comprised of Pan-Protestantism, Republican values, and core Anglo-American values, especially the ability to speak English.[25] Alternative forms of cultural identity, especially those based on Catholicism, non-English languages, and Mexican cultural traditions, in turn, were either devalued or viewed as being incompatible with American ideals and traditions and had to be replaced.

The subtractive character of public education in Houston was reflected in the English-language policy discussed earlier and in the textbooks used in the schools. These textbooks were distinctly partial toward Protestant Anglo culture. They, in other words, were "Anglo-centric" and provided the perspectives, events, and cultures of the dominant Anglo population group while excluding or demeaning those of the Mexican group.[26]

Texas history books illustrate the subtractive nature of the public school curriculum in the Houston Independent School District. History books, which began to appear a decade after the Mexican American War of 1848, contained only disparaging comments about the Mexican presence in the Southwest. These books, noted the historian Carlos E. Castañeda, consistently denounced the character of the Mexican people and stressed the nobility of the Texans and their cause.[27] Most of them also had a narrow scope of Texas history and omitted or minimized the cultural contributions of Spain and Mexico to the development of Texas. According to the authors of these history textbooks, little or nothing transpired in Texas worthy of record before the coming of the first Anglo settlers from the United States. The trivialization of Spanish and Mexican contributions to Texas in the history books existed into the 1930s. The following quotes from a popular state-adopted textbook illustrate the continuity of this narrow scope of Texas history. The widely used history text entitled *Lone Star State* was written by Clarence Wharton and published in 1932. The author's view of early Texas history is reflected in the following comment on Anglo-American colonization: "We are now at the real beginning of Texas history. All that happened in 300 years after Piñeda sailed along our shores and Cabeza de Vaca tramped from Galveston Island to the Rio Grande was of little importance."[28]

The Anglo-centric perspective can be observed in another popular history textbook used in the public schools throughout the state and most likely in Houston. This textbook was written by G. P. Quackenbow. Although published in the late 1800s, it was still used in most of the public schools until the 1940s. In the struggle for Texas independence this popular history painted a picture of a battle between "jealous" Mexicans and "prosperous" Anglo settlers. Quackenbow's description of the events leading to the Texas Revolution of 1836 further illustrates the predominance of the Anglo-centric view of Texas history. He summed up this history as follows: "In 1835, the Revolution began with the battle of González in which 1,000 Mexicans were defeated by 500 Texans. Goliad, and the strong citadel of Bexar known as the Alamo were soon after taken and the whole Mexican army was dispersed. On the 6th of March, 1836, however, Santa Anna, having raised a new force of 8,000 men, attacked the Alamo, which had been left in charge of a small but gallant garrison. All night they fought but superior numbers triumphed. Every man fell at his post but several, and these were killed while asking quarter."[29] Another popular history book used in the schools described the Battle of Mier that the Mexican troops won in the following manner: "at this point, where Mexican valor failed, Mexican trickery succeeded. . . . They indicated that a reinforcement of eight hundred fresh men were expected every moment; that the general admired the bravery of the Texans and wished to save them from the certain destruction . . . it seems strange that the Texans had not learned by this time never to trust the Mexicans, promises or no promises."[30] In the textbooks quoted above Mexicans have few positive attributes. Anglos, on the other hand, are portrayed in glowing terms with few negative characteristics.

Despite the exclusivity and Anglo character of schools, some Mexican students succeeded in school and utilized it for improving their economic opportunities and for becoming productive citizens in their barrios. A few, in other words, managed to succeed despite the structural barriers of inequality and the subtractive curriculum. Edna Luna, for instance, managed to graduate from Jefferson Davis High School in 1928. Estella Gómez followed in her footsteps and graduated from Sam Houston High School in 1929.[31] A handful of other students attended Rice Institute, including P. L. Niño and Francisco Chairez, who earned degrees as engineers in 1928. These individuals and their educational achievements were touted by the Mexican community as examples for the youth to emulate.[32]

The presence of a small group of individuals who succeeded in school raises questions about the popular and historical interpretation of the Mexican experience in education. This general interpretation posits the view that all Mexican-origin children were nonachievers and that their performances in the schools were solely part of a history of underachievement as reflected in low scores on tests of reading, math, and general knowledge, as well as in enrollment, attendance, and attainment rates. Historically, this is an inaccurate portrayal of this community's performance in the schools. The existence of successful individuals suggests a more diverse pattern of school performance. This history, I would argue, is actually one of skewed performance that is characterized by a dominant tradition of underachievement and a minor one of school success, as is supported by the above evidence.

Most Mexican-origin individuals, however, did not succeed. They experienced much failure in the schools. Poverty, ignorance of American laws, the need for child labor, and severe overcrowding and inadequate attention to the cultural and linguistic needs of these children encouraged

most of them to drop out of school after several years.[33] The school experience in many cases reinforced their subordinate status by reaffirming
their lack of success in the larger society.

EXPANDING PUBLIC
EDUCATIONAL OPPORTUNITIES, 1930 – 60

The pattern of increasing albeit unequal educational opportunities was
strengthened in the years from 1930 to 1960, when school segregation expanded to the higher grades, and when institutional discrimination became more pervasive and scholastic performance more skewed. The pattern of separate and unequal schooling gradually expanded and increased
into the secondary grades after the 1930s as a result of Mexican student enrollment. In the Magnolia Park area Mexican-origin children began to
enroll in larger numbers at Edison Junior High and at Deady Junior High
during the years from 1930 to 1960. Those who finished these grades continued into Milby High School. Mexican-origin children residing closer
to what is now the Gulf Freeway attended Jackson Junior High and the
Stephen F. Austin High School. The Mexican children in El Segundo barrio at times enrolled at Sam Houston High School, which used to be located around the downtown area. In the Northside, Mexican children attended Marshall Junior High and then Davis High School.[34] Although data
is lacking, it is possible that Mexican-origin children attended secondary
schools in parts of the city that were outside their barrios.[35]

As in the case of the elementary schools, some of these secondary
schools eventually became segregated as a result of various forces, including population shifts. But public prejudice was an important influence in
ensuring that the schools remained segregated. One example illustrates the
role of community prejudice in strengthening the pattern of segregation.
In the mid-1930s the Settlement Association of Houston established an
educational and social facility in the 5500 block of Canal Street. This was a
cooperative project between local school officials and the Houston Settlement Association. Its purpose was to provide English, citizenship, pottery,
and other types of classes for Mexican adults and children. The facility was
at the edge of the Mexican district in Magnolia Park and was opposed by
many homeowners in the predominantly Anglo residential section. On
opening night many of these individuals "swarmed in the streets, calling
the Mexicans insulting names and trying to drive them away." The president and director of the association, a Miss Bailey (no first name avail-

able), called the police, who quieted things down by midnight. The police promised increased protection, but association officers, scared by the anti-Mexican sentiment of the community, decided to leave the area and relocate in another part of the neighborhood. The president of the association thought that it would be unfair to the Mexican youth and adults to subject them to the "possibility of a recurrence." An educational and social facility was later founded in the heart of the Mexican community.[36]

Public prejudice also encouraged the principal of Hawthorne Elementary to promote segregation within this predominantly Anglo school. In the early 1930s the principal of Hawthorne approached the Houston Settlement Association for assistance in establishing programs and activities for its students. These children, however, had to meet in separate groups so as not to disturb the existing patterns of social relations based on segregation.[37]

Another incident illustrates the role of bias in the maintenance of school segregation. In the mid-1940s De Zavala Elementary School was condemned as a fire hazard. School board members began to discuss the construction of a new school to replace it and where to send the existing children. Because of bias in the community, they decided to send them, not to the neighborhood school closest to them, a predominantly Anglo school, but rather to the Mexican school closest to De Zavala. Bias in school official actions thus contributed to the maintenance and strengthening of the Mexican school phenomenon in Houston.[38]

The earlier pattern of institutional discrimination continued and became more pervasive during the decades from 1930 to 1960, but there were some slight changes. For example, during the late 1940s the school district began to hire some Mexican American teachers. This action served to modify the pattern of structural exclusion at this level. By 1958 approximately twenty-five persons of Mexican origin were employed as public school teachers.[39] No clear reason has been found to indicate why public school officials began to hire Mexican American teachers. It is possible that the increasing number of Spanish-speaking children in the schools created the conditions for their hiring, but more research needs to be conducted in this area.

Despite these positive steps, local officials failed to hire Mexican-origin administrators for the elementary and secondary grades. Structural exclusion of Mexican Americans thus continued to be the pattern at this level. The first Mexican American principal was not hired until the mid-1960s.[40]

The first district-level administrator was not hired until 1971 and as a result of political pressure from the Mexican-origin community.[41]

Other exclusionary practices continued during this period. Local officials continued to mount a campaign against the use of Spanish in the schools and to neglect the needs of barrio schools. They also failed to encourage or support the election of Mexican-origin individuals to the school board. By 1960 the pattern of exclusion, although modified, was still intact.[42]

In addition to continued institutional exclusion, there was also a pattern of discrimination reflected in local school decisions about the Mexican schools and the Mexican population. For example, during the 1930s local school board members, in response to Depression woes, used the schools to encourage repatriation of the Mexican population.[43] While a few members of the Mexican-origin community supported this effort in the early decades of the Depression, repatriation became a symbol of America's mistreatment of this population group.

The campaign to systematically deport Mexican immigrants was part of a larger movement aimed at blaming them for unemployment and for high relief rates caused by the Great Depression. The official purpose of this campaign was to improve occupational opportunities for Anglos and to remove Mexican-origin individuals from the welfare and relief rolls by either deporting or repatriating them. But it quickly became part of a general campaign of fear and intimidation of unwanted Mexican immigrants and also led to widespread denials of basic constitutional and human rights.[44]

The 1940s brought an end to these types of discriminatory actions but not to the pattern of discrimination. The Mexican schools such as Lubbock, Jones, Rusk, and De Zavala Elementaries, continued to be inadequate, substandard, and in need of repairs. In 1945 De Zavala was overcrowded and, as noted earlier, condemned as a fire hazard. Despite the objections of Anglo parents residing in the community surrounding the school, the local board decided to expand the school by providing a new wing. A decade later Rusk Elementary, located on Maple Street, was condemned by the school district due to overcrowdedness and inadequacy of the facility. This old school was razed and a new one constructed at the corner of Garrow and Page, near Settegast Park, but it took the district four years to build it. The new Rusk Elementary relieved overcrowded conditions at Lubbock and Jones and served the children of Clayton Homes, a new housing project located several blocks from the school.[45] In the mean-time other schools failed to obtain adequate resources to instruct the in-creasing numbers of Mexican-origin children enrolled in them.

The pattern of discrimination also became more pervasive during these decades largely as a result of the emergence of new assessment methods, placement practices, and curricular changes during the early decades of the twentieth century.[46] Many of these school reforms were developed as part of a national movement to improve the efficiency and effectiveness of public education in the United States.[47] Houston school officials joined this national movement in the 1920s as it expanded educational opportu-nities for most children from ages five to twenty, reorganized elementary and secondary education, and revised curricula. In an effort to meet the needs of students with varying abilities they assessed their abilities, es-tablished a special curriculum—e.g., trade, vocational, and industrial courses—and then placed them in these classes.[48]

These "progressive" reforms, once implemented in the schools, had a negative impact on the education of Mexican-origin children since it led to their misdiagnosis and to their classification as intellectually inferior, culturally backward, or linguistically deprived. Once classified as inferior, these children were systematically placed in "developmentally appropri-ate" instruction groups, classes, or curricular tracks. In the elementary grades the "developmentally appropriate" classes were slow-learning or special-education classes, and in the secondary grades they tended to be either vocational or general education classes.[49]

This process of labeling and placement at the elementary grade level occurred as early as 1908 when local school officials classified Mexican children as "subnormal" and provided them with a special class at Rusk Elementary. An ungraded class was also established at Dow Elementary for students with special needs, including a delinquent child, a bright child who disliked school, a blind child, and a non-English-speaking child. These types of classes were expanded during the next three decades.[50]

At the secondary level the process of labeling and tracking began by the third decade of the twentieth century and expanded in the post–World War II period. Generally speaking, administrators assigned Mexican-origin children to vocational or general education courses or tracks and discouraged them from taking academic classes. This vocationalization of the curriculum began as early as the 1930s when some of the schools in the Mexican community developed vocational training for boys and domestic science for girls.[51] Some historians have argued that vocational education was a negative experience for the Mexican-origin population because it did not promote mobility or advancement. Vocational education, according to most historians, reinforced the existing subordinate position of the Mexican-origin population by limiting rather than broadening employment opportunities. More specifically, it trained Mexicans to be docile workers employed in semiskilled or unskilled labor.[52] Because of the dearth of studies dealing with the placement of Mexican children in vocational education, it is not possible to determine whether vocational education actually trained these students to be docile workers or provided them with work skills necessary for advancement.[53] Evidence, however, suggests that vocational education was used by educators to limit the educational opportunities of Mexican-origin students by placing an inordinate amount of emphasis on the vocational aspect of instruction in the barrio schools at the expense of academic subjects. The greater emphasis on vocational education in the predominantly Mexican American schools led to an imbalance in the curriculum and foreclosed most possibilities for increased academic instruction among members of this minority group.[54]

The discriminatory treatment of Mexican-origin children was also apparent in their interactions with instructional staff. Generally speaking, local educators provided these children with schools that were staffed by insensitive instructors who were oblivious to the cultural and special educational needs of these children. Although some of these teachers cared, most had low expectations of the children's learning abilities and discouraged, at times unwittingly, Mexican children from achieving. They also ridiculed them for their culturally distinctive traits. Many a Mexican child was punished simply for speaking Spanish at school or in the classroom.[55] Teachers also interacted with Anglo students more and had less praise for Mexican children.[56]

The policies, procedures, and practices utilized by school administrators to assess and classify students, place them in classes, and promote them through the grades served to stratify the student population according to various categories and to reproduce the existing relations of social and economic domination in the classroom.[57] The major educational consequence of inferior schooling as well as unfavorable socioeconomic circumstances was the strengthening of the pattern of skewed academic performance developed in the early part of the twentieth century.

A dominant tradition of underachievement and a minor one of success, as mentioned earlier, characterized this pattern. Although no concrete data exists on the number of Mexican-origin children who scored poorly in school, scattered evidence suggests that this was the case. In the early 1950s, for instance, the Houston Settlement Association conducted a study of the Mexican school in El Segundo barrio and found that large numbers of children were not even enrolled. A study of Hawthorne Elementary indicated the magnitude of the problem of underachievement. In this study investigators found that out of 238 Mexican children in the elementary grades 90, or approximately 38 percent, were one year below grade level and 57, or about 24 percent, were two years below grade level. Thus, out of 238 children 147, or 62 percent, were below grade level in their academic work.[58]

Poor attendance record and low achievement usually led to high dropout rates. The pattern of poor school achievement is reflected in the low median number of years of schooling completed by Mexican-origin individuals twenty-five years old and older. As of 1950 the median number of years of schooling completed by the Mexican-origin population in Houston was 5.2. For Anglos and African Americans the rate stood at 11.4 and 7.6, respectively. Some change occurred by the following decennial, as indicated by the increase in the median number of years of schooling completed by this population group. In 1960 Mexicans had 6.4 median years of school completed. The median years of schooling also increased for the other two groups but at varying rates. In general the gap between the Mexican-origin population and Anglos decreased, whereas that between Mexicans and African Americans remained constant.[59]

Despite the gloomy picture of underachievement there was an unnoticed increase in academic excellence. This was reflected in the number of Mexican-origin children who were advancing to the senior grades, completing high school, and enrolling in college. High school enrollment and completion slowly increased between 1930 and 1960. At Austin High, for instance, only one Mexican American made it to the senior grade in 1938. The number remained unchanged in 1945. By 1955 the number had increased slightly to ten. Five years later there were forty-four Mexican-origin pupils attending Austin.[60] The figures for Davis High were also low, but they showed a slight increase. Mexican students comprised less than 4 percent of the total student population in 1945 and 1949. By 1951 approximately 9 percent of the Davis student population was Mexican American.[61] A similar development occurred at Milby and at Reagan High. In the former, Mexican-origin pupils comprised about 6 percent in 1951 but approximately 11 percent in 1960. In the latter, Mexican Americans comprised less than 1 percent in 1951, but their numbers increased five years later so that slightly over 6 percent of the total student population was Mexican American.[62] Enforcement of school attendance laws, new curricular programs, declining economic opportunities for youth, and increased desire for learning by the community led to the enrollment of larger numbers of Mexican-origin children in the secondary grades.

Census data for 1950 and 1960 indicate that a small proportion of Mexican-origin individuals were completing high school and attending college. According to the 1950 census 16 percent of the Mexican-origin population had completed between one to four years of high school and close to 4 percent had completed one to four years of college. These percentages increased ten years later when 21 percent had completed one to four years of high school and slightly over 7 percent had completed one to four years of college.[63] This group formed part of the emerging middle class that was to play an important part in the community's struggle to achieve equality, justice, and equal opportunity in Houston.

CONCLUSION

Public education for Mexican-origin children, then, was a twentieth-century phenomenon. In the century's early decades they were provided increasing albeit inequitable access to the public schools. This public schooling, however, was of inferior quality, as evidenced by school segregation and administrative mistreatment. Segregation originally was found only in the elementary grades, but over time it expanded to the secondary level. Administrators consistently diagnosed Mexican children as being intellectually inferior, channeled them into low-track classes, and deprived them of opportunities for success. Discrimination in educational administration eventually led to the tracking and channeling of these children into slow-learning classes at the elementary level in the early part of the century and into general education and vocational classes by the post–World War II era.

Mexican children in Houston likewise received English-only instruction, were punished for speaking Spanish, were discouraged from maintaining their cultural heritage, were coerced into speaking English, and were discriminated against by school board members, administrators, and teachers. In other words, they were provided with demeaning educational experiences and a subtractive curriculum. Although public education experienced significant innovations during the first half of the century, little change occurred in the subtractive curriculum, in the treatment of Mexi-

can children, or in the structural exclusion of the Mexican-origin community during these decades.

The major educational consequence of inferior schooling was a pattern
of skewed academic performance, characterized by a major tradition of
underachievement and a minuscule one of school success. Over the years
an increased number of Mexican Americans managed to advance through
the grades and succeed, but the vast majority continued to be low achiev-
ers because of structural inequalities and inadequate schooling opportunities. Throughout this entire period members of the Mexican-origin
community in Houston adapted as best they could to these school policies
and practices. Occasionally they took actions against institutional discrimination.[64] In most cases, however, they creatively adapted to the limited
opportunities provided by local school officials.

CHAPTER 3

Community Activism
and Identity in Houston

Mexican-origin involvement in politics appeared in the early decades of the twentieth century and increased over time.[1] Prior to 1930 it was limited primarily to the social and civic arena, but after 1930 it expanded and became more diverse. The increase in political involvement is indicated by the renewed activity of existing organizations and by the establishment of many new ones.[2] In general, these organizations assisted the population in adapting to American life. Occasionally they protested, challenged, or opposed the continuing social and political deprivation of the Mexican-origin community. Political involvement was not limited to one particular class or gender. Individuals from all social classes and of both genders were involved in this process. The following documents the nature of political involvement by members of the Mexican-origin community in Houston from the early 1900s to around 1960.

POLITICAL INVOLVEMENT IN THE BARRIOS, 1907–30

Mexican-origin individuals began to get involved in the political affairs of their communities as early as 1907, but this involvement was limited primarily to civic and social affairs. Generally speaking, there was no visible participation by Mexicans in the electoral arena during the early decades of the twentieth century. Although they comprised anywhere from 2 to 5 percent of the total population during this period, they did not run for or support candidates for political office. Neither were they involved in party politics in the city. This lack of electoral involvement differed significantly from the experiences of Mexicans in other parts of the state.[3] The immigrant status of this population, their small size, and the citizenship and language requirements for voting acted as barriers to electoral participation in Houston.[4]

There also was no visible political participation by Mexicans in the workplace. Mexican-origin individuals comprised a significant proportion of workers in key industries such as the railroads, but they did not participate in any significant unionizing activities.[5] A conservative southern political culture and discrimination from the few unions in existence discouraged labor involvement. Most preferred to adapt to their working conditions or to resist in more casual methods that have not been uncovered by historians.[6]

One area of active political involvement was in the social and civic affairs of the community. Political involvement in this area appeared in the early 1900s and increased appreciably in the 1920s. Its increase was due to many factors, including immigration, urbanization, and the emergence of an immigrant leadership within the community that the historian Mario García refers to as the "Immigrant Generation."[7] This new generation of community leaders was born in Mexico and came to the United States for various reasons. The vast majority of them were, in the words of De León, "poor folk," but there also were small and influential groups of upper-class *ricos* (wealthy individuals), middle-class professionals, and religious exiles.[8]

Mexican immigrants, in general, tended to view themselves as *Mexico de a fuera* (Mexico from the outside) and hoped to return to *la patria* (the motherland) as soon as conditions allowed. Their leaders had a "Mexicanist" identity and shared certain ideas about ethnicity, politics, and society.[9] This identity was complex and comprised of at least four distinct intellectual strands: cultural nationalism, structural accommodationism, social reformism, and conventionality.

The Mexicanist identity, for instance, was nationalistic.[10] It stressed loyalty to Mexico and Mexico's patriarchal and cultural ideals.[11] Those with a Mexicanist identity held ambivalent attitudes toward or had reservations about American cultural forms.[12]

The Mexicanist identity was structurally accommodationist. Mexican immigrants who shared these ideals sought accommodation with, not integration into, the established socioeconomic and political structures of American society. Although they sought equal access to and equitable treatment by institutions such as public schools, they were not interested in becoming American citizens.[13] Nor were they interested in joining the American mainstream.[14]

Those with a Mexicanist identity likewise were interested in social reform, but only minimally because of their limited stake in American society.[15] The idea of minimal social reform and collective action was based on what the historian Emilio Zamora calls an ethic of mutuality. Those involved in the community, in other words, were motivated by a prevailing sense of altruism, fraternity, and camaraderie. They shared a sentiment that derived from their common identity as Mexicanos, a bond with their community, and the mutual experience they shared as targets of racism and discriminatory treatment in Texas society.[16]

Finally, the Mexicanist identity was highly pragmatic. Those who believed in it used whatever tactics were available to achieve their ends. Activists in the workplace used mostly direct action and confrontation tactics. Those organizing in the community around social and electoral issues turned to the Mexican consulate for assistance or used conventional methods of struggle such as lobbying, petitioning, and litigation.[17]

Mexican-origin leadership in the United States was not solely comprised of immigrants; nor was the Mexicanist identity the only set of ideals in the barrios. Mexican Americans—that is, Mexican-origin individuals born or raised in the United States—were also part of this leadership group. But Mexican Americans and their distinct ideals were few in number and influence during these decades.[18] Immigrants were the dominant social group in the community during the early decades of the twentieth century, and the Mexicanist mentality was the dominant set of ideals.

In Houston, as in other parts of the country, Mexican immigrants provided most of the leadership in the community. These leaders founded their own organizations to promote their particular interests or concerns. Many of these groups were multipurpose in general, whereas others were devoted primarily to meeting the cultural, recreational, or civil rights of the Mexican-origin community. Some of the most important organizations founded or expanded during this period included masonic or fraternal lodges, *sociedades patrioticas* (also known as *juntas patrioticas*), *mutualista* societies, and social clubs.[19] Masonic or fraternal lodges provided insurance and other social needs. Sociedades patrioticas, or juntas patrioticas, sponsored festivities for Mexican Independence Day, Cinco de Mayo parades, beauty contests, speeches, and debates about general social and political issues. Mutualista societies generally provided funeral and illness benefits, collective support, group defense, cultural recreational services, and sometimes employment referrals. Social clubs were more general in nature and included those aimed at promoting recreation, leisure, and entertainment activities.[20]

Immigrants began to organize around their particular social concerns as early as 1907.[21] Within a twenty-five-year period they established a variety of organizations and provided for the health, recreational, and social services of other immigrants residing in Houston. These organizations in general made life more tolerable for Mexican immigrants who had decided to make Houston their home.[22]

Although it was rare, some members of the community engaged in struggles against discrimination and injustice. Some of these struggles were initiated by existing or new organizations or by prominent individuals, usually those with access to the print media.[23] This is the case, for instance, with the Agrupación Protectora Mexicana, an association dedicated to the defense of Mexicans in Texas. Its members displayed an awareness of discrimination and commitment to struggle on behalf of civil and human rights. The commitment of these members was shown in 1911 when a delegation from Houston attended the Primer Congreso Mexicanista, a meeting being hosted in Laredo. This statewide conference was organized in order to inform the Mexican-origin community about the problems confronting it. More specifically, the conference encouraged discussion of the lack of legal justice, social and educational discrimination, labor exploitation, cultural retention, and the need for unity.[24] The Houston delegation to this conference played a key role in speaking out against all forms of discrimination and for cultural maintenance. J. J. Mercado, especially, took a leading role in the deliberations by denouncing judicial injustice against Mexicans in Texas and expressing his concern over the linguistic deterioration occurring within the Mexican community in Texas.[25] Other members of the organization protested the problem of exclusion and discrimination in the public schools, the loss of the Spanish language and Mexican culture through the assimilationist public school, and the inferior quality of education for Mexican-origin children. As a way of resolving these issues, the Houston delegates proposed sending a letter of protest against segregation to the state superintendent of public instruction. They also supported the establishment of *escuelitas,* or community-controlled schools that would teach the Spanish language and preserve the

Mexican culture, and promoted the hiring of Spanish-language teachers from Mexico for instruction in the public schools.[26]

Members of the activist community in Houston also supported other civil rights causes. For instance, they supported Gregorio Cortez's efforts to get paroled from Texas prisons after his encounter with the law. They also supported Aniceto Pizana and Luis de la Rosa's popular uprising in the Lower Rio Grande and Venustiano Carranza's efforts in northern Mexico to oust the tyrant Victoriano Huerta, who in 1913 had usurped the presidency from Francisco I. Madero.[27]

Most organizations and individuals during the early decades of the twentieth century did not engage in civil rights activities because of their immigrant status, limited resources, and lack of political power. Some, however, supported cultural maintenance efforts in the schools or sought to keep themselves informed of important issues such as educational discrimination. For example, in keeping with the critique of assimilation and "de-Mexicanization," Mexican-origin clubs presented plays and other forms of cultural activities at Rusk Elementary. This was a means for ensuring that "lo mexicano" was preserved in the schools as Mexican children learned "lo americano." [28] Because of the immigrant status of the population, the Mexican consul also was invited to address the community on issues pertinent to them, including those pertaining to inequality in education. In this way the Mexican consul played an important role in the education of the population attending the segregated Mexican schools.[29]

As indicated above, then, most immigrants were interested in surviving, not challenging, the new environment. Adaptation to new conditions thus became the dominant means of political activity in the colonias during the early decades of the twentieth century.

POLITICAL INVOLVEMENT IN THE BARRIOS, 1930–60

During the years from 1930 to 1960 political activity within the Mexican-origin community increased and expanded to the electoral arena. Several significant factors contributed to this activism, including fluctuating economic conditions, public education, the impact of American consumer culture, a more differentiated class structure within the Mexican community, increased institutional mistreatment, and the emergence of a new generation of community leaders.[30] The latter were members of the Mexican American Generation. These activists were born or raised in the

United States and became involved in civil rights, labor organizing, and electoral activities during the years from the late 1920s to the early 1960s.

This new American-born generation of Mexican-origin leaders held distinct and, in contrast to the Immigrant Generation before them, different ideas about ethnicity, politics, and society. Theirs was a Mexican Americanist rather than a Mexicanist identity.[31] The Mexican Americanist identity, while ideologically complex and highly evolutionary, was, like the Mexicanist one, comprised of at least four unique but dissimilar intellectual strands: cultural pluralism, structural integration, reformism or moderate reforms of the existing social order, and accommodationism or the use of conventional means to realize social reform.[32]

The members of the Mexican American Generation, for instance, were not assimilationists or *vendidos* (sellouts), as many scholars argue.[33] They believed in cultural pluralism, a complex set of ideals that embodied distinct notions of culture, race, class, and gender. Culturally speaking, these individuals urged acculturation, or the adoption of selective aspects of the dominant culture into the existing Mexican culture.[34] They sought what the historian Richard García calls a synthesis of lo americano and lo mexicano. The former, however, became dominant over time as a result of living in the United States.[35] It is interesting, and probably in keeping with their desire to assimilate, that most members of the Mexican American Generation also viewed themselves as members of the Caucasian or white race, although they were primarily a racially mixed or mestizo group.[36] They aspired to middle-class status, looked to middle-class role models, and promoted the establishment of male-only organizations.[37]

Members of the Mexican American Generation additionally believed in structural integration or in gaining access to mainstream institutions. For this reason they were extremely loyal to the existing social order and to the ideological rationalizations for maintaining these structures.[38] In most cases they believed in integrating on their own terms, but because of their lack of significant political and economic clout this was usually done on Anglo terms.[39]

Despite support for the social order, members of the Mexican American Generation were aware of continuing inequities such as racial discrimination, unequal treatment, poverty, and institutional insensitivity. These indicated that the society was imperfect and in need of moderate change. The goal of members of the Mexican American Generation thus was to support moderate social change that would improve, not replace, the existing social order.[40]

Their appreciation of American institutions, ideas, and behaviors likewise encouraged them to utilize mostly conventional strategies and tactics such as education, litigation, and lobbying to realize their social change goals.[41] In general, Mexican American activists vehemently rejected violence and direct action as legitimate forms of struggle. The LULAC constitution for the state office was adamant on this issue: "We shall oppose any radical and violent demonstrations which may tend to create conflicts and disturb the peace and tranquillity of our country."[42] Occasionally Mexican American organizations used direct action, but the vast majority of these social activists emphasized conventional means, especially litigation.[43] Litigation strategy during these years generally sought treatment of Mexican Americans as part of the Caucasian or white race in order to achieve social equality. This not only was the most effective means for challenging discrimination against Mexican Americans but it also complemented the white ethnic identity of the activists in the community.[44]

Members of the Mexican American Generation were in the forefront of efforts to better life for the Mexican community during the years from 1930 to 1960, and they were responsible for the increase in electoral and community involvement. They, in essence, initiated and led the campaign for Mexican American civil rights in the United States.

The new generation of middle-class Mexican American leaders was also active in Houston. These leaders established new types of organizations and expanded activism to include social protest and electoral activities. They established two basic types of organizations: those aimed at meeting the needs of Mexican immigrants and Mexican Americans; and those aimed at meeting the needs of Mexican Americans only.[45] The former was what Arnoldo De Leon called "transitional" in nature. They lasted for only a few years and appealed, for a short period of time, to Mexican nationals and the more Americanized members of the Mexican-origin community. They represented a historical link between earlier types of Mexican-origin organizations and the emerging Mexican American ones. They also helped bridge the transition from the Mexicanist to the Mexican Americanist identity.[46]

Three important "transitional" organizations were founded in Houston during the Depression: El Club Femenino Chapultepec,[47] the Federación de Sociedades Mexicanas y Latino Americanas (FSMLA),[48] and La Unión Fraternal.[49] Although they had different objectives, they became involved in meeting the needs of the Mexican and Mexican American population and in protesting various forms of institutional discrimination, including school segregation. However, because of their short duration, they only had a limited impact on barrio life and institutional discrimination.

The most significant organizations were those founded by Mexican Americans for Mexican Americans. In Houston the leading organization founded by this new generation of leaders was the League of United Latin American Citizens (LULAC), including Council 60, the Latin American Club (LAC), and Council 22.[50] LULAC and its different councils best represented the Mexican Americanist identity in Houston because it articulated the new ideas about being Mexican in the United States and sought to integrate the population into this country's mainstream institutions.[51] One of the central reasons for the establishment of LULAC, for example, was "to study the laws of local government, and to induce the Latin people of Houston to understand the government, to partake of voting privileges, and thus to become better citizens."[52] Emilio R. Lozano, president general of LULAC, reiterated this purpose when he urged the membership in a May, 1935, meeting in Houston to "exercise our American citizenship properly" in order to receive better treatment at the hand of Anglos. He also urged all "American citizens of Latin extraction" to pay their poll tax, be independent financially, and be "good, true, and loyal American citizens."[53]

The Latin American Club (LAC) had similar integrationist goals. According to its constitution, the organization's basic purposes were to protect "Latin American Citizens" of this country, to teach them the importance of United States citizenship, and to study the laws of local, state, and national government. Most important, LAC encouraged the "Latin American" people to understand the government and to partake in voting and all other privileges extended to them by the United States.[54] LULAC, LAC, and other similar organizations became highly active in promoting active citizenship among their members. The ultimate result was an appreciable increase in electoral and civic activism.[55]

Different types of electoral activities were promoted during the 1930s. LAC, for instance, initiated a series of campaigns for payment of the poll tax and hosted demonstrations of new voting machines.[56] In 1935 LAC endorsed a bond election that would be used to improve recreational facilities in several of the barrios in the city.[57] Three years later the Texas American Citizens of Magnolia Park, a group similar to LAC, hosted a meeting of Anglo politicians running for office. In November, 1940, another organization, the Latin Sons of Texas, endorsed a slate of candidates for political office in Houston.[58] In this same year two additional organizations in the Magnolia Park area, the Pan American Political Council and the Cooperative Club of Latin American Citizens, held rallies for Anglo candidates.[59]

In one instance LAC and Council 60 threatened to withdraw their political support for an Anglo city councilperson by the name of S. A. Starkey unless the derogatory remarks he had made about Mexicans were withdrawn.[60] The president of LAC, John Duhig, chided Starkey and threatened to vote against him in the next election unless he showed "the Latin American citizen, who has done his duty in placing him in office" some respect. LAC claimed to have over fifteen hundred poll taxes to battle the commissioner and even proposed putting up a candidate of its own against him. Although Starkey offered no apology and merely stated that he had been misquoted on the issue, this incident served to inform the dominant society that Mexican Americans were emerging as a political force to be reckoned with.[61]

Most of these electoral efforts focused on promoting active citizenship and encouraging support for Anglo candidates. In one particular case in 1947, however, John J. Herrera, a prominent member of LULAC Council 60, ran for a special senatorial race in Harris County. Although he lost, running seventh among forty-two candidates, it was the first time that any Mexican American had run for political office in the county.[62]

Despite the increase in electoral activity, no Mexican Americans were elected to office from 1930 to 1960. The lack of Mexican Americans in elective office indicated that the pattern of political powerlessness established in the early decades of the twentieth century remained intact during the years from 1930 to 1960. The Mexican-origin population, in other words, remained without any significant political power and influence.

Civic involvement in the Mexican-origin community also increased in the 1930s and became more assertive and diverse during the next two decades. During the Depression organizations such as LULAC, LAC, and Club Chapultepec promoted a variety of activities, including the payment of poll taxes, naturalization, and an end to discrimination in hiring, social services, and the treatment of Mexican-origin workers.[63] None of these activities, however, focused on eliminating discrimination in the schools. This did not mean that these organizations and individuals belonging to them were not interested in education; rather they were. But because of the effects of the Depression, activists focused on supporting the schools or on providing services to students and parents.

Although minimal then, there was some involvement in the schools.

LAC, for instance, participated in health education drives in the community and in the schools during the 1930s. Because of the large number of
Mexican workers contracting contagious diseases such as tuberculosis,
LAC in May, 1938, helped to sponsor "Latin American Health Week."
Health education activities, comprised of lectures and free moving pic-
tures on tuberculosis and other phases of health conditions, were held in
several Mexican schools during an entire week in early May.[64] During the
mid-1930s LULAC also sponsored activities aimed at keeping youth in
school and out of trouble. It formed a Boy Scout troop for Mexican Americans, supported the passage of recreation bonds to improve recreational
facilities in several barrios, and organized the Club Recreativo Tenochti-
tlán.[65] This club worked on projects to get the city's parks and recreation
department to improve school playgrounds.[66] In 1940 FSMLA promoted
health education by sponsoring a variety of exhibitions informing members of the community on ways to avoid or control such diseases as syph-
ilis, cancer, and tuberculosis.[67]

The campaign for barrio betterment and especially for civil rights increased appreciably during World War II. The federal government's involvement in promoting understanding between the United States and
Latin America during an international conflict provided a stimulus for
increased civic involvement. This climate emerged as part of the Good
Neighbor Policy aimed at promoting better relations between Mexicans
and Anglos in the Southwest during the war years in the early 1940s. The
Mexican-origin population in Houston as well as in other parts of the state
and country took advantage of this favorable political circumstance to attack discrimination in all its institutional forms. The emphasis of this effort was on informing the Anglo community about the detrimental effects
of discrimination and segregation and on encouraging their elimination.[68]
Of particular importance was the role that La Union Fraternal and FSMLA
played in this civil rights campaign. In the early 1940s, for instance, both
were involved in protesting school segregation in Houston and in the surrounding communities.[69]

In the mid-1940s LULAC Council 60 joined them.[70] In 1944, for example, it formed the Anti-Segregated Mexican School Committee to combat discrimination and segregation.[71] Between 1945 and 1947 Council 60
also worked with local officials in Pearland to eliminate school segregation.
Pearland was a small community located about eighteen miles southwest
of Houston. In early 1945 a complaint of discrimination from Pearland

came to John Herrera, district governor of LULAC. According to this complaint, Spanish-speaking students were forced to attend a dilapidated one-
room, one-teacher Mexican school while Anglos had a modern school
plan. This Mexican school had fifty-one students in grades one through
five and was two miles from the Anglo school on the edge of the city limits. In the fall of 1945 Manuela González attempted to enroll her daughter
in the San Jacinto Elementary School, the school for Anglo students. She
immediately received opposition from parents, teachers, and school administrators. She then called John Herrera for assistance. LULAC appealed
to the board and complained that school officials "had no right to separate
these children two miles away from the other children and put them all in
one room with only one teacher for five grades and to share a playground
fenced with barbed wire." This appeal, however, apparently had no effect
on the local school board.[72]

LULAC, with the entire support of the Mexican-origin community,
then boycotted the schools. For eight months the community protested.
During the 1946–47 school year local officials, at the insistence of the state
superintendent of public education, L. A. Woods, integrated the schools
and moved the Mexican school to the central campus.[73]

In addition to participating in the struggle against educational segregation, Mexican American groups also promoted stay-in-school activities.
In the mid-1940s the Good Citizens League, an organization containing
prominent leaders of the Mexican-origin community, supported a campaign to keep youth in schools and to teach them useful trades and how to
become "better citizens." The ultimate purpose of these efforts was to reduce the amount of juvenile delinquency in the barrios.[74] FSMLA likewise
promoted sports activities as means of reducing delinquency and increasing school attendance.[75]

After the war Mexican American participation in civic issues in general
and in civil rights activities in particular heightened. Transitional organizations such as La Union Fraternal, FSMLA, and Club Chapultepec either
became defunct or disbanded. Mexican American groups such as LULAC,
however, became more widespread. In fact, LULAC became the leading
organization engaged in civil rights. It was assisted tremendously by the
emergence of the Ladies LULAC Council.

During the 1950s a newly reorganized and reanimated Ladies LULAC
Council 22 engaged in many social activities aimed at improving conditions in the community and in the schools.[76] In the mid-1950s, for in-

stance, it established a variety of programs benefiting children in the community. Two important programs affecting schoolchildren were the Milk Fund and the Eye Glass Fund. As part of the former program Council 22 purchased milk tickets for needy children whose parents were victims of tuberculosis. The Eye Glass Fund was developed to provide glasses for underprivileged schoolchildren.[77] Additionally, this council supported the establishment of an English-language-based nursery school for Spanish-speaking children, provided libraries at Lubbock and Dow Elementary, and helped with a Latin American exchange-student program. Janie Tijerina, wife of longtime Council 60 member Félix Tijerina, was one of the most active members of the Ladies Council.[78]

LULAC Council 60 accelerated its involvement in the post–World War II era. In the late 1940s and early 1950s it supported a campaign to reduce the dropout rate and to end juvenile delinquency in the community through three types of activities: increased parental involvement in the schools, the development of sports teams, and the establishment of a Boys' Club.[79] In the early and mid-1950s Council 60 supported the development of job training for dropouts, the establishment of a library in Anson Jones Elementary, and increased school attendance.[80] To promote the latter, Council 60 printed and distributed "Back to School" pamphlets in Houston's barrios and made announcements on KLVL radio, the only Spanish-language media in the city. It then held rallies in late August or early September to encourage increased enrollment in the schools.[81]

Toward the end of the decade LULAC took steps to establish one of its most well known projects, a preschool for non-English-speaking children. The inspiration for this special educational program came from several sources. First, Council 60 learned of the success of Council 22's support of a language-based preschool program in the early 1950s. Second, two LULAC members were informed about a successful program in Freeport, a small community located in the Houston area. In 1955 Oscar Laurel and Howard Ruhlman of Council 60 were invited by the Brazosport Chamber of Commerce to attend a fund-raising fiesta for La Escuelita, a preschool program established by the Freeport Chamber of Commerce to teach English to Spanish-speaking children. These individuals were impressed with its success and encouraged LULAC to sponsor similar efforts.[82] Third, Alfred Hernández got the idea of developing a preschool program for Spanish-speaking children in the mid-1950s after speaking to a psychologist from the University of Houston concerning the cultural biases in the aptitude tests given to incoming soldiers. As part of the solution to these low test scores, they discussed developing an intensive language program for quickly learning English. Hernández worked with this idea and began to consider how it might be applied to children so that they could learn a second language through a small, basic vocabulary.[83]

The idea of a preschool program for Spanish-speaking children, however, did not become a LULAC project until Félix Tijerina embraced the idea. Tijerina was the president of LULAC from 1956 to 1960. In 1957 he became convinced of the importance of this type of program after talking to Isabel Verver, a teenage girl who had taught at a preschool in Ganado and in Edna, Texas, based on the principal of teaching English to Spanish-speaking children using a basic vocabulary.[84] These experiences eventually led Tijerina to develop an experimental preschool program that eventually came to be known as the Little School of the 400.[85] The name came from the list of four hundred basic English words that formed the core of the curriculum. The Little School of the 400 became one of LULAC's most important projects in the latter part of the 1950s and the early 1960s.[86] These activities indicate that Mexican American involvement in civic matters increased appreciably during the years from 1930 to 1960 and that women also played a key role in this process.

The actions by the local LULACs to improve the schooling of Mexican children differed from the approach taken by the state office. At the state level LULAC focused primarily on eliminating school segregation through litigation. It initiated this effort in 1930 with the filing of an antisegregation lawsuit against local officials in Del Rio, Texas. Although LULAC lost the case, the courts ruled that segregating Mexican children on the basis of race was unconstitutional.[87] From 1948 to 1957 LULAC filed discrimination charges against many local school districts throughout the state. John J. Herrera, one of Council 60's most prominent members, played a key role in initiating the rash of antidiscrimination activity in Texas during the post–World War II period. In 1948 he participated as a lawyer in a lawsuit against the local school officials from Bastrop, a small rural community in central Texas.[88] In *Delgado v Bastrop Independent School District* the parents of school-age Mexican-origin children alleged that school officials in four communities in central Texas were segregating their children contrary to the U.S. Constitution. The U.S. District Court agreed with the plaintiffs and ruled that placing students of Mexican ancestry in different buildings was arbitrary, discriminatory, and illegal. Judge Ben H. Rice also

permanently restrained and enjoined the local school board and the local superintendent from segregating these students in separate schools or
classes.[89]

The *Delgado* decision was an extremely important case for several reasons. First, it helped to clarify several of the constitutional issues not answered by prior rulings.[90] Second, it determined how far school authorities
could go in grouping Mexican-origin children in separate classes within
the same school.[91] Third, it clarified the responsibility of state school officials with respect to the establishment and maintenance of segregation.[92]
Finally, and most important, it provided a psychological boost to the fledg-
ling Mexican American civil rights movement in education and led to the
development of a systematic campaign to eliminate school segregation in
the entire state.[93] Herrera's role in this lawsuit was of extreme importance
and helped to lay the foundation for the growth of the post–World War II
Mexican American civil rights movement.

After *Delgado,* the LULAC state office encouraged and worked for the
passage and implementation of antisegregation school policy at the state
level. It pressured the state board of education and the commissioner of
education to issue policy statements in opposition to segregated schools
for Mexican-origin children.[94] In some cases LULAC filed administrative
complaints against local districts that refused to eliminate segregation.[95]

By the mid-1950s, however, LULAC resorted again to litigation because
of the ineffectiveness of administrative remedies and the continued failure
of local districts to eliminate segregation. As part of the litigation campaign
at the state level, civil rights activists within LULAC developed a legal strategy that sought to have the Mexican-origin population declared part of the
Caucasian or white race.[96] This legal strategy was in keeping with the juris-
prudence of the time. For instance, most federal and state documents before 1954 mandated or sanctioned the separation of blacks and whites, but
they did not stipulate that members of the same race could or should be
segregated. Mexican-origin civil rights lawyers thus sought acceptance of
their own group as Caucasian or white in order to prove that in the absence
of a statute allowing segregation of Mexicans, any attempt by local school
officials to separate them would be a violation of law.[97] Although the courts
made inconsistent rulings on the racial status of Mexican Americans, the
trend in federal decisions between 1930 and 1960 was to classify them as a
distinct class of whites for constitutional purposes.[98]

This legal strategy was largely in response to the rise of anti-Mexican sentiment in the state and the efforts by the dominant society to disfranchise Mexican Americans or to target them for discrimination based on a change in racial classification from white to nonwhite. As early as 1896 members of the dominant society began to challenge the white racial status of the Mexican American population in order to disfranchise them politically.[99] That these discriminatory efforts continued into the twentieth century is illustrated by a 1936 incident in which a federal agency changed the racial status of Mexican Americans. That year the newly established Social Security Board called upon Mexicans in the United States applying for social security to designate themselves as a race other than "white." Some of the designations from which they could choose were Mexican, Chinese, Japanese, Indian, and Filipino. Mexican Americans from LAC and from Council 60 as well as other LULAC councils in the rest of the state responded vociferously to this policy change. Fearful of increased racial discrimination and insulted by being labeled as nonwhite by federal officials, they initiated an aggressive letter-writing campaign to their representatives in congress and to federal officials protesting this action and demanding its rescission. Representative of the sentiments of most Mexican American leaders in Houston was the letter sent by one of LULAC's members to Joe H. Eagle, Houston's congressman from the Eighth District. After complaining about this change in policy he stated: "We are NOT a 'yellow' race, and we protest being classified as such, and ask that the classification be corrected to eliminate such classification for the Latin American Race."[100] Others wrote similar letters to government officials and reminded them that Mexicans were white since they were descendants of the Spaniards.[101] This political pressure eventually led to the rescinding of the designation.[102]

The white status of these individuals was a departure from the identity of those who belonged to the Immigrant Generation. Most of the leaders during the early decades of the twentieth century, especially those in the 1920s, viewed themselves as descendants of indigenous people and tended to promote "native" values, *mestizaje* (mixed blood ties), and various forms of an emerging cultural nationalism.[103] Their veneration of the Indian Virgen de Guadalupe and of Benito Juarez, Mexico's first Indian president, reflected this belief in what José Vasconcelos, the most prominent Mexican intellectual of the 1920s, called "indologia" or "la raza cosmica."[104] Members of the Mexican American Generation rejected this identity and acquired a new one based on *la raza blanca* (the white race).

This racial status was quickly incorporated into the emerging ethnic identity of the Mexican American Generation and became the guiding post for civil rights activity for the next three decades.

CONCLUSION

During 1930 to 1960, then, there were significant political developments in the Mexican-origin community. First, there was a trend toward increased political participation in the electoral and civic arenas. Second, there was a shift in the ethnic identity of the community's leadership from a Mexicanist to a Mexican Americanist one and from an indigenous to a white racial status. This racial classification served as an important means for challenging institutional discrimination and anti-Mexican sentiments in the years from 1930 to 1960. However, the designation came to haunt the community in the late 1960s as local officials used the white label to desegregate the schools. In response to this new form of discrimination, members of the Mexican-origin community abandoned its white identity and acquired a new one based on minority group status in the United States. They became brown, not white, as noted one of the slogans used during the late 1960s and early 1970s. The following chapters explore the forces and events that led to this shift in the community's identity from white to brown and to their increased mobilization over the issue of school segregation during the height of the Chicano movement years.

PART II

Rumblings and Early School Activism, 1968–70

CHAPTER 4

THE COMMUNITY IS
BEGINNING TO RUMBLE

"The Mexican-American community is beginning to rumble," noted Ben Canales, an official with United Organizations Information Center, a community-based group located in the Northside barrio of Houston. This comment was made before a Houston Board of Education committee meeting in October, 1969. It aptly reflected the community's increased dissatisfaction with the local district's unwillingness to improve the conditions under which Mexican American children were educated in particular and the growing restlessness among middle- and working-class Chicanos over the neglect of their interests and needs by political leaders at all levels of government in general. Since 1960 Chicanos in Texas, especially the older and more established middle-class individuals who were members of existing organizations such as the League of United Latin American Citizens (LULAC), the American G.I. Forum, and the Political Association of Spanish-speaking Organizations (PASSO), had worked to elect liberal politicians, to enact federal legislation aimed at meeting the educational and vocational needs of Mexican American children, and to ensure the passage of important civil rights measures. Despite their involvement in the political process, Mexican Americans continued to be neglected by authorities and agencies at all levels of government.[1]

Failure to impact significantly the dominant society's view of Mexican Americans laid the groundwork for the further radicalization and increased political mobilization of the community. The 1966 farmworkers' strike in the Rio Grande and its brutal suppression by the Texas Rangers and state police as well as the Minimum March of that summer accelerated this process. They radicalized existing organizations and unleashed a series of new ones with notions of ethnic identity, political culture, and social change different from those of the Mexican American Generation. These energized groups mobilized an increasing number of community people and mounted a vigorous campaign against all forms of discrimination in American institutional life, especially public education.[2] Canales's statement refers to the complex process of ideological fermentation, organizational development, and political mobilization occurring in the Chicano community in Houston and throughout the state.

EARLY ACTIVISM AND SCHOOL REFORM, 1960–66

Although Mexican Americans had a rich legacy of activism in the schools in the early 1960s, it was subdued and narrowly focused. Activism in the schools focused on four areas of activities. First, sporadic efforts were made to improve the treatment of the Mexican American children in the schools and the quality of their education. For instance, in the summer of 1961 parents from the Clayton Home area in the Second Ward met to discuss conditions in their local schools. They also set up committees to improve the quality of the school facilities provided for their children. Although no information is available on what happened to these recommendations or what further actions the Clayton Home tenants took, their efforts indicated a deep concern for quality education.[3]

At times specific incidents of discrimination were challenged or contested. One such incident occurred in early 1960 when the school board engaged in a debate over the need for free lunches. One school board member remarked that "Mexican American children did not need free lunches because they would rather eat 'pinto beans.'"[4] This comment incensed the community and led to the study of and support for a free-lunch program in the Houston Independent School District. LULAC, the American G.I. Forum, and the Civic Action Committee sponsored this study.[5]

The second major focus of Mexican American activism during this early period occurred at the University of Houston. In 1963 Mexican American students at the University of Houston founded a PASSO chapter on campus to promote awareness of the community's diverse interests and to endorse candidates who best represented them. Under the leadership of Samuel S. Calderón and Manuel Crespo, the UH-PASO conducted voter registration drives, informational workshops on the community's needs, get-the-vote-out campaigns, and analyses of political campaigns. For several years this organization was an important instrument of political awareness and social change on campus.[6]

Third, and probably most important of all, was LULAC's Little School of the 400, a specific educational experiment aimed at improving the scholastic achievement of Mexican Americans. This concept was the brainchild of Félix Tijerina, a local member of LULAC. In 1960 Tijerina, who had just stepped down as national LULAC president, feverishly promoted the Little School of the 400 program in that city and throughout the state, and during the legislative session in 1959 he and LULAC lobbied on behalf of state support for the concept. This project was Tijerina's way of improving the education of Mexican American school-age children and reflected his personal philosophy toward underachievement. Tijerina believed that the lack of facility with English in the early years of child development was at the heart of the high failure rates of Mexican Americans in the schools. He felt that the solution to this problem of underachievement was English-language instruction at the preschool level. His strategy thus was to change the child, not the school. In 1957 he established the Little School of the 400 with this objective in mind. The program's primary objective was to teach Mexican American preschool children four hundred essential English words that would provide them with a better opportunity for completing the first grade of school and for advancing through the grades.[7]

The state legislature agreed to fund this project in 1959 and implement it in the summer of 1960. Tijerina and LULAC promoted, publicized, and helped implement this educational innovation. The success of this promotional campaign was apparent when on June 1, 1960, the first 614 schools opened their doors to 15,805 Spanish-speaking children. By 1967 over 150,000 Spanish-speaking children had taken part in the program.[8]

The program was relatively successful in increasing school achievement among Mexican American school-age children entering the first grade.[9] Despite its apparent success, prominent scholars such as George I. Sánchez, Herschel T. Manuel, and others heavily criticized the Little School of the 400. This program, they noted, ignored the positive role that the children's native language played in their intellectual and psychological development. They also felt that it was based on unsound educational assumptions about language teaching and learning.[10] This criticism, coupled with the development of similar and new federal programs such as Title I and the Head Start project in the mid-1960s, contributed to its diminished importance in the community and its expiration by 1967.[11]

In addition to supporting the Little School of the 400 Tijerina also ran for the school board in 1960. He ran on an independent platform and promised to represent all his constituents "fairly and honestly." He said nothing about his ethnicity and, despite his promotion of the preschool English program for Mexican Americans, promised no significant changes in education if elected to the school board.[12] He failed to be elected.

Fourth, existing organizations such as LULAC and the American G.I. Forum (AGIF) took advantage of the new federal legislation and developed innovative educational and work-training programs for the community's benefit. One such program was Jobs for Progress, sponsored jointly by LULAC and AGIF. The idea of a job-placement referral service originated in the LULAC organization during the spring of 1964 and in the context of a national war-on-poverty program. The National LULAC office endorsed this idea in February, 1965. Two months later, in April, LULAC Council 60, one of Houston's most active chapters, opened the first Jobs for Progress placement office in the nation. In June, 1966, Jobs for Progress received federal funding.[13] It provided education to adults and helped place them in meaningful jobs.[14]

These educational efforts by LULAC and AGIF, however, did not go far enough in bringing about change in the schools or in society. They were based on changing the individual rather than the society and its discriminatory practices.

THE RISE OF THE CHICANO MOVEMENT, 1965–69

During the middle and late 1960s the character and pace of Mexican American activism in Houston changed, largely as a result of the impact of the emerging national Chicano movement. Some historians argue that the Chicano movement was primarily comprised of youth in search of an identity and power; others argue that it was a diverse movement of mostly working-class men and women aimed at improving the social, economic, and political status of Mexican-origin individuals.[15] The Chicano movement, in my view, was a complex set of increased political and cultural activity on the part of diverse sectors within the Mexican-origin community.[16] Professionals, campesinos, students, barrio youth, women, and many other middle- and working-class groups participated in the Chicano movement. Although each of these groups had distinct ideas about how to challenge Anglo hegemony and improve Mexican American life, the majority believed that the political methods of moderation and the cultural identity of the Mexican American Generation were ineffective and no longer viable.

The Chicano movement produced what the historian Ignacio M. García calls a militant ethos—that is, "that body of ideas, strategies, tactics, and rationalizations" that the activists utilized in dealing with the problems plaguing Mexican Americans and the solutions proposed to deal with those problems. This militant ethos, he argues, encouraged Mexican American activists to accept Chicanismo, a complex set of ideas that included cultural nationalism, self-determination, militancy, and the politics of opposition.[17]

During the Chicano movement era two distinct patterns of political activism emerged. First, established middle-class leaders became more militant in their criticism of governmental policies and practices and in their tactics. A few even abandoned the politics of accommodation and embraced direct action strategies utilized by civil rights activists. In 1966, for instance, a group of middle-class leaders expressed their frustration and anger at the federal government by conducting a walkout at a national hearing on employment being held in Albuquerque, New Mexico. The following year, in October, another group of individuals walked out on a federal hearing conducted by cabinet members of the Johnson administration. These actions resulted from the frustrations felt by established middle-class leaders when federal officials continued to ignore their political and cultural interests and exclude them from federal policies and programs that called for "maximum citizen participation."[18]

The increasing dissatisfaction of established middle-class leaders led to the development of a new style of politics that emphasized a more militant approach to governmental neglect. This new militancy was clearly expressed in 1966 by Dr. Hector P. García, founder of the American G.I. Forum, when he warned the White House that "Mexicans were prepared to march in the streets if that were necessary to reach their goals."[19]

The second major pattern of activism was the emergence of a new type of national leadership that went beyond the politics of opposition already used by the disenchanted middle class. These new leaders encouraged the organization and mobilization of previously uninvolved sectors of the Mexican-origin community and directly or indirectly rejected the cultural identity of the Mexican American Generation. They also contested the integrationist and reformist goals of this earlier generation of activists.

The first, and probably most important, leader was César Chávez, a union organizer for the California farmworkers. He used both traditional union methods and civil rights tactics to publicize his struggle in the fields. In 1965 Chávez, for instance, conducted a boycott of grape growers in California. The following year he engaged in a protest march to Sacramento, the state capital, and took steps to organize an international boycott of table grapes. Chávez effectively used Mexican cultural and religious symbols, especially La Virgen de Guadalupe, Mexico's patron saint, in this effort. Through his use of cultural symbolism—i.e., *Mexicanidad* (nationalism)—a Catholic religious orientation, and a philosophy of nonviolence, Chávez provided inspiration to thousands of Mexican Americans throughout the country interested in social justice and equality.[20]

The second important leader to emerge during the mid-1960s was Reis Tijerina. He formed the Alianza Federal de Pueblos Libres in New Mexico to fight for land grant rights and used violence and confrontation to achieve his goal. In 1966, for instance, he "occupied" the Echo Amphitheater, a campground in the Kit Carson National Forest, to illustrate the rights of grant heirs. As part of this strategy a forest ranger was "tried" and a Forest Service truck impounded. The following year, on June 5, 1967, his group engaged in a shoot-out with Tierra Amarilla county authorities after several members attempted a citizen's arrest of the local county attorney for interfering in the organization's affairs. Through these and other acts Tijerina became a symbol of direct and revolutionary action.[21]

The third major leader to emerge in this period was Rodolfo "Corky" González. Corky, as the historian Ignacio García notes, provided a comprehensive ideology against urban ills. In 1963 he formed a community group to fight police brutality. This group eventually became the "Crusade for Justice" in the latter part of the 1960s. Through this group Corky provided the ideals of cultural nationalism and an action plan for achieving "Chicano" liberation in this country.[22]

The fourth major leader of this period was José Angel Gutiérrez. He provided pragmatism and the politics of confrontation.[23] Gutiérrez was one of the founders of the Mexican American Youth Organization and La Raza Unida Party in Texas. These two organizations mobilized thousands of youths and adults and promoted social, education, and political change in the state and the Southwest.[24]

These leaders and the organizations they established led many of the struggles against discrimination, exclusion, and assimilation in the Southwest and other parts of the country during the 1960s and early 1970s. Collectively and individually they mobilized different sectors of the Mexican-origin population such as professionals, students, youths, women, and both middle- and working-class individuals in the barrios.

The most powerful sector of the Chicano movement, however, was comprised of the young people, who expanded its base and contributed to its radicalization.[25] The Chicano youth movement was comprised of both male and female organizations from the barrios and the universities. The members of barrio organizations were basically lower-class individuals who coalesced around different community issues, one of them being education. The student organizations' memberships were primarily middle-class, and their major issues revolved around education. The National Chicano Youth Liberation Conference, held in Denver, Colorado, in March, 1969, brought both of these youth groups together. The manifesto emanating from that conference, "El Plan Espiritual de Aztlán," provided the youths with an ideology of cultural nationalism and a specific plan of comprehensive action for achieving "Chicano" liberation. This new "Chicano" identity, or at least distinct elements of it, was soon adopted by thousands of barrio residents throughout the country.

MIDDLE-CLASS ACTIVISM IN HOUSTON

The pattern of increasing middle-class militancy and the emergence of a new type of leadership were reflected in Houston school politics by the late 1960s. Established middle-class leaders in Houston, for instance, increased their criticism of the Houston Independent School District and more vigorously challenged discriminatory policies, programs, and practices.

An example of the renewed assertiveness on the part of middle-class activists in the community occurred in the fall of the 1969–70 school year when a few of these leaders went before the local school board and leveled charges of inferior education and discrimination against HISD. On Wednesday, October 1, 1969, Leonel Castillo, local director of Services, Employment, and Redevelopment, a federally funded training agency, went before the school board's compensatory education committee. This committee was established in the fall of the 1968–69 school year to recognize officially some of the problems facing the district in educating Mexican Americans and to take corrective action.[26] Although the committee had taken some steps to improve the schools, these did not deal directly with the problem of discrimination and unequal education.[27]

Castillo charged that Mexican American students were getting an inferior education in Houston. These comments were based on his experiences with some students who participated in a college-bound summer school program. These youths, who came from several junior high schools including Hogg, Marshall, Edison, and George Washington, had been identified by several educators involved in the summer school program as potential college material and selected to participate in this summer program. Upon their arrival, however, the organizers of the program found that the reading levels of these students were so low that the curriculum had to be revised downward. A majority of the approximately 120 male participants were reading at either a second- or third-grade level. These students, noted Castillo, "had received their education, since the first grade, in the Houston public schools." He also charged that the administrators had a bad attitude toward the Mexican American students and no desire to improve educational programs and that they did not want to motivate those students to learn.[28]

Ben Canales, an official with United Organizations Information Center (UOIC), charged that in some schools, such as Jeff Davis and San Jacinto High, Mexican American students were constantly harassed by teachers.[29] He added that the community was fed up with the local officials' neglect of these students' needs and stated, "We know that principals and teachers in schools with predominantly Mexican American enrollments are inferior to their counter parts in Anglo schools and they wouldn't make it in Anglo schools."[30]

As part of their presentations, community leaders made specific recommendations for school reform.[31] Antonio Criado, vice president of UOIC, made three specific recommendations for change. These recommendations reflected a mixture of new and old ideologies pertaining to language and culture in the schools: a compensatory view of language as a "handicap"; an emerging pluralist notion of language as asset; and a civil rights perspective of language as an instrument of discrimination. Specifically, Criado proposed that school officials (1) recognize a language barrier as a handicap, "just as deafness and blindness are handicaps," and take steps to help students with this; (2) alter history and other courses that make Mexican American students feel inferior and ashamed of their heritage; and (3) recognize that Mexican Americans cannot be treated like Anglo-Americans in measuring ability by testing. The latter recommendation was most likely based on the emerging view among activist educators that there were inherent cultural and language biases in standardized evaluation instruments.[32]

Ben Canales also added that the district should hire Mexican American principals, counselors, and teachers in those schools with large numbers of Mexican American students. Additionally, he stated that the professional staffs of these schools should be sensitized to the needs of these students through in-service programs.[33]

Probably because of the seriousness of the charges, the general superintendent of HISD, Glenn Fletcher, agreed to call a meeting of principals, assistant principals, and counselors of some schools with large numbers of Mexican American students so that they could discuss these problems with community representatives. "We recognize that problems exist and we are working on them," he added.[34]

On October 13, 1969, the meeting between top personnel from twenty-five Houston public schools and a panel of Mexican American adults was held. Although intended to be a meeting, there was no discussion of the issues. The group of educators merely heard a panel of Mexican American leaders level charges against HISD. José Rojo, an attorney with the Houston Legal Foundation, presented a position paper prepared by UOIC. He argued that there was a pattern of discrimination and harassment against Mexican Americans in the school district. More specifically, he argued that the general feeling by students was that Mexican Americans were fair game for mistreatment or different treatment by teachers and administrators "without fear of retribution." Corporal punishment, for example, was administered too frequently against Mexican Americans and without sufficient reason. Some teachers had a negative or hostile attitude toward Mexican American students and called them names. One junior-high coach, for instance, called Mexican American students "hoods" and "punks." Also teachers, principals, and counselors were insensitive to Mexican American problems.[35]

In addition to evidence of discrimination Rojo provided data indicating the low median years of schooling for the Mexican American population and especially the high rates of student dropouts. According to him 89 percent of the Mexican American pupils in Houston dropped out without finishing high school. This, he said, proved that the district's educators were not doing an adequate job.[36] He recommended the establishment of a task force of educators, parents, student leaders, and others to investigate these charges.[37]

The HISD administration did not immediately respond to these charges at the meeting, but one of its token Mexican American representatives did. Rosemary Saucello, a Houston school district graduate who earned a law degree, disagreed with Rojo's charges and blamed the parents of Mexican American pupils, not the school administration, for the problems of underachievement and high dropout rates. She said heavier penalties should be dealt parents who permitted their children to be absent from school. "Let's do something about the dropout rate even if we have to put the parents in jail," she said. A good number of the HISD-appointed parents, staff, and administrators at the meeting heartily applauded her remarks.[38]

Several days later the HISD administration responded to the charges of discrimination and harassment. The staff vehemently denied the charges of inferior teachers. J. Paul Rodgers, principal at Jeff Davis, stated that teachers at his school had to have the same requirements and qualifications as teachers in other schools. Ken Mueller, principal at San Jacinto, said, "If anyone can cite one instance of discrimination I will personally apologize to the students." "It's too bad the critics don't see what we are doing here before complaining," noted Rodgers.[39]

A select group of Mexican American student leaders at several of the mentioned schools also denied the charges leveled against HISD by middle-class community leaders. Ramiro Marin, age seventeen, senior class president at Jeff Davis, for instance, said he had never been discriminated against in the Houston public schools. Robert Casares, sixteen, junior class president at Jeff Davis, said no junior had ever complained to him about discrimination and harassment. "I feel I'm getting a good education. I respect the school," he noted. Christina Uride, eighteen, a senior and president of the Future Teachers Association at San Jacinto, said she knew of no harassment or discrimination. "I think I'm getting a good education here," she said. José Garza, seventeen, president of the Spanish Club at San Jacinto, stated, "I think the teachers here are good and would teach anywhere." Gracie Solíz, seventeen, a National Honor Society member at San Jacinto, said that she had received encouragement from the teachers. Finally, Delia Salas, seventeen, secretary of the Spanish Club at San Jacinto and student council representative for two years, felt that Mexican Americans got a good education at the school.[40]

Principals Mueller and Rodgers noted how they had tried to institute special courses aimed at Mexican American students. San Jacinto had a Texas history course that emphasized the contributions of "Spanish-speaking citizens" and recently had tried to start a Spanish-language business education course but could not locate a bilingual teacher. Jeff Davis had bilingual courses in Latin American and Mexican history.[41]

School administrators noted that during the current school year they had begun a pilot program in bilingual education in six elementary schools. Both Ben Canales and Antonio Criado, members of UOIC, maintained that these efforts were not enough. "They are trying pilot programs when they should be trying mass programs," Criado said; he added, "The dropout rate for Mexican American students is a crisis and the school administration doesn't recognize it."[42]

Despite the seriousness of these charges, no specific measures were taken to address them by either the board of education or the superintendent. The specific request made by Rojo on October 16, 1969, for the establishment of a task force of educators, parents, student leaders, and others to investigate these charges likewise was ignored. Community leaders found out that local officials were not genuinely interested in addressing the issues of underachievement and discrimination in the schools.

The increased militancy and participation of middle-class leaders were also reflected in the school board elections of November, 1969. Prior to this year only one Mexican American activist, Félix Tijerina, had run for a position; in 1960 he had been an unsuccessful candidate for the school board. His ideological orientation was representative of the Mexican American Generation's thoughts. He said nothing about ethnicity and was opposed to militancy, mass-based mobilization, and radical reform.[43] In November, 1969, when four Chicanos ran for the school board, the election reflected the diverse changes occurring in the Mexican American community and the impact of the emerging Chicano ideology on cultural identity.[44] All of these individuals, for instance, ran as "ethnics," i.e., as Mexican Americans, interested in serving the community. At least three of them believed in the need for more rapid change and in the use of direct action.[45]

Despite these shared sentiments there were also many differences between them and in their personalities. Abraham Ramírez, an activist lawyer and certified public accountant, ran for position one. Also running for the same position was Raul Gutiérrez, a newcomer to Houston who had just retired from the armed forces. He had recently been elected as a representative of the poor to the Harris County Community Action Association Board and was a ROTC teacher at Wheatley High School. He was one of the founders of a grassroots organization that encouraged the use of aggressive tactics in promoting school reforms. Rev. James L. Novarro, a social, civic, and religious leader and founder of *El Sol,* a community newspaper in Houston, was a candidate for position two. Although a political conservative, he supported mass actions, as indicated by his leadership role in the minimum-wage walk conducted on behalf of the south Texas farm-workers in the summer of 1966.[46] The final candidate was Juan Coronado. He originally filed for position three on the ballot but for some unknown reason switched to position four. In the former position he had no significant minority opposition, while in position four he competed with another minority candidate who had a great deal of public support, Rev. Leon Everett.[47]

The desire to influence school policy in general and to address the concerns of discrimination and neglect were the major reasons for running for the school board positions.[48] However, the central issues of discrimination and institutional neglect were immediately forgotten in the battle for votes. The key conflict was between Abe Ramírez and Raul Gutiérrez. The middle-class members of the United Organization Information Center backed Ramírez. This group in turn was part of the political machine of Lauro Cruz, the first Chicano to get elected to the state legislature in 1966. Business and professional organizations and individuals living in the suburban areas of the city thus supported Ramírez. Raul Gutiérrez, on the other hand, was supported by a variety of barrio organizations from the Northside, Second Ward, and Magnolia Park; the Harris County Democrats also supported him. The Ramírez candidacy supported by professionals and businesspeople confronted the Gutiérrez organization supported by the masses of working-class individuals from the barrios. It was a "knocked down, dragged out confrontation" between both individuals and groups who were vying for political hegemony in the community.[49]

Coronado's candidacy was drowned out by Rev. Leon Everett's popular support. Reverend Novarro, in an editorial in *El Sol,* commented on the impact of this conflict on the Mexican American quest for power: "We are seeing a war of fratricide that is splitting the Mexican-American community and creating wounds that will be hard to heal. . . . The turmoil, the conflict and the confusion created by the various personality cults developed and later clash of petty interest is most tragic and indicative of a political infantilism of those that are responsible for this tragedy." "*El Sol,*" Novarro added, "cannot condone nor justify the undermining, character assassinations, fratricidal methods, maneuvers and schemes being carried out expediently and unscrupulously by petty individuals, under the cloak of given organizations."[50]

None of the four individuals who ran for school board positions won. Although all made a "fine showing," the reality indicated that "no one came even close to winning," according to Novarro. In addition to the in-fighting this loss was the result of other more important factors, especially the lack of registered voters. According to most sources, there were from 125,000 to 150,000 Mexican Americans in the metropolitan area. Yet out of that total number only slightly more than 14,000 of them were registered to vote. In addition, all indications were that less than 50 percent actually voted in any one election. According to Novarro, "this reduces the political power of the Mexican-American group as such, to a very small percentage of the total vote that any candidate needs to win a city wide election." "This in itself," he added, "should be a tremendous eye-opener to all self appointed leaders of the Mexican-American destiny in Houston."[51]

THE NEW VOICES OF PROTEST IN HOUSTON

New leaders and new organizations also were founded in Houston during the late 1960s. The new activists began to organize and speak out against discrimination in education in 1967. The initial emphasis of this new type of leadership was evident at the University of Houston campus when several students formed the League of Mexican American Students (LOMAS).[52] LOMAS sought to increase awareness of Chicano issues among students and worked to formulate an intellectual foundation for the emerging activism by students. It brought Chicano leaders such as Corky González to campus and established an intellectual ethos critical of mainstream scholarship concerning Mexican Americans.[53] For several years in the late 1960s LOMAS was an important instrument of consciousness raising and political organizing on the University of Houston campus.[54]

In 1968 militant activism expanded to the nonuniversity community as a result of a Raza Unida Conference held in Houston in April of that year. This was one of a series of conferences organized by the statewide Mexican American Youth Organization (MAYO) to promote awareness and encourage activism in different parts of the state.[55]

MAYO, according to Navarro, was the most effective youth organization in Texas because it brought together barrio youth and students and made them significant forces of change. Its primary purpose was to foster social change in the barrio and to challenge the political, economic, and cultural hegemony of the Anglo ruling elite.[56] MAYO transformed itself into La Raza Unida Party in 1972 and focused entirely on electoral efforts. In the late 1960s, however, MAYO was a significant source of youth and student mobilization and of social and political change.

The MAYO conference in Houston was hosted and planned by Joseph Rojo and George Rivera. Its specific purpose was to bring together leading activists from across the city and to agree on goals and tactics for increasing social change. One of the major outcomes of this highly publicized meeting was the collective call for a "peaceful revolution" for Mexican Americans in Houston and for aggressive action on behalf of *la causa* (the cause).[57]

Although details on who attended, what specific workshops were held, and who spoke are lacking, this conference was successful in directly or indirectly encouraging the founding of Advocating Rights for Mexican American Students (ARMAS) and Las Familias Unidas de Segundo Barrio. The former, probably established in the fall of the 1968–69 school year, was an organization of junior and senior high school students. Its purpose was to bring about school changes that would increase the achievement of Mexican American students.[58] Las Familias Unidas (LFU) de Segundo Barrio, a grassroots organization, was founded soon after the Raza Unida Conference. In the summer of 1968 LFU took up the "revolutionary" cause by protesting the poor city services that plagued that area.[59] The era of radical protest by a new type of grassroots leadership had begun in Houston.

In public education the era of militant protest in Houston began during the 1968–69 school year. Protest activity was initiated by ARMAS, but the context for its actions was shaped by militant developments in other parts of the state. Of particular importance was the walkout by students in south Texas. In the fall of 1968, 192 Chicano students walked out of Edcouch Elsa High School in Hidalgo County because the school board refused to listen to a list of fifteen demands. Sixty-two of the students were expelled, and the newly formed Mexican American Legal Defense and Education Fund (MALDEF) filed suit charging that the expulsion was unconstitutional and violated the students' rights to protest. MALDEF and the students won the suit in December of the same year.[60] In that same month the United States Commission on Civil Rights held several days of hearings in San Antonio, Texas. These hearings focused national attention on the invidious discriminatory practices utilized by most social institutions against Chicanos and Chicanas. A multitude of school policies and practices, especially no-Spanish-speaking rules and tracking, came under sharp criticism at these hearings.[61]

Youth activists supported and publicized these events through several community newspapers, including *El Yaqui, The Compass,* and *Papel Chicano.*[62] In December, for instance, Raul Gutiérrez wrote in support of the

Edcouch Elsa boycott in the first community newspaper established by young people in this period—*The Compass.* Gutiérrez complained that although conditions such as those at Marshall Junior High were bad, "nada [nothing] is being done in Houston." According to him, at Marshall the principals failed to meet on time with parents, there was an intimidating presence of "police protection" at parent meetings with the principal, and the school ignored parental demands, especially one directed at a teacher who was molesting young women. There was neither a Parent-Teacher Association nor a student council. He urged that militant action be taken to correct these injustices. The recent walkout in Edcouch Elsa, he noted, was a reminder for youths in Houston to "do our share."[63]

Several months later ARMAS did take action, marking the students' entry into the local Chicano movement of that era and reflecting an increasing militancy among young people. This moved student activism beyond the politics of accommodation and integration that had been shaped by the Mexican American Generation and the community's middle-class leadership.

ARMAS's first action occurred in March, 1969, after the school board forced cuts in the free lunch program that affected four thousand Mexican children. Mexican American parents protested this action and demonstrated in front of the school administration.[64] ARMAS supported the parents and passed out leaflets in some of the schools. These leaflets asked everyone—"Mothers, high school students, office workers, laborers"—for their support.[65] Although additional funds were eventually provided, local officials did not address the issues of discrimination in the schools and inferior education. This prompted ARMAS to take more radical action.

Sometime during early September, 1969, ARMAS drafted a list of demands for presentation to the HISD administration. This list reflected the new consciousness of cultural nationalism, especially increased racial and cultural pride. It specifically demanded fair treatment for Mexican Americans, the inclusion of Mexican American history and culture in the schools, and the hiring of Chicano counselors "who understand the special problems of Chicanos in high school."[66] In order to gain support and publicity for their demands ARMAS planned a demonstration and a general walkout of the schools.[67] A decision was made to initiate these actions on September 16, a traditional holiday celebrating the anniversary of Mexico's independence from Spain. On this day Chicano students, symbolically speaking, would celebrate their independence from Anglo America.[68]

On Tuesday, September 16, 1969, ARMAS demonstrated in front of Jefferson Davis Senior High School. The principal at Davis, J. Paul Rodgers, requested that they not trespass on school property. The group complied with this request but only after they had read their list of grievances and demands. The demands made by ARMAS were as follows:

1. Initiation of courses on Chicano history and culture, taught by Chicanos, into the regular school curriculum.
2. Stopping the practice of "push-outs"—that is, when counselors whose main concern is to keep order in the school advise students who are disciplinary problems to drop out of school.
3. Hiring of more Chicano counselors, who understand the special problems of Chicanos in high schools and who understand why only 2 percent of the students at the University of Houston are Chicanos while Chicanos comprise over 14 percent of the city's population.
4. Elimination of the "pregnancy list" at Davis High School, a publicly posted list of all girls who have left school because of pregnancy—a vicious form of personal degradation.
5. Lengthening the twenty-minute lunch break allowed at Marshall, since all other schools get at least thirty minutes.[69]

ARMAS members then encouraged students from Davis to join them as they moved their demonstration off school property. Approximately one hundred students walked out of Davis.

Students in support of the ARMAS demands walked out of other schools. At Marshall Junior High approximately seventy-five students walked out, forty students left Hogg Junior High, twenty walked out of San Jacinto Senior High, and twenty left Booker T. Washington Junior-Senior High. A few brave souls from Reagan High also walked out.[70] They all met at Moody Park for a rally to discuss the success of the walkout and to plan for the future.

The principals and faculty at these schools reacted in various ways, most of them negatively. Some principals threatened all the students participating in the walkout with expulsion. A few teachers threatened to use physical force to keep the students in class and viewed the students' demands unworthy of consideration. At San Jacinto Senior High uniformed and plainclothes cops "were everywhere, shouting insults at the students and spoiling for a fight," noted one observer.[71] Some of the teachers grabbed students and shoved them back into classrooms, while others tried to intimidate them by taking down the names of those who were walking out. Other schools, namely Reagan High and Marshall Junior High, were locked up completely and nobody was allowed to go outside.[72] "The students who did escape, however, marched around the high schools encouraging those in sympathy to join them," reported one journalist. Although most students were intimidated by the faculty threats as well as by teachers, many of them expressed verbal support for the walkout.[73]

The walkouts, according to one source, were well planned and executed.[74] They helped ARMAS attain one of its primary goals: to gain support from other students for its demands. According to one source, for instance, more than five hundred students walked out in all and many others showed their support by staying home that day.[75]

But the walkouts failed to have any significant impact on the schools or on the community as did others in different parts of the state or the Southwest. In Los Angeles, for instance, the student strikes of March, 1968, resulted in significant political developments beyond the issues of school reform and contributed to the further enhancement of community organizations. They also acted as the catalyst for the formation of a Chicano student movement as well as the larger Chicano movement of which it became the most important sector.[76] In Crystal City the walkout led to significant reforms in the governance, administration, and content of the public schools as well as to the formation of La Raza Unida Party and the political control by Chicanos of the city and county governments.[77]

Several possible reasons account for this lack of impact on the local community. First, the Houston walkout failed to disrupt the educational process significantly. Few students, in other words, participated in this action. Second, there was no significant leadership or guidance from university students or from seasoned activists in the community. Third, there was little, if any, support from parents and community members in general. A few parents supported the students, but the vast majority of individuals in the community were not even aware of this action taking place. One of the more prominent and active members of MAYO, Poncho Ruíz, for instance, expressed mild surprise years later that ARMAS had conducted a boycott of the Houston public schools in 1969. He did not know that this action had taken place.[78]

Although the boycott was not a catalyst to significant school and social reforms in Houston, it did have some limited impact on community awareness and political mobilization. The greatest impact of the boycott, however, was confined largely to the junior and senior high school students themselves. One observer felt that the students learned an important lesson from these actions: they learned that "if they act together, they can force the administration to acknowledge their demands and respect their Mexican American heritage."[79] But this is misleading, for the school board essentially ignored the issues raised by the students' boycott. Punitive actions were taken against the leaders and followers by expelling or suspending some of them, but nothing was done to acknowledge or address their demands.[80]

Several months after the student boycott a new community group committed to mobilizing against discrimination in the schools was formed. This group, under the leadership of Raul Gutiérrez and Daniel Reséndez, was called Barrios Unidos.[81] On February 13, 1970, this group charged HISD with discrimination, inferior education, and insensitivity toward Chicanos. Barrios Unidos presented the local board with thirteen demands for improving the education of Mexican Americans. Unlike the one drawn up by ARMAS, this list was more comprehensive in proposing changes. It included taking punitive actions against school staff having "negative attitudes toward Mexican American students" (numbers 1 and 2), eliminating the no-Spanish-speaking practices (number 11), and opposing the integration of schools with students who are Mexican American and African American (number 9).[82] Barrios Unidos's list of demands was submitted by Raul Gutiérrez, president, and Daniel Resendez, spokesman, and included the following:

1. Be it understood, where individual negative attitudes toward Mexican American students may prevail among teachers, principals, and counselors [sic], those offenders should not be assigned to a teaching environment where they may directly or indirectly react from such attitudinal conditioning.

2. Appropriate personnel action . . . reprimand, probation, dismissal . . . should be initiated against those persons committing acts of mistreatment and abuse of civil rights of Mexican-American students.

3. Community voice and control of parents' school groups should not be watchdogged by principals and teachers nor should principals have the ultimate power over the parent groups' decisions.

4. Schools should be utilized for community use. Either a junior or senior high school should remain open in each barrio after normal school activities. Barrios Unidos is prepared to sponsor community activities at Marshall and George Washington Junior High Schools.

5. Immediate implementation of a method and schedule by which successful Mexican-Americans and representatives of LOMAS (League of Mexican-American Students) from the University of Houston may address junior and senior high school assemblies in predominantly Mexican-American schools. Identification of students with these persons would serve to improve their aspirations.

6. Curriculum and textbooks should reflect the contributions of Mexican Americans in the Southwest and the country as a whole. We want courses in Mexican-American history, cultural development, and art studies. Works of Mexican-Americans should be placed in the libraries.

7. Accelerate the implementation of bilingual education. Advertise and conduct a sincere recruitment campaign for qualified bilingual teachers, counselors, and principals to be assigned to predominantly Mexican-American schools. Such a recruitment campaign should not be limited to presently employed bilingual teachers of whom many are not assigned to predominantly Mexican-American schools.

8. Begin an immediate replacement of all teachers and principals who have reached retirement age or have served the required number of years toward retirement; and who are now employed at predominantly Mexican-American schools; younger qualified teachers are needed instead of older and mediocre teachers and principals.

9. A school should not be considered integrated where the majority of students are Mexican-American and Negro. The statistical practice of labeling Mexican-American students white is misleading and serves as a technique to disguise minimum efforts in meeting federal integration guidelines. It also serves to isolate two minorities. By practicing ethnic isolation, the school district is creating and ignoring a problem of racial conflict between the two groups. This problem is promulgated by the principals' and teachers' attitude of fear of what the black students might do and indifference towards what the white students do. The result is a manifestation of abuses against Mexican-American students.

10. Senior students unable to financially meet all the unnecessary graduation expenses should not be threatened by the principal with suspension and no diploma. They should be allowed to graduate without all unnecessary expenses.

11. The present practice of punishing and suspending Mexican-American students for speaking Spanish or, as commonly referred to by teaching personnel, "a foreign language," should cease immediately. No school

principal should prohibit Mexican-American students from speaking Spanish on school campus.

12. Eliminate as much as possible at the Junior and Senior High School level, South American, Spain's and Mexican history, replacing it with MEXICAN-AMERICAN HISTORY. . . . CHICANO HISTORY. WE HAVE MUCH TO OFFER.[83]

The demands for school reforms were not presented for the purpose of gaining publicity, noted *El Yaqui,* the newsletter for Barrios Unidos, but "because our children are recipients of very poor quality education, and are the subject of the worst discriminatory practices in [*sic*] the part of teachers, principals, and other students." "Barrios Unidos," it continued, "fully intends to pursue this issue until a balanced educational attitude and program has been developed that will enable the Chicano student to receive quality education, and the treatment and dignity to which he is entitled."[84] As in prior cases, the local board refused to acknowledge these demands and to address them. Once again the Mexican American community was ignored.

CONCLUSION

In Houston, then, school activism in the early 1960s was ad hoc in nature and limited to mostly middle-class organizations. By the end of the decade school activists, especially those from middle- or lower-middle-class organizations, became more militant in their approach. New groups of activists such as barrio youths, students, and grassroots individuals joined the struggle for improved education. Unlike activists from the early 1960s, those in the latter part of the decade criticized established school practices and policies and sought to promote reforms aimed at changing the institution of schooling rather than the child. They condemned discriminatory practices and promoted a variety of reforms aimed at making the schools more humane and more diverse in their curricular offerings, personnel, and governance.

Much of this change resulted from the impact of the Chicano movement. This *movimiento* encouraged increased militancy among established middle-class groups, the formation of new voices of protest, and the promotion of systemic school reform. Despite the increased militant ethos and participation of existing and new groups of activists, local school officials remained indifferent to Mexican American concerns. One of the reasons for this indifference was the lack of unity among activist groups. Each group acted independently of the others and failed to form coordinated actions against school discrimination. The school board's refusal to recognize and tackle the problem of institutional discrimination raised by these activists only increased their disillusionment with public school officials and laid the groundwork for their further radicalization and mobilization. All that was needed was a catalyst to unify them.

Federal court decisions regarding integration during the summer of 1970 provided this catalyst. These federal decisions set the stage for a vigorous response by a united Mexican American community in Houston that would last for the next two years. Local school district intransigence and insensitivity ironically served to sustain the new activism motivated by these unjust federal court rulings. The rumblings of the Mexican American community during the 1960s, then, were a prelude to the coming explosion of political activism of the following decade that quickly developed into a movement of catastrophic proportions.

CHAPTER 5

PAWNS, PUPPETS, AND SCAPEGOATS

Despite the increased involvement of some barrio youth and grassroots activists and the militant rhetoric of the established middle-class groups, in the late 1960s activism in the politics of education was characterized by a lack of unity and limited community involvement. During the summer of 1970 both of these conditions were dramatically transformed as activists focused on the issue of school integration and as significant political unity and mobilization occurred within the Mexican-origin barrios of Houston. Integration not only brought unity to the ideologically diverse activist community, it encouraged all those involved to accept a new ethnic identity and new forms of struggle.

COMMUNITY RESPONSES TO
LOCAL DESEGREGATION POLICIES

The decisions by the federal judiciary and local school board members in a local school integration case, *Ross v Eckels,* were catalysts for the unity of the diverse Mexican American activist community as well as its rapid acceptance of a new racial and political identity. On May 30, 1970, U.S. federal district judge Ben Connally ordered the implementation of an integration plan for Houston that allowed students to attend the schools nearest their homes. This plan, officially known as the equidistant zoning plan, called for the shifting of attendance zones to facilitate integration. The students affected, approximately 40,000 of the district's 245,000 school-age children, would be required to attend schools within the new attendance zone for the 1970–71 school year.[1]

Blacks initiated the Houston integration case in response to the *Brown v Board of Education* decision of 1954. The Ross case, as it was known locally, had been in court for approximately fourteen years. During that entire period the court approached the problem of integration as a black-white issue. For desegregation purposes Mexican American school-age children were officially considered by the court to be "white."[2] The May, 1970, ruling continued this practice despite a growing recognition by various branches of the federal government that these children were an identifiable minority group.[3] In keeping with legal tradition Judge Connally viewed Mexican Americans as white and ruled that they, not Anglos, would have to be integrated with African Americans in the north and east sides of town.

In the initial weeks after the ruling the majority of activists and community members ignored its significance. Unlike in other cities of the Southwest, in Houston school integration and the politics associated with this reform were not important issues in the Mexican American community. As events during the months prior to the May 30 ruling indicated, Mexican American activism in education was focused on obtaining equitable and quality instruction in the schools.[4] The court ruling was viewed as primarily affecting African Americans and Anglos, not Mexican Americans.

By the latter part of June a few activist members of the Mexican American community became aware of the meaning of integration on the east side of town. These activists responded in two major ways to this ruling: one group pursued a legal route; and another group of activists, comprised of grassroots individuals, conducted an intensive educational campaign in the community, informing the parents about the injustice of the court's decision and the need to have it changed. Regardless of the approach taken, it took several weeks for many in the community to realize the unjust nature of this integration plan. Ironically, barrio youths and students were either unaware of the importance of this decision to the Mexican American community or decided not to take any action against it. Barrio-MAYO (Mexican American Youth Organization), between February and April, 1970, was heavily involved in a series of dramatic episodes in the community that took most of its time. In February, for instance, Barrio-MAYO took over the Juan Marcos Presbyterian Church for thirteen days, complaining that the church's program for the barrio was too spiritual and did not address its members' full needs. The following month the organization demonstrated in front of the First Presbyterian Church and disrupted its church services to protest the church's failure to develop programs to meet the social needs of the barrio. During April the group interrupted a LULAC political rally at Our Lady of Guadalupe Church, jeered Gov. Preston Smith at the annual San Jacinto ceremony honoring the victory of Texan troops over Mexican troops in 1836, and disrupted a University of Houston law school conference on Mexican American affairs.[5] On the other hand, members of University of Houston–MAYO (UH-MAYO) and probably of ARMAS as well had just begun their summer vacation and were not enrolled in any classes at the university or in the public schools. For these and probably other unknown reasons the most militant members of the Mexican American activist community did not immediately respond to this court decision.

Community awareness of injustice in education increased toward the latter part of July and early August. This awareness was influenced by a multitude of actions on the part of a few community activists, local school officials, and the federal courts. Abraham Ramírez, Jr., was particularly important in increasing community awareness of the unjust nature of integration. Ramírez was a well-known activist lawyer in the Mexican American community and had run for the school board in November, 1969. He upheld the ideals and politics of the Mexican American Generation but was willing to use more assertive strategies and tactics in school reform.[6]

The *Cisneros v Corpus Christi Independent School District* case particularly influenced Ramírez. Mexican American and African American labor activists from the Corpus Christi area filed this case in 1968.[7] These minority parents complained that the local district was discriminating against both groups by maintaining a segregated school system and by integrating blacks with Mexican Americans. With respect to the latter charge the parents complained that "the district violated court orders by mixing their children in classrooms, but not Anglo children."[8]

Unlike the activists of the past, the lawyers in the *Cisneros* case sought to take advantage of the legal principles developed since *Brown* was decided in 1954 and to apply them to Mexican Americans. They abandoned the "white" legal strategy used by LULAC and the American G.I. Forum during the 1940s and 1950s to eliminate segregation and substituted the equal protection argument used in black desegregation cases. Most federal, state, and local policies before 1954 mandated or sanctioned the separation of blacks and whites but said nothing about same-race segregation. Mexican Americans thus sought acceptance of their own group as Caucasian or white in order to prove that in the absence of a statute allowing segregation of Mexican Americans, any attempt by local school officials to separate them would be a violation of law.[9]

In order for Mexican Americans to apply the *Brown* findings of Fourteenth Amendment violations to themselves, they had to win judicial recognition as a separate class or as an identifiable minority—that is, a group classified as having unalterable congenital traits, political impotence, and the attachment of a stigma of inferiority. Despite overwhelming evidence that they constituted a separate class of whites throughout the Southwest, the Supreme Court had not made significant rulings to that effect.[10] The lawyers for the Mexican American community thus had to gain court recognition of this status. Once they established this classification, they could proceed to establish a prima facie case of discrimination based upon direct evidence of segregative state action and statistical evidence of an unconstitutional degree of segregation.[11]

Mexican American plaintiffs in *Cisneros* effectively argued these issues and laid the basis for changing the legal framework under which future desegregation cases would be decided. In early June, 1970, Judge Woodrow Seals found that on the basis of their physical characteristics, Spanish language, Catholic religion, distinct culture, and Spanish surnames, Mexican Americans were an identifiable ethnic minority group for desegregation purposes and that *Brown* applied to them. Judge Seals also ruled that Mexican Americans and blacks were unconstitutionally segregated "in all three levels of the school system" and that state action was responsible for this.[12] In direct reference to the issue of integrating Mexican and African American children, but not Anglos, the court ruled: "The court is of the opinion that by placing Negroes and Mexican-Americans in the same school does not achieve a unitary system as contemplated by law. A unitary school district can be achieved here only by substantial integration of the Negroes and Mexican American with the remaining student population of the district."[13] He then ruled that an appropriate desegregation plan that included Anglos, Mexican Americans, and blacks be submitted to him as soon as possible.[14]

This finding was a significant one for educational equality since it introduced a new group into the national desegregation process. Federal courts now had to consider Mexican American students in determining whether a unitary school system was in operation.

Abraham Ramírez, Jr., saw the implications of this finding on the local desegregation case. A week after the *Cisneros* decision he wrote to Mario Obledo, general counsel of MALDEF in San Antonio, Texas, that the local federal court in the *Ross* case had failed to "recognize the Mexican American as a minority." Failure to consider this group a minority led to the development of a desegregation remedy that was discriminatory since it paired "white" Mexican Americans with African Americans. "I feel that your office should immediately study the court's opinion and file an appeal, if necessary, without delay," he added.[15]

Three days later Obledo responded that a lawyer would be assigned to study the opinion. In late July, Alan Exelrod, the lawyer assigned by MALDEF to investigate this issue, wrote to Ramírez requesting materials for making a presentation to the Fifth Circuit Court of Appeals. He acknowledged that the equidistant plan of the school district made no differentiation between the Anglo and the Mexican American "in the white category." "In order to show the effect of the equi-distant zoning plan [*sic*] on Mexican Americans," he noted, "we need the absolute numbers and percentage of Mexican Americans in the white category for each school in the district." He further added: "If the school does not have this information, then try to determine whether they have a list of students which will be attending each school. Should this list exist, the Spanish surnames can be counted and a relatively accurate figure for Mexican-American concentration of students can be determined." Exelrod realized that he was asking a lot of Ramírez, "but it is the only way we can help the Court of Appeals understand the situation."[16]

In response to his request Ramírez compiled a report on the numbers and percentages of Mexican Americans in the schools.[17] In this report Ramírez provided enrollment data for the elementary, junior high, and senior high schools on the basis of race and ethnicity.[18] He also made some observations on emerging Mexican American complaints, on the dilemma of Mexican American parents who could not get transfers out of their minority schools due to the particular provisions of the integration plan, and on the advice he had been giving to Mexican Americans who called him on these issues.[19] He paid close attention to the possible impact integration might have on the predominantly Mexican schools and on the predominantly African American schools.

According to Ramírez, there were forty-eight elementary schools in which the fall, 1969, enrollment was predominantly Mexican American, but in only ten of these was there an increase in black enrollment. At the

Table 2. Actual and Proposed Black Enrollment in Predominantly Mexican American Schools for Fall, 1969, and Fall, 1970

School	% Mexican American	No. of blacks enrolled fall, 1969	No. of blacks enrolled fall, 1970*	Increase in black enrollment
1. Bowie	n/a	696	809	+113
2. Milam	n/a	77	213	+136
3. Rusk	98	0	53	+ 53
4. Crockett	91	13	68	+ 55
5. Lee	91	7	49	+ 42
6. Dow	85	51	334	+283
7. Sherman	82	132	153	+ 21
8. Eliot	78	80	892	+812
9. Pugh	72	11	86	+ 75
10. Port Houston	65	27	66	+ 39
Subtotals:		1,094	2,723	1,629
11. Edison Junior High	n/a	45	129	+ 84
12. Davis High	n/a	298	544	+246
Subtotals:		343	673	330
Totals:		1,437	3,396	1,959

*Numbers in this category are estimates.

Source: Abe Ramírez, letter to A. Exelrod, Aug., 1970, Abe Ramírez Collection, Box 1, No. 22, HMRC.

junior high level there were three schools that were predominantly Mexican American—Edison, Marshall, and McReynolds Junior High Schools. Only Edison had an increase in the number of blacks enrolled as a result of the equidistant plan. At the high school level only Davis High School would get an increase of blacks.[20] These schools and their increases in black enrollment are shown in table 2.[21]

In sum, Ramírez found that the numbers of black students in some of the predominantly Mexican American schools were projected to increase with the implementation of the equidistant plan. Because of the imprecise nature of his data, he had less success in determining how many Mexican American students would be enrolled in predominantly black schools. "Sometimes it is impossible to guess what the Mexican American enrollment is going to be under the Equidistant Plan [sic]," he noted. In the case of Harper Elementary School, for instance, the principal reported a black enrollment of 361 African Americans in the fall of 1969 and no Mexican American or other white students. The equidistant plan, however, projected an enrollment of 296 black students and 245 whites. Were the latter Mexican Americans or Anglos? "Definitely, the HEW report gives us no basis to even guess or estimate a working figure," noted Ramírez.[22]

Despite the inaccuracy of the figures, Ramírez argued that in his view "white" was synonymous with Mexican American. Although he had "nothing to back my statement," Ramírez did indicate that the housing patterns of the last decade in Houston were such that they "would give some credence to the integration of Mexican Americans and blacks in the schools."[23]

Once MALDEF received this report the decision was made to get involved in the Houston case. The data as well as the arguments and conclusions reached by Ramírez were eventually incorporated into a formal appeal that was then filed on August 11, 1970. On this date MALDEF filed an amicus curiae (friend of the court) brief with the U.S. Fifth Circuit Court asking that the disputed Houston school desegregation plan take into account Mexican American students. Upon filing the legal brief Ramírez said, "We want to know where we stand." "For instance," he continued, "if a school is to have 555 Negroes and 395 whites, we want to know— whites or Mexican Americans?"[24]

The suit contended that Mexican Americans comprised over 13 percent of the student population. However, there was no attempt to develop for the Houston Independent School District (HISD) any information concerning where the Mexican American children attended school; whether school zone lines were drawn, intentionally or unintentionally, to segregate Mexican Americans and blacks; or whether segregated housing patterns "inhibited the Mexican American's exodus from the barrio."[25] More specifically, the suit argued that Mexican Americans comprised a distinct, identifiable minority group; that this group had suffered discrimination in the schools throughout the Southwest; that the conditions existing in other parts of Texas also existed in HISD; and that there were philosophical and psychological reasons for including Mexican Americans in the desegregation of schools. The suit offered no specific desegregation plan but asked that the present plan before the Fifth Circuit Court be remanded for additional hearings.[26]

Community awareness of injustice in the integration plan emerged gradually. It began after the school board reprinted, "as a public service," thousands of copies of the court's implementing decree on June 30, 1970. This decree provided the school district with instructions on how to implement the desegregation order. It delineated the roles and responsibilities of local officials and stipulated what needed to be done in several areas, including faculty and staff, transportation, school construction and site selection, attendance outside of established school zones, extracurricular activities, student assignment, and transfer policies. The decree also ordered the establishment of a court-appointed Bi-Racial Committee to oversee this implementation. Under the decree each student, with some exceptions, was to attend a school nearest his or her residence but a different one from the year before. Most important for the Mexican American community, the decree discontinued transfers from the schools in the new zones to any other schools within the district.[27]

The elimination of these transfers had a significant impact on a few select parents and students. Prior to this plan an undetermined number of Mexican American parents sent their children away from the neighborhood schools to attend schools with more resources in the Anglo community. Under the desegregation mandate a student was allowed to transfer voluntarily "from a school in which his race is in the majority to the nearest school in which his race is in the minority."[28] In practice this meant that Mexican Americans, who were legally defined as "white," could only transfer to "black" schools in which their race was in the minority. They were forbidden to transfer from a predominantly Mexican American school to an Anglo school. These new restrictions meant, then, that Mexican American students, for the most part, now had to attend schools within the zones defined by the local board, even if those schools were inferior ones in the ghetto.[29]

Some of the parents affected by this decree began to complain privately. A few took their complaints to Abraham Ramírez, Jr., as he was collecting data for MALDEF's appeal to the Fifth Circuit Court.[30] Most of the other parents and students in the community became aware of the unjust nature of desegregation in early July when local officials redrew the new attendance zones to reflect the court's mandate and listed the new schools that students were supposed to attend during the 1970–71 school year. With these actions minority parents and students realized that in their neighborhoods black-white integration meant the placement of Mexican American students with African American students. Mexican American parents opposed this type of integration in their community and began to complain. Probably because of his role in the collection of data for MALDEF, Ramírez received many of these individuals' complaints.[31] In a letter to MALDEF on August 2, 1970, he noted that Mexican American parents were claiming that "they are being forced to send their children to Black schools." These schools, he added, had "inadequate facilities, supplies, [and] equipment."[32]

In addition to their concern that their children would be attending sub-standard schools, the parents were also worried that their children had to go into the black ghettos. "While this is not bad on the surface, the situation is horrible taking in consideration the Black militant confrontation with the Houston police," noted Ramírez. "There have been killings and fights already in the Black community, and the situation promises to get worse," he added.[33]

While some parents complained, others organized and raised questions about the content of the integration plan. They reached the conclusion that local school officials were using Mexican Americans for political reasons. Their growing consciousness was in all probability influenced by Ramírez's research and arguments as well as by their own meanings and reflections.

Representative of the community's interpretation of the desegregation plan were the comments made by Lorenzo P. Díaz. Díaz was a community activist from the Northside, one of the barrios most affected by the court's plan. Davis Senior High and Marshall Junior High, both located in the Northside, for instance, were two of the schools receiving significant numbers of African American students under the district's desegregation plan.[34] Díaz was incensed by this ruling and accused the local school board of using Mexican Americans as "pawns, puppets, and scapegoats" just to make it appear as if HISD were abiding by the Supreme Court mandate to integrate the schools. "All HISD is doing in the Northside is integrating two minority races, Mexican Americans and negroes, while in other areas it still left some schools almost all anglo or all black," Díaz stated.[35]

In many respects Díaz's perspective was similar to MALDEF's, but his was more poignant. He articulated a clear and coherent interpretation of the district's political uses of Mexican Americans embodied in the integration plan. White political leaders, especially the "liberal" slate of school board members, were publicly committed to complying with integration but did not want to inconvenience Anglo parents and students. A partial solution to this dilemma was found if they used the "white" status of Mexican Americans to integrate the public schools. Labeling Mexican Ameri-

cans white and integrating them with blacks eased the burden of involving greater numbers of Anglo children in the desegregation remedy. The
other white population thus would not be greatly inconvenienced in the
process.[36]

Mexican American groups and individuals, such as MALDEF, Díaz,
and others in the community, were not fooled by the school board's strategy. They realized how they were being used and urged the community to
mobilize against this treatment. However, not all individuals responded
vocally and publicly to the injustice of the integration plan. Some responded in highly personal ways. David Ybarra, a student who lived in El
Segundo barrio and attended Jackson Junior High, for instance, was dis-
appointed with the decision. Under the integration plan he was supposed
to attend E. O. Smith or Lyons, both predominantly black schools. "But
I'm not," he noted; "I'm going to try to move into the Jackson area." He
further noted that if he could not move into this area he would "stop going" to school. Mario Torres, who attended one of the predominantly
Mexican schools in the Denver Harbor area, noted that he was supposed
to attend Wheatley under the integration plan. "Too many Blacks," he argued, stating that if the Mexicans enrolled in that school, "there's going to
be trouble. Fights." [37]

The editorial staff of *Papel Chicano,* a newly founded community newspaper that expressed the sentiments of barrio youth activists, quickly challenged sentiments of defeatism and withdrawal.[38] The publication specifically urged all students and parents to speak up about the injustice of this
integration plan and to oppose its implementation. "This issue cannot be
faced by dropping out," students and parents were reminded. "Go back to
school and fight for our rights to a decent education and not be used as the
flunkies of the school system." [39]

One group of individuals took this advice seriously and founded a new
organization to channel their frustrations and to challenge the integration
plan. In early August, Mexican American parents and students from the
Looscan Elementary School area in the Northside barrio organized the
Northside Mexican American Civic Organization (NMACO). This group,
according to the chairperson, was organized in order "to use every legal
way to fight the injustices committed by the plan against the Mexican
American." The chair added, "We will work with any group that will help
our cause." In its efforts to fight the integration plan the organization set
out to unite community groups from other parts of town, including Magnolia Park, Denver Harbor, Bonita Gardens, and Manchester.[40]

During the month of August the Northside group engaged in a variety of educational and protest activities. On August 12, 1970, for instance, a meeting was held to inform the community about the pros and cons of the desegregation plan and the options available. At that meeting Abraham Ramírez, Jr., encouraged a variety of organized actions against the integration plan, including a legal strategy aimed at recognizing Mexican Americans as an identifiable minority group for desegregation purposes.[41] Five days later, on Monday, August 17, NMACO took to the streets. With the support of about one hundred Mexican American parents and students the group picketed Looscan Elementary School to protest the equidistant zoning plan.[42] On August 24 NMACO held another informational meeting at Saint Patrick's Church hall. At that meeting Ramírez informed the group that Chicanos from the Sixth Ward and Denver Harbor would boycott HISD. "What followed," noted one of the participants, "was una cosa de unidad [a thing of unity]." Lorenzo Díaz, chair of NMACO, voiced support for the boycott and the willingness of the group he represented to engage in oppositional actions in order to protest the integration plan. "It's time for us to dissent in a proper manner," he noted; "moving and running away is not the solution to the problem." Díaz concluded that if a boycott occurred it would be against the equidistant plan, not against equal integration.[43]

The conditions for assuming a new identity and for utilizing more radical means to fight injustice in the integration plan were present. What was needed was an additional catalyst to enhance this process. This occurred in late August with the ruling by the Fifth Circuit Court on MALDEF's petition.

THE FIFTH CIRCUIT COURT AND COMMUNITY RESPONSES

After August 25, 1970, the dynamics of community involvement changed rapidly. On this date the U.S. Fifth Circuit Court denied MALDEF's petition for intervenor status and ignored its arguments for considering Mexican Americans as an identifiable minority group for desegregation purposes.[44] That court also modified the lower court's ruling and ordered the pairing of twenty-five elementary schools.[45] The ruling ironically exposed, in starker terms, the unjust nature of the Houston integration plan, since it specifically identified the schools to be paired. As community members quickly found out, they were mostly minority schools, fourteen of which

Table 3. List of Schools to Be Paired, August 25, 1970

Predominantly Black Schools		Predominantly Mexican American Schools
Ryan and Ross	pair with	Looscan
Bruce	pair with	Anson Jones
Atherton	pair with	Eliot*, Scroggins*
Burrus	pair with	Roosevelt+
Crawford	pair with	Sherman*
Dodson	pair with	Lantrip
J. W. Jones	pair with	Fannin
Henderson	pair with	Pugh*
Pleasantville	pair with	Port Houston*
Rhodes	pair with	Frost
Sanderson	pair with	Easter and/or Chatham
Poe++	pair with	MacGregor++

* a school most affected by boycotts in September, 1970
+ a predominantly Anglo school
++ a predominantly black school

Source: Ross v Eckels, 434 F.2d 1140 (Fifth Cir., August 25, 1970).

were predominantly black while nine were predominantly Mexican American (see table 3). One of these schools, Roosevelt, was predominantly Anglo, although it did enroll some Mexican American students.

This pairing decision incensed most sectors of the Mexican American activist community as no other single event had done and served to unite them around the issue of integration. Moderate middle-class activists, militant youths, and grassroots individuals as well as many members of the Mexican-origin community not actively involved opposed this decision. Martin G. Castillo, chair of the president's Cabinet Committee on Opportunity for the Spanish Speaking (CCOSS) and a moderate middle-class activist, best expressed the community's sentiment when he criticized the Houston integration plan as "indefensible from an educational and legal point of view."[46] He noted, "There can be no enrichment or equality of opportunity in a situation which requires consolidating two disadvantaged groups" and further added: "The Spanish-speaking child has suffered too many years from linguistic isolation and unrealistic educational techniques. The Black child has suffered too many years of segregation and educational deprivation. To expect that anything resembling education can result from joining these tragic consequences under the guise of desegregation is asking too much." [47]

Other moderate and militant activists in the community criticized the integration plan and argued that the pairing plan was unjust in two major respects. First, it integrated blacks with Chicanos—two relatively powerless groups attending similarly inferior schools. Second, it excluded Anglos from the integration plan in the east side of town. For instance, "In the Looscan pairing," noted one of the activists writing for the community newspaper, "an all Anglo school close by was completely left out while Looscan was paired with two black elementaries." [48]

MAYO responded by arguing that while the district simply declared Mexican Americans white for the purpose of integration, Chicanos knew that they were not white. He said, "They can tell by looking in a mirror." Chicanos, however, were intelligent and knew what the district was doing to them. "They also have pride in themselves and enough courage not to let this great whitewash game be run on them," MAYO stated. [49]

Students and parents from the community also were angry over the integration order. Some high school students from Denver Harbor and Magnolia Park were upset that large numbers of them were being forced to attend Wheatley High, a predominantly black school. Other students complained that "Manchester and Looscan [Elementary] communities were chopped down the middle for integration purposes." In many cases, one of them said, "parents were very upset about difficult transportation problems because of railroad tracks, freeways, busy streets, and general problems of inconvenience for their children." [50] Lorenzo Díaz complained that the integration plan "just disturbs the educational life of the people and serves no purpose at all." [51]

Community responses to the court ruling suggest a coalescing of the various strains of activist thought and action in the Mexican-origin community. All those involved in the community— students, barrio youths, middle-class leaders, and working-class individuals—as well as those not previously involved in social change came together on this issue. Their actions also suggest another trend: the rejection of the community's white racial identity and the acceptance of a new one. The content of this new identity, however, was in doubt and varied between groups and individuals. Lawyers argued for an identity based on legal principles. Castillo aptly expressed this sentiment when he stated that the courts should recognize that, for educational purposes, Mexican American and African American children were part of two distinct minorities. "We need the highest courts of the land to put all speculation on this point to rest," he further noted.[52] MAYO members such as Gregory Salazar and Poncho Ruíz, however, argued that Mexican Americans were of indigenous origin; they were "brown," not white. Other individuals, especially those who had not been active before, simply argued that they were "Chicanos" or Mejicanos.[53] Although disagreement existed on the contents of the new identity, most if not all of the activists agreed that the label "white" was not accurate anymore.

In addition to rejecting their white status, many activists also abandoned the politics of accommodation utilized by members of the Mexican American Generation. The vast majority of the activists involved in integration came to accept the legitimacy of direct action tactics such as demonstrations, protest, and pickets. The formation of the Mexican American Education Council (MAEC), a community organization of individuals from many of the barrios impacted by the desegregation plan, became important in the acceptance of this new identity and in the rejection of the politics of accommodation. Once formed it became the mechanism for expanding and diffusing the new racial and political identity of the Mexican-origin community in the barrios of Houston. More specifically, MAEC provided collective definitions of conditions as unjust and mutable and strengthened collective perceptions of efficacy by creating awareness of the large number of actual and potential supporters. MAEC not only identified the institutional wrong, it also developed effective and assertive cultural and political strategies for correcting that wrong.

MAEC AND THE PROMOTION OF A NEW IDENTITY

A variety of individuals incensed by the Fifth Circuit Court's pairing order called for a citywide community meeting on Thursday, August 27, 1970, to decide what action they might take. A large number of individuals representing a variety of barrios and both moderate and militant organizations attended the meeting. Out of twenty known members, eleven of them were women.[54]

Several key decisions impacting the education struggle were made at this meeting. First, those assembled decided to form a new organization comprised of all the community groups affected by the integration plan. The name chosen for this group was Mexican American Education Council, or MAEC.[55] Five barrios or neighborhoods were represented in the organization: El Dorado, Manchester, Denver Harbor, Northside, and Clayton Homes. In the coming days additional barrios would be added to the group. Also represented were the militant groups within the city, including two chapters of MAYO and Barrios Unidos. Membership of MAEC was listed as follows:

1. El Dorado barrio: Juanita Hernandez, Isidro Meze
2. Manchester barrio: G. Guzman, Mario Quinones, Elvia Quinones, Mrs. Margaret Guzman
3. Denver Harbor barrio: Martha Gonzalez, Virginia Pena, Ben Reyes, Tony Reyes, Eva Gonzalez, Ernest O. Garcia (?)
4. Northside barrio: Maria Resendez, Carmen Beltran, Marcelina Diaz, Lorenzo P. Diaz
5. Clayton Homes barrio: Josephine Rodriguez (?)
6. Unknown: Bill Gutierrez, Mr. and Mrs. Abe Ramirez
7. Barrio-MAYO: Gregory Salazar and Yolanda Garza Birdwell
8. UH-MAYO: Jaime De La Isla
9. Barrios Unidos: Abel Alvarez.[56]

Besides the MAYO chapters and Barrios Unidos, no other organizations participated in an official capacity in MAEC. While middle-class organizations such as LULAC, the American G.I. Forum, and PASSO were not officially represented, individual members from these organizations were actively involved in MAEC.[57] A major reason for their lack of formal participation was MAEC's structure, which was organized on the basis of barrios and individuals representing those residential areas. If middle-class individuals such as Abe Ramírez, president of LULAC Council 60, participated in MAEC, it was as a barrio representative rather than as a member of an established community organization.[58]

The purpose of MAEC was to promote education in the community, but in actuality it served to develop a united and organized response to the desegregation decision. MAEC also served as a basis for articulating issues and for formulating and implementing varied strategies for ensuring educational justice. MAEC soon came to dominate the struggle against unjust desegregation. Those at the meeting also decided to support the legal challenge to the *Ross* case, and Abe Ramírez would be in charge of the lawsuit.

Finally, the group agreed to meet with the board and to negotiate members' concerns. A list of demands was drawn up to be presented to the board for resolution. Although this list included twenty demands, the key demand was recognition of the Mexican-origin population as a distinct minority group. MAEC also drew up a press release announcing the formation of the organization and its effort to seek "active participation in the integration plans in the School District." [59]

The following day MAEC met with several school officials to present its concerns and list of demands. Between two hundred and three hundred Mexican American parents and children demonstrated in front of the school district central administration building, and several members of the council met with school board members. [60] The picketers, many of them mothers, carried signs demanding "justice" for their children and declaring themselves to be "Brown, not white." While in the picket lines they chanted "We're a minority too" and "We want justice or we won't go to school." [61]

Inside the administration building several MAEC members, including Abe Ramírez, Leonel Castillo, Mrs. Marcelina Díaz, Mrs. Elvia Quiñones, Bill Gutiérrez, and Gregory Salazar, met with three school officials. [62] The majority of these individuals were moderates or novice activists; Salazar was the only militant voice in the group. They met with Dr. Leonard Robbins, president of the school board; George Oser, chair of the board's desegregation committee; and Dr. George G. Garver, general superintendent of HISD.

During the meeting community members voiced their complaints to the board. Mrs. Díaz from the Northside focused on the problem of transportation. According to the integration plan, most Mexican American children paired would not be provided free transportation. They either had to walk to their new schools or the parents had to provide them with transportation. She explained the danger to the children when they had to cross railroad tracks, busy streets, and other dangerous crossings. She also tried to explain how difficult it would be to provide transportation to the children in communities where cars were often unavailable. Mrs. Elvia Quiñones emphasized again the difficulties of transportation and the separation of families with several children in the elementary schools. Bill Gutiérrez asked questions about the legal aspects of the integration order and referred them to the *Corpus Christi* decision in which the courts ruled that Mexican Americans were identified as a legal minority with the rights of a minority. Gregory Salazar spoke about the cultural differences and how few teachers were available who understood the problems and culture of the Chicanos. He also pointed out the difficulties in establishing special programs such as bilingual education at the new schools.[63]

After the community members spoke Abe Ramírez presented a list of MAEC's four major demands: (1) increase Mexican American representation on the court-appointed Bi-Racial Committee that had five Anglos and five blacks; (2) increase Mexican American representation on the HISD integration committee; (3) file a legal appeal of the pairing plan; and (4) declare Mexican Americans a legal minority "with the rights that accompany a minority."[64]

Responses by the school board members and the superintendent were, in the words of two community members, "negative and uncooperative."[65] The school board members, for instance, "hemmed and hawed" about the first three demands.[66] All three stated that they would not consider helping with transportation problems despite the difficulties faced by poor families. Oser said that considerations were being given to the nominations of Mexican Americans to the court-appointed Bi-Racial Committee but not as many as MAEC requested. Abe Ramírez said that MAEC wanted three or four of the white members of this committee to be Mexican American, but Oser disagreed with this recommendation. He also noted that two Mexican American representatives were members of the board-appointed desegregation committee. MAEC apparently did not feel that this was an adequate number or that these Mexican Americans represented the community's interests.[67]

The superintendent argued against the appeal. He said that the school administration could not change the directive of the U.S. Fifth Circuit Court of Appeals to pair twenty-five elementary schools nor did the district have unlimited discretion to change zone boundaries. Of the twenty-five schools to be paired under the higher court directive, fifteen of them were predominantly black, nine were predominantly Mexican American, and one of them, Roosevelt, was predominantly Anglo. The total number of students to be involved in the pairing decision was unavailable, but most understood that while large numbers of minority students would be affected, only a few Anglos would be. According to one estimate, at least 5,657 Mexican American students would be affected by the pairing order.[68] Despite the large number of blacks and Chicanos affected, the administration was unwilling to consider modifying the ruling or appealing it.[69]

Oser likewise flatly rejected the fourth demand to declare Mexican Americans a distinct minority. His answer to this demand was, as reported in *Papel Chicano,* "a flat no." Board president Leonard Robbins for the most part opposed these demands and during the discussion walked out of the meeting.[70]

After the official meeting was over about twenty-five MAEC members caucused at the administration building. Angered by the school board's unwillingness to meet their demands, they unanimously decided that the only alternative available to them, other than to file a legal suit in the courts, was to engage in radical action. After much heated debate the group unanimously decided to "advise Mexican American parents to keep their children home from school on opening day Monday to protest pairing of 25 elementary schools." Ramírez added, "The Mexican American children would stay home as long as necessary to see if the administration will respond with the proper solution."[71]

Those present agreed to announce the boycott at a press conference the following morning and to call for a mass meeting of Mexican Americans at 4 P.M. Sunday in the El Dorado section of northeast Houston to explain their decision to the community.[72] The most militant members of MAEC—two members from MAYO and two from PASO—agreed to conduct the press conference. After some objections from Lucy Moreno about the lack of females on the roster, she was asked to be there.[73]

Despite the unanimity of the decision, some MAEC members did not want to boycott the schools. They told Castillo and Ramírez, who were acting as spokespersons for the group, that this was not a good idea after all. "The worst thing to do," one person noted, "was to take kids out of school." The group should reconsider their decision, another person said. None of these comments, however, was said in front of the militants for fear of being reprimanded by them.[74] Rather, they were "whispered" to Castillo and Ramírez after the meeting ended. After listening to these concerns Abe Ramírez and Leonel Castillo began to have doubts about the boycott and thought that maybe they should reconsider this decision. Ramírez also voiced his concerns to Leonel Castillo about what the militants might say at the press conference on Saturday morning. He convinced Castillo to dissuade them from holding the press conference on Saturday. However, Castillo arrived at the event late because of a prior commitment, and by the time he got to the press conference it had begun. Unable to encourage its cancellation, Castillo joined in and became a part of the event. There was no backing down now; MAEC was committed to boycotting the public schools.[75] Toward the end of the press conference the participants announced the rally to be held on Sunday, August 30, 1970, at El Dorado Park where further information would be provided to the Mexican American community.

Under cloudy skies on Sunday afternoon between one thousand and four thousand Chicanos showed up at Saint Philip of Jesus Catholic Church grounds for a rally in support of the boycott.[76] Its purpose was to protest the pairing plan to equalize the racial balance in the schools. Rally speakers included Leonel Castillo, Gregory Salazar, Lorenzo Díaz, Abe Ramírez, Tina Reyes, and a spokesperson from the University of Houston MAYO.[77] Before the rally began those in charge argued that MAEC needed a chairperson. The only person who had time to lead such a group was Leonel Castillo. He worked with the Catholic Diocese and had some "free" time. Although he had plans of going to law school that fall, Castillo was chosen temporary spokesperson of MAEC until the group could meet to choose a permanent one. Once this decision was made, the rally continued.[78]

Bill Gutiérrez served as master of ceremonies and conducted the rally "with poise and dignity as people climbed on and off the stage and speakers came and went." Those present at the rally knew the seriousness of the decision to boycott the schools. "Most were committed and determined," noted one of the observers, "but each had their [sic] own fears and hesitations, and each hoped that the Raza that was not affected directly, would stand behind their own children in the struggle for recognition."[79]

Leonel Castillo began the event by explaining the school board's refusal to recognize Chicanos as a separate ethnic group and the reasons behind the boycott. "This is a very serious thing—we understand that—and we are committed to go ahead with it," he said to "thunders of applause." "How many of those paired schools (in the integration order) are Anglo?" he asked the crowd. "Zero," the audience responded. He pointed out that out of the twenty-five schools paired, nine of them were predominantly Mexican American and fourteen were predominantly black. "So who's being integrated?" he asked.[80]

Abe Ramírez followed Castillo and discussed the legal aspects of the boycott. He told the crowd that parents could not be arrested for keeping their children out of school. State law required that children attend school for 165 days a year, but according to him, it did not say which days or which schools. Private school attendance was an acceptable option.

Tina Reyes, newly appointed chair of the huelga school committee, then explained the program of private schools, called huelga *escuelas,* that MAEC would establish. Huelga schools were community learning institutions whose purpose would be to continue the children's education during the duration of the boycott.[81] Reyes noted that many volunteer teachers had already been contacted. She urged the parents, especially mothers, to take their children to libraries and to educate them at home, "especially during the first part of this week while the MAEC schools are being organized." A spokesperson for University of Houston MAYO informed the cheering crowd that college students would be available as tutors.[82]

Others briefly expressed their thoughts on the boycott and explained what their own communities were doing. Lorenzo Díaz, speaking on behalf of the Northside Mexican American residents, charged HISD with a history of discrimination and spoke of the new integration plan as "the last straw." "We can take no more—we're going to do something about it," he declared at the rally. Gregory Salazar also drew cheers when he charged that the school administration was classifying Mexican American children as white to effect integration with blacks without inconveniencing Anglos. "Now, because it is convenient to them," he argued, "we're white." "But what about when you apply for a job?" he asked; "what color are you then?"[83]

At the rally approximately $571 was collected for operating the huelga schools. Names and addresses of volunteer boycott workers were also gathered. MAEC informed the crowd of the planned activities for the following day. The first day of the boycott would include picketing of the school administration building and several Mexican American schools, morning and evening outdoor rallies, and an attempt to pack the Monday night school board meeting. All were encouraged to participate, and the rally ended on an exuberant note.[84]

CONCLUSION

The first major action in the contemporary struggle against unjust integration had been taken. The seeds of disillusionment of the past two years now burst forth and rapidly grew to become a united but tension-riddled movement of mass protest against educational inequality. During the next several weeks the community's level of participation in this major event exploded as MAEC brought together moderate, militant, and novice activists to lead one of the largest mass actions against educational inequality in the city's history. The challenge in the weeks to come was keeping all these diverse strains of activism united and focused on winning the struggle for recognition. The boycott and its associated activities provided the first great challenge to MAEC and its leadership. The following chapter discusses the initial actions taken during the first three weeks of the boycott and how MAEC's leadership balanced the diversity of activist thought in the struggle for recognition in the schools.

Pairing for whom? Men, women, and youth picketing HISD on behalf of
MAEC's demand for recognition, Friday, August 28, 1970. Courtesy *Houston
Chronicle,* Houston Metropolitan Research Center.

MAEC press conference calling for boycott of public schools, Saturday,
August 29, 1970. (*left to right:* Raymond Rodríguez, David Ortiz, Leonel Castillo,
Gregory Salazar, Jaime de la Isla, Lucia R. Moreno.) Courtesy *Houston Chronicle,*
Houston Metropolitan Research Center.

Viva La Raza! A huelga school class, September, 1970. Courtesy *Houston Post*, Houston Metropolitan Research Center.

Yolanda Flores teaches a huelga school class at North Side People's Center, September, 1970. Photograph by Othell O. Owensby. Courtesy *Houston Chronicle*, Houston Metropolitan Research Center.

A huelga school class with several tables of children, September, 1970. Courtesy *Houston Post,* Houston Metropolitan Research Center.

The MAYO 9, September 15, 1970. (*left to right:* José Francisco Campos, Idelfonso "Poncho" Delgado Ruíz, Hector Almendárez, Carlos Carrizal Calbillo, Santos Hernández, Anthony Merced López, Gregory Salazar, Walter Birdwell, Yolanda Garza Birdwell.) Courtesy *Space City News,* Houston Metropolitan Research Center.

"To hell with H.I.S.D.," May, 1971. Courtesy *Houston Post*, Houston Metropolitan Research Center.

Four speakers addressing the Moody Park rally, Sunday, August 15, 1971. Courtesy *Houston Chronicle,* Houston Metropolitan Research Center.

Crowd at Moody Park rally (between 2,000 to 5,000 attended), Sunday, August 15, 1971. Courtesy *Papel Chicano,* Houston Metropolitan Research Center.

PART III

The Struggle for Recognition, 1970–72

CHAPTER 6

RAIN OF FURY

On the first day of school in the autumn of 1970, the Mexican American
Education Council (MAEC) protested unjust integration orders by organizing and conducting a boycott of the public schools involved in the proposed pairing order. The school boycott lasted for two and a half weeks—
from August 31, 1970, to September 16, 1970. In total over 3,500 students,
or over 60 percent, of the 5,831 students affected by the original pairing order of August 24, 1970, participated in this action.

In addition to the boycott and related activities, MAEC also developed
a network of huelga schools.[1] Officially called Huelga Enrichment Centers
because they were not licensed, these schools were located in the area where
the Fifth Circuit Court ordered the pairing of the elementary schools.

MAEC's challenges during these three weeks were formidable. The organization had to develop a plan for protesting school board actions, provide leadership to a diverse group of activists, establish huelga schools,
organize rallies in different parts of town, negotiate with local school of-
cials, and coordinate boycott activities. However, MAEC's primary challenge was to make sure that all sectors of the activist community—militant barrio youths and students, novice political actors, and moderate
middle-class and lower-middle-class activists—worked in unison to resist
an unpopular decision by the courts and the schools. The organization's
work was facilitated by the emergence of strong leaders at the barrio level
who organized most of these boycott or huelga school activities.

These actions symbolized the community's willingness to unify around
a specific incident of discrimination on the basis of a new identity and a

new politics. In other words, the unjust decision not only brought activists together but also encouraged them to accept the Chicano ideology of militancy, a nonwhite racial identity, and cultural pride. This chapter traces the evolution and dynamics of collective unity, identity shift, and political mobilization during this three-week period. For narrative purposes, it is divided into two major parts, the establishment of huelga schools and the evolution of boycott activities.

THE HUELGA SCHOOLS

Two MAEC members were given the responsibility for establishing a network of huelga schools—Sister Gloria Gallardo and Tina Reyes.[2] Sister Gloria, a Roman Catholic nun assigned to the Bishop's Committee for the Spanish Speaking, assumed primary responsibility for public relations and for establishing huelga schools throughout the city. Reyes, an activist from the Second Ward, assumed primary responsibility for ensuring that these schools had sufficient resources.[3]

The purpose of these educational institutions, as mentioned earlier, was to provide students with adequate instruction while they were boycotting the schools. In addition to the traditional three R's, these schools were to teach courses on Mexican American culture and history. Certified teachers and volunteers from the University of Houston would teach the basic skills classes, and MAYO would teach the historical and cultural aspects of the huelga school curriculum.[4]

Before instruction could begin Sister Gloria had to overcome several major problems, including the location of school sites, staffing, and registration. At least six locations had been found prior to the first day of the boycott and twenty-five others were under consideration. But a dispute between federal officials at the state and local levels over whether MAEC could use federal funds to establish private schools in antipoverty agencies emerged and cast doubt on some of these additional facilities.[5]

The use of church facilities and the Young Women's Catholic Association (YWCA) also was controversial. Helen Grant, executive director of the metropolitan YWCA, defended this decision to locate a huelga school at one of its local branches in the Magnolia Park barrio. She argued that the YWCA's decision was not an endorsement of the boycott action: "We decided to make it available to them [Mexican Americans] for community purposes."[6] Mario Quiñones, one of MAEC's local leaders and a member of the Harris County Community Action Association in the Port Houston

Table 4. Enrollment in the Huelga Schools, Wednesday, September 3, 1970

Name	Address	Enrollment
1. Denver Harbor Facilities		2,000
Facility #1	6323 Force	
Facility #2	1146 Gazin	
2. Port Houston HCCAA	1821 Daugherty	126
3. San Felipe Church	9800 Wallisville Rd.	500
4. Juan Marcos Presbyterian Church	3600 Fulton	177
5. Northside People Center	1501 Brooks	50
6. Saint Joseph's Church	1505 Kane	25
7. Our Lady of Saint John	7500 Hirsch Rd.	70
8. Magnolia Park Branch YWCA	7305 Navigation	45
		Total: 2,993

Source: "Chicanos Sign 3,000," Houston Post, Thursday, September 3, 1970, p. 13A.

area, argued too that the willingness of these agencies, centers, or churches to provide space for the establishment of huelga schools was not a statement of support for the boycott. "They are just giving space to get the kids educated," he said.[7] Despite this dispute, Sister Gloria was able to use some of these facilities as sites for the huelga schools. By the middle of the week at least nine of them were secured.[8]

Staffing was as problematic as site location. MAEC planned to staff the schools with regular teachers working after hours and with volunteers from local universities. Teachers from HISD and from local universities as well as undergraduate and graduate students volunteered their services, but this was inadequate to meet the great demand for huelga school instruction. Initially MAEC leaders expected about one thousand students to enroll in these schools. Their expectations were too low, as indicated by registration figures.[9]

Registration for the schools began on Tuesday, September 1. Slightly over two hundred students registered that day. On Wednesday, however, enrollment quickly jumped, closing with three thousand students registered. Much of this explosion in enrollment was concentrated in the Denver Harbor barrio, as indicated by the following table showing the names of the facilities, if any, the addresses, and the enrollments (see table 4).[10]

Because of demand for secondary instruction, Sister Gloria made plans for the opening of at least one senior high huelga school. Registration for this school was held on Friday evening at Saint Joseph Church on Kane Street.[11]

During the second week of the boycott the number of huelga schools doubled. Seven additional elementary schools were opened on Monday, September 7, and one senior high school was opened the following day.[12] State representative Lauro Cruz, the first Mexican American legislator from the Houston area and a strong supporter of the boycott, said that MAEC might have to open a second high school to accommodate the striking students. "This is because of sympathy for our cause and because of low quality education in the Houston schools," he said.[13] On Tuesday, MAEC leaders called for additional retired teachers to join the huelga schools because of the large numbers of Mexican American students enrolling.[14]

During this same week, the number of volunteer certified teachers increased to eighty-five. At the senior high huelga school alone there were thirty-five volunteer certified teachers at the first session. These teachers were aided by more than sixty-five University of Houston upperclassmen and graduate students as tutors in special subjects. Sister Gloria reported that some of the teachers were leaving Houston schools to help in the boycott. Others were retired schoolteachers who volunteered their services.[15]

Although no data is available on enrollment, it is likely that the number being served increased significantly during the second week, anywhere from five hundred to one thousand more students than the week before.[16] At the senior high huelga school, for instance, more than four hundred students enrolled in the first session.[17]

Most huelga school instruction in general focused on teaching the three R's. In practically all of the classes lessons in reading, writing, and occasionally arithmetic were offered.[18] At the senior high huelga school the curriculum was more innovative and "enriching." There the school taught a variety of traditional and nontraditional classes on subjects such as contemporary social and economic problems, the fundamentals of aeronautics, art appreciation, music, and public health, as well as college-level courses "redesigned" for high school students. Classes were small and did not exceed twenty-five students.[19]

The principal of the large senior high huelga school was Eliseo Cisneros. He had taught senior high foreign languages and journalism in a suburban school district the year before. Cisneros held a degree from the University of Texas, probably a bachelor of science in foreign languages, and was a substitute teacher for the Houston Independent School District during the regular academic year.[20]

A curriculum committee headed by Dr. Edward González, a biochemistry professor at the University of Houston campus, planned the high school's courses. This committee planned a program to fulfill all requirements for senior high students in the Houston schools. "Most of the teachers here are not political," said Dr. González. "We are concerned about educating the students who are staying out of school [because of the boycott]."[21]

In addition to the three R's, the huelga school instructors also taught history and culture classes in general and "the political aspects of the boycott" in particular.[22] This instruction occurred but, according to one source, was not effective. Of particular importance was the knowledge taught about the reasons for the boycott. Evidence from several sources suggests that children were taught why the community was boycotting the public schools. Some of these students, especially those from the elementary grades, only obtained a rudimentary knowledge of why they went to huelga schools. "We go to huelga school," reported one student from the San Felipe Church school, "because we are protesting." Another said that they were boycotting because "We have better teachers [at the huelga school] and have lunch and air-conditioning."

Older students gained a better understanding of the meaning of the boycott. One of these students was Jaime Díaz, a ninth grader. In a paragraph on why he was boycotting he wrote: "I am boycotting because I am not a white. I am a Chicano and I'm brown. The School Board considers me white now and that's because they are integrating the schools, you know blacks with whites. Well, I'm no white and I will stand up and show my color. The integrating of schools have [sic] taken place in most Chicano schools, you know, putting us as whites. Well, that's the reason I'm boycotting."[23] Another ninth-grade student, Irene Peña, also showed a good understanding of the meaning of the boycott. She stated that Mexican Americans were being denied their rights and discriminated against by the local school board. "Now the time has come to show the people of the U.S. that we are not someone people can toss around as if we were nobody," she argued, adding, "We are showing them we can stand on our own two feet." "I think we chicanos [sic] are boycotting," noted another ninth-grade student, "because we don't like the idea of the school board using us as whites."[24] Another unnamed ninth-grade student noted that

Chicanos were boycotting because "we can't just let ourselves be thrown around and called white, when we're not—we're BROWN!"[25]

At the senior high huelga school instructors tried to make their classes "more relevant to the Chicano." In a course on business law, for instance, students discussed the unfairness of the legal system and how it treated politically active people such as Huey Newton, leader of the radical Black Panther Party, and Reis Tijerina, a leader of the militant land rights group in New Mexico.[26] A social problems class taught by a MAYO member discussed the farmworkers' strike in California and Texas. There was also an informal discussion in that class about what students should be learning in the huelga schools.[27]

These examples suggest the existence of some political instruction in the huelga schools at the elementary and secondary levels. The effectiveness of this instruction, however, was questionable, as indicated by Cam Duncan, a supporter of the boycott. She observed and commented on the organization, staffing, and content of the huelga schools. Her visit probably took place toward the end of the second week of instruction. In general she argued that the schools were run by inexperienced individuals, the curriculum was narrowly confined to the three R's, and instruction, especially of the political aspects of the boycott, was ineffective.[28]

During her observations she noted that there were nearly twenty elementary "freedom schools" held in churches and community centers, staffed by volunteer teachers and funded by donations. Although Sister Gloria reported that all the schools had some books and supplies by Tuesday of the second week of the boycott, Duncan noted that there were few textbooks and school supplies. She explained that "this will certainly change if the schools become permanent."[29]

Duncan visited a huelga school at San Felipe Church off Wallisville Road in the El Dorado barrio. The school had an enrollment of two hundred first-through-eighth graders and was coordinated by a nineteen-year-old student. Classes in this school differed little from the standard three R's, although some classes used copies of *Papel Chicano* in their reading and writing lessons. Some political instruction was taking place, but it was not effective. "The students I talked to expressed little understanding of the demands the MAEC is fighting for and of the consequences of the present pairing plan," she noted.[30]

In the evening she visited the senior high huelga school at Holy Name School, 1913 Cochran. The original plan was for the school to open at Saint Joseph's Church, but it was then moved to the Holy Name School, a "newer, well-equipped" Catholic facility. The school had about five hundred students and twenty-five teachers. Classes were held from 6:00 to 10:00 P.M. daily, and most courses offered by HISD were taught there, as well as classes in social problems and Chicano history.[31]

The school's principal, Eliseo Cisneros, insisted that the school was apolitical and existed merely to keep the boycotting students from falling behind in their public school classes. Some of the teachers and many of the older students, however, felt that the huelga school was providing a political curriculum. Despite this instruction, Duncan noted, students were not being provided with a full understanding of the boycott, especially the reasons for the boycott and the underlying racism of many students.[32] She wrote:

> Despite the fact that the MAEC has taken every opportunity to announce publicly that the reason for the boycott is not to prevent the transfer of chicanos to black schools and vice versa, it appears that the huelga schools are not dealing effectively with the racism of many students and parents, nor educating the people on all of the issues in the strike. Like talking about why blacks are not boycotting, about what a really progressive education could be offered at huelga schools, about what community control of schools means, and how it could be achieved.[33]

Leonel Castillo later admitted that the huelga schools were not doing all they could to eliminate these racist sentiments. He attributed many of the difficulties to the incredible administrative problems involved in setting up a volunteer school district for over thirty-five hundred students in one week.[34]

The huelga schools remained in existence for the entire duration of the boycott. Although it is unclear who actually attended, what was taught, and who taught in them, they served to remind the community that Chicanos and Chicanas could shape their educational destiny. The schools were an extension of the community's political involvement and served to further unite the various activist strains found in the barrios and to inspire them to continue the struggle.

THE BOYCOTT — WEEK ONE:
MONDAY, AUGUST 31–SUNDAY, SEPTEMBER 6

The huelga schools were an extension of the community's political involvement. Most of this involvement centered on the radical measures taken by various sectors of the Mexican-origin community to protest the school's proposed pairing order. The first week of militant activism began on Monday, August 31, with thousands of students heeding MAEC's call to protest the proposed court-ordered pairing of mostly Mexican American schools with predominantly black schools.[35] On the first day about 3,500 Mexican American students boycotted the schools.[36] In the barrio schools of the Northside (Looscan and Sherman Elementary Schools), Denver Harbor (Scroggins and Eliot Elementary Schools), Port Houston (Port Houston Elementary), and the Second Ward (Lantrip and Anson Jones Elementaries) the boycott was 75 percent effective. Some of the schools in El Dorado barrio reported about 90 percent of the students absent due primarily to the boycott.[37] The mainstream media reported that at Ryan Elementary in the Northside only 111 of 258 Mexican Americans registered at that predominantly black school showed up.[38] Although not included in the pairing order, the students at the combined junior-senior high school at Furr supported the boycott; about 300 Mexican American students expected to attend classes there did not appear.[39]

Mexican American parents, all members of MAEC, took the lead in supporting the boycott effort in their local communities. They tried to enroll their children in predominantly Mexican American schools, picketed schools, or demonstrated in front of the administration building. At Sherman Elementary, located in the Northside, parents briefly blocked the driveway to keep teachers and students from attending the school. They advised the elementary-school children to go home.[40] Mexican American parents reportedly took their children out of Kay Elementary School, a formerly predominantly African American school.[41] Other parents picketed outside Eliot Elementary, located in the Denver Harbor barrio, and at J. P. Harris Elementary in the East End barrio.[42] Over one hundred parents marched and demonstrated in front of the school administration building while collectively chanting "Brown, Brown, We're not White, We're Brown."[43]

Despite these actions, the local board reported that the majority of parents and children were complying with school board guidelines as "dictated" by the federal courts. School board officials noted that the district opened its 232 schools "with pockets of dissent prevailing to disrupt education." The boycott, officials acknowledged, was most keenly felt at Pugh, Scroggins, and Port Houston. According to Dr. Charles R. Nelson, deputy superintendent of elementary schools, these schools reported absenteeism of 25–50 percent, a figure much less than that reported by Mexican

American sources.[44] The principal of Eliot Elementary, Courtney Parks, reported that the "brown boycott" was sharply felt at his school since only about one-third of the expected student body enrolled for classes.[45]

Later in the day MAEC held a mass meeting at Moody Park to report on the status of the boycott. Over six hundred individuals attended this rally. Several, including Mr. B. Mega from El Dorado barrio and Andy Guerrero from the Second Ward, reported favorably on the day's boycott activities.[46]

After these initial reports individuals voiced their support for the boycott. One speaker urged that even the Chicanos not affected by the pairing decision should boycott the schools. Any Chicano who did not want to support the boycott had "better get out of the way," he added.[47] This as well as other comments reflected several aspects of the new Chicano ideology, including awareness of an institutional wrong that could be changed through the promotion of a collective minority group identity and the willingness to confront existing school authorities through militant means to correct an injustice. Abel Álvarez, representative for the Barrios Unidos organization formed in January, made reference to one aspect of this ideology when he said, "It's obvious they're [the school board] using Mexican Americans for integration purposes." He further commented that Chicanos wanted to be considered as an ethnic group distinct from whites.[48]

Gregory Salazar, a MAYO member, voiced the opinion that Chicanos had always been considered a separate ethnic group for housing and jobs, "but we are now considered white for integration purposes." Both he and Yolanda Birdwell, another member of MAYO, urged the crowd to continue the boycott. They argued that people should stay out of the schools, not for racial reasons but to protest the poor education Chicanos were receiving in the schools and "because they were being used as white only for the convenience of the racist school board."[49] This latter statement was aimed at discouraging racial prejudice against African Americans and at challenging the underlying racism in many of the students' decisions to boycott the schools.

Racial prejudices between Mexican and African Americans, a topic generally unexplored by scholars, was very much a reality in the barrio. The proposed pairing of these two groups in the schools and the tensions raised by the boycott apparently encouraged individuals to express these racist sentiments. One of the students in the elementary grades, for instance, was reported to have said that he wanted to go to the huelga school because "there are no colored people" there. A ninth-grader was more explicit; he was boycotting because "the niggers always get what they want—chicanos never do!" Other students were afraid of going to schools that were pre-dominantly black because "black kids are always bossing us around, pick-ing fights."[50] Adults also expressed these sentiments at meetings and in private conversations with some of the MAEC leaders.[51] Salazar's com-ments sought to counter these attitudes and remind the community about the true reasons for the boycott—discrimination against Mexican Amer-icans, not racial prejudice against African Americans.[52]

Not all the speakers at the rally were Mexican Americans. One, Curtis Graves, an African American state representative from Houston, was a political ally of the Mexican American community and a close personal friend of state representative Lauro Cruz from Houston. Cruz was the first Mexican American elected to the state legislature from the Houston area. His support of the boycott was welcomed by MAEC because he gave it an aura of legitimacy. But, as will be shown later, his support also complicated MAEC's leadership because Cruz acted independently of the organization. He had his own political reasons for supporting this effort and did not gen-erally consult with or seek the approval of the MAEC leader. Still, MAEC leaders welcomed his support.

Cruz was probably the one who invited Curtis Graves to attend the rally and issue a statement of support, which Graves did gladly.[53] "Congratula-tions on coming together as a united race," Graves stated to the gathering. He told them that racist elements were trying to integrate Chicanos as whites with the blacks and said, "This is a travesty on justice and you should not stand for it. You have been used." He reminded the crowd: "You are not white, but you are Chicano." Finally, he agreed with the Mex-ican American community's efforts to bring to the attention of the district the "unfair integration policies of HISD."[54] He argued, "The black man in this community stands with you. Don't stop the boycott until you have reached 100 percent."[55]

Graves's appearance was a positive sign of support from the African American community for the boycott. This support, although welcomed, was limited since no other major political leaders issued a statement of support. A few, such as school board member Rev. Leon Everett II, sup-ported the Mexican American community's effort to gain legal recogni-tion as an ethnic minority group but opposed the boycott. "They are to be commended for their belated thrust," Everett said.[56] Still, the comments by Graves projected a public image of minority cooperation on this issue and indicated that this boycott was not merely a Mexican American issue but one of concern to minorities and those interested in justice. His appearance and comments also challenged the public perception that racism against African Americans was an important motivation for the boycott.

On the second day of the boycott between seventy-five and one hundred Mexican American mothers and some fathers picketed at Pugh, Scroggins, and Eliot, all located in the Denver Harbor area. The rains came that day but did not discourage the mothers, a large number of whom marched and chanted in front of these elementary schools: "Rain, rain go away, La Raza wants to picket today." Others yelled, "Brown, brown, we're not white, we're brown." Chicano mothers rallied in answer to the city-wide Chicano boycott of HISD schools. "We as Chicanos must fight for our schools," stated Mrs. Ernest Sauseda [sic]. "We are protesting the busing of only Chicano children to the black schools, we're not white," she added. Several other mothers—Mrs. Edward Salazar, Mrs. Mario Peña, Mrs. Manuel del Campo, and others—pleaded for *ayuda* (assistance) and asked families to keep their children out of the schools. "Put them in the huelga schools," most of them advised.[57] Another parent, Mrs. America García, reinforced these comments when she said, "Chicanos must stick together and support an all-out Chicano boycott." Mrs. García contributed to this effort by providing child care and making her home available to some thirty-three boycotting minors so that their mothers could protest the pairing of the schools.[58]

Youth activists in the community agreed with the mothers of Denver Harbor. One of them argued that Chicanas and Chicanos did not like the idea of integrating only minorities. "If you're brown, you will boycott schools, if you are brown and don't boycott," this person argued, "you are placing an injustice upon your raza." The activist urged readers to "boycott Raza, boycott now."[59]

By the third day the boycott seemed to be attracting larger numbers of students. MAEC encouraged their participation in many of these activities and also urged them to attend the huelga schools. In the meantime parents, especially women, were asked to march and picket in front of several schools. At Jackson Junior High, one of the schools picketed, the principal locked the gates and remained in front of the school while the teachers patrolled the hallways.[60] Once the mothers began to picket the school, however, students began to "blow out," or leave the school. An additional catalyst to "blowing out" was the brave action of one *bato* (young male) who jumped from a second-story window and joined the picket line. Soon five Chicana students—Tina Campos, Linda Sánchez, Sara García, Yolanda García, and Jerry Rodríquez—"blew out." So did two Chicanos from the

Jackson Football B team. "They knew that they might be kicked off the team pero [but] for the Raza, it was worth it," noted one of the activists. By the end of the day about 250 Chicano and Chicana students had walked out of school and joined the picketers. Because of school regulations those on the picket line could not chant, so they simply communicated with the other students in the school by showing "the Chicano Power fist signs." [61]

The boycott at Furr Junior-Senior High and the "blowout" at Jackson Junior High indicated that the boycott was beginning to spread to the higher grades and that parents were using more militant methods. On Friday the week's activities culminated with a "picketing tour" of several Houston schools. [62] About 250 Mexican American children and parents traveled by cars and a bus to a school, marched around it, then moved on to another school. Some of the schools picketed in this manner were Jeff Davis High, Edison Junior High, Austin High, and Jackson Junior High. [63]

By the end of the week at least four individuals were arrested for boycott activities. One mother from the Denver Harbor barrio was arrested for trying to convince another parent not to register her child in the HISD school. Three MAYO members—Andy Guerrero, Mike Almendárez, and Hector Almendárez—were arrested for using a bullhorn without a permit; they were announcing the boycott and encouraging students not to attend. "Raza be careful," warned an activist, "but make a stand on the issue of the boycott." He further stated, "Ponganse alalva [sic] [be on guard]." [64]

On Friday evening a meeting of over 700 Mexican Americans was held at Saint Joseph's Catholic Church to discuss the achievements and problems of the past week as well as how to continue the efforts. Elva González noted that only 205 of over 1,600 students had reported to Port Houston Elementary School. Gregory Salazar stated that not enough people were boycotting junior and senior high schools. Guillermo Gutiérrez stated that chairs were needed for the huelga school at the Northside People's Center. Toward the end of the meeting one woman suggested that it might be better to move out of Houston, but the majority rejected this idea. One of the activists, impressed with the community's mobilization, reported that "for the first time in 100 years the Chicano is really starting to unite." [65] Another rally to discuss the status and future plans was called for Sunday afternoon to be held at Eastwood Park on the east side of Houston.

A variety of speakers including state representative Lauro Cruz, Abe Ramírez, and Leonel Castillo spoke at the Sunday rally attended by about three thousand individuals. They provided a status report of the boycott and the huelga schools.[66] Emphasis quickly shifted to the topic of what needed to be done the following week. Rally speakers encouraged Mexican American parents to keep their children out of public schools until the district declared them a minority group. "All Mexican Americans, on this issue, stand together," said Cruz.[67] He also proposed expanding the boycott to include those not directly affected by the pairing order. More specifically, he called for a "sympathy" boycott on Friday of all students still in school.[68] This sympathy boycott would coincide with the school administration's announced plans to observe El Día de la Independencia (Mexican Independence Day) on September 16.

Abe Ramírez supported Lauro Cruz's statements and encouraged the crowd to continue the boycott. "It is an effort supreme to any other issue now before us," he said.[69] Leonel Castillo, chairperson of MAEC, told the crowd that talks with the school administration would begin Tuesday. "We will argue only one point—that is that we are an identifiable ethnic minority group," he said, adding, "It will probably be a short meeting."[70] After several more speakers and a great deal of clapping and chanting, the rally ended on a positive note.

WEEK TWO: MONDAY,
SEPTEMBER 7–SUNDAY, SEPTEMBER 13

During the second week of the boycott community leaders continued to picket, to encourage nonattendance in the paired and nonpaired schools, and to focus on educating in the huelga schools those boycotting the schools. Community leaders made plans to negotiate with school officials. The first meeting, with Superintendent George Garver, took place on Tuesday, September 9.[71] Five MAEC members as well as state representative Lauro Cruz met with him on this day.[72]

The group raised several concerns. One pertained to intimidation by school officials. Cruz and Ramírez specifically charged that some truant officers and principals told parents that they would be forced to pay fines if their children continued to boycott the schools. A second and more important concern was recognition by the board of Mexican Americans as an identifiable minority group for purposes of desegregation. Superintendent Garver sympathized but told them that the identification of Mexican Americans was a policy matter for the school board and not an administrative one. Leonel Castillo then asked to meet with the board in order to get "a policy decision" before discussing any further issues of triethnic desegregation.[73]

Once other members of MAEC were informed of the meeting's results, they were angry. Abel Álvarez probably best summarized their sentiments when he said, "Our pleas have fallen on deaf ears." "We have no alternative but to go to the people, unite them and continue with the boycott," he added.[74] Mexican American leaders then went ahead with the proposed plan to encourage all HISD students to boycott classes Friday, September 11, as a gesture of sympathy with the strike against the schools. A second day-long statewide boycott was called for Friday, September 18.[75]

Later that day Dr. Leonard Robbins, board president, stated that the recognition of Mexican Americans as an identifiable minority group could be granted only by the courts, not by the Houston school board. He also told MAEC members that a lower court decision declaring Mexican Americans an identifiable minority group in Corpus Christi was "not germane to Houston."[76] State representative Cruz and Abe Ramírez criticized this position and said that the school board should "do more to get another ruling." Dr. Robbins defended the principals' actions pertaining to truancy, stating that state law required children to attend accredited schools until they reached the age of seventeen or else the parents would face charges of truancy and fines.[77]

These comments only served to fan the flames of anger toward the presumed intransigence of the local school district. The following day, Wednesday, Cruz and Ramírez, acting without official authorization of MAEC but supported by its chairperson, held a press conference. They called for a general one-day boycott of the Houston schools for Friday, September 11, as a gesture of sympathy for the estimated thirty-five hundred Mexican American students who were protesting the pairing order. They called for an additional general boycott of Houston schools to be held on Friday, September 18. This would be coordinated with a statewide boycott of schools called by MAYO and other members of the Mexican American community. Cruz and Ramírez also stated that MALDEF was planning on filing a suit in federal court embodying a twenty-step plan for racial integration of the Houston schools.[78] Leonel Castillo later said that the proposed twenty steps could not be divulged because "other Mexican American leaders had not approved all of them."[79] These actions, they argued, were necessary due to the negative attitude of school officials and to their failure to meet the demand of MAEC and other community organizations for a change in the legal classification of Mexican Americans.[80]

At the press conference Cruz also stated that he planned to meet with Gov. Preston Smith on Friday to see whether Smith would assist the Mexican American community's efforts to be declared an ethnic minority group. In a related issue Ramírez reported that MALDEF was beginning to document cases of intimidation of Mexican American students by teachers and other school officials.[81]

On Thursday, September 10, Superintendent Garver, probably in response to the possibility of escalation of boycott activity and in order to encourage dialogue between HISD and the leaders of the Mexican American boycott, issued a statement recognizing Mexican Americans as an "identifiable minority group within the total community." "This recognition," the statement read, "should not be confused with the legal recognition of an ethnic minority. Legal recognition can only be granted by a Court." Since Mexican Americans were a distinct minority, the statement implied that "they may have special educational needs." According to Garver, "It is, therefore, vitally important that any effective educational system address itself to meet adequately the needs of all children." In a concluding statement the superintendent encouraged the participation of the Mexican American community in resolving the issue of integration: "In recognition of the special educational needs that Mexican-American children may have, the School district will continue to attempt to work with representatives of the Mexican-American community, including parents and other interested groups, to determine their suggestions and recommendations which can be implemented or submitted to the Board of Education for their consideration."[82]

Members of the Mexican American community viewed this statement as a positive sign and decided to meet with Superintendent Garver that Thursday afternoon.[83] In a meeting that lasted more than five hours state representative Lauro Cruz and MAEC members discussed the group's twenty-step plan. Among other things, MAEC wanted school officials to do the following: (1) recognize Mexican Americans as an identifiable minority group; (2) place eight Mexican Americans in responsible positions within the school administration; (3) refrain from punishing or reprimanding Mexican American students boycotting the district; (4) grant all usual privileges of school activities to boycotting students when they returned to class; and (5) have proportionate representation by Mexican Americans on all study groups and commissions appointed by the district.[84]

Garver told MAEC representatives that parts of their plan were "workable" and promised to support them in a meeting with the board to be held on Friday.[85] Despite the favorable reaction by the superintendent to their "concerns," MAEC, after the meeting, reissued the call for a one-day general sympathy boycott for Friday by all students.[86]

The organization's response was issued in the context of two other actions taken by more radical students and by a new conservative Mexican American group. First, there was a press conference held by some fifty Mexican American junior and senior high school students that Thursday. Militant students involved in the boycott activities called the press conference. Although they did not obtain MAEC's authorization, the students were supported in their efforts by the chairperson and the group's membership. These students reported that doors and gates were being locked at certain schools and that principals and coaches were threatening and intimidating those who joined the boycott. Gregory Salazar, a representative of MAYO who also spoke on behalf of this group, said that the students believed they were being threatened with arrest by police officers. When asked about the superintendent's statement, he said, "The administration doesn't have the power to set policy. They only carry out policy." The superintendent disagreed with this sentiment, stating, "While this is a statement by the general superintendent, it is the policy of the school district until changed by board decree." Salazar, however, was not hopeful that anything significant would occur unless the school board took further action. "I hope that the school board will file an appeal and that the ruling will be favorable," he said.[87]

The second incident dealt with formal opposition to the Mexican American community's boycott of the schools by a conservative group headed by John Coronado, editor of the Spanish language newspaper *Observatorio Latino*. Coronado was the spokesperson for more than four hundred Mexican American business leaders in Houston and founder of the Mexican American Chamber of Commerce. He felt that the courts should settle the issue of ethnic identity raised by MAEC. Those seeking recognition as a separate ethnic group "have a genuine case," he noted, "but they shouldn't play political football with those kids." He urged all the parents to attend the public schools and not to be "misled by political agitators." He noted that he would appear before the school board on Monday night to voice his objections to the Houston school system.[88]

No additional voices of support or opposition to MAEC or its issues emerged during this crucial period. "Old-guard" organizations such as LULAC and new ones such as PASSO were strangely silent and did not take a public position on this burning issue.[89] These organizations, for the most part, opposed the tactics and the new racial identity promoted by MAEC and were unwilling to endorse these actions officially.[90]

The following day, Friday, September 11, a group of Mexican Americans met with the school board while another group went to court to file a lawsuit asking for intervention status in the *Ross* case. About twenty members of MAEC were present at the meeting with the board and the superintendent at which the twenty-point plan was presented to them.[91] Following is the list of demands presented by the Mexican American Education Council to the Houston Independent School District, September 1970:

1. The School Board should immediately and officially recognize the Mexican American as an identifiable ethnic minority group, subject to the due protection of the law and that the School Board immediately implement this policy.

2. The School Board should immediately file an appeal to the Fifth Circuit Court on the basis that the proposed desegregation plan is a sham while [it] emphasizes the pairing of the Mexican Americans and Blacks.

3. The School Board should immediately place eight (8) Mexican Americans in responsible positions within the administration of the District. At present there is not a single Mexican American administrator with any real responsibility.

4. The School Board should immediately assure the Mexican American Education Council that the school children and parents who participated in the boycott will not be punished or reprimanded in any way by any school officials.

5. Students who participated in the boycott will be granted the usual privileges and rights in school activities, extra-curricular activities and all other school related activities.

6. The School Board should have proportionate representation of Mexican Americans on all committees, commissions and study groups appointed by the District. Particularly important in this regard are the Desegregation Committee, the Legislative Committee and the Financial Committee.

7. The School Board will publicly guarantee the Mexican American Education Council that the bilingual education programs and other pro-

grams designed for the Mexican American will not be diluted, decreased or hurt in any way by any desegregation plan.

8. All poor children, regardless of the area in which they live, will be assured free and safe transportation to school. Low-income neighborhoods present more safety hazards to parents and children and therefore there is a great need for assistance in assuring free and safe access to school.

9. The School Board will not pair or group any schools until a reasonable plan for pairing or grouping has been developed. Elements of a reasonable plan include:

   a. Identification of the Mexican Americans as a separate ethnic minority group.
   b. Transportation or assistance through or around hazardous streets and areas.
   c. Notification, in Spanish, if necessary, and full discussion with the parents of the children to be grouped or paired.
   d. Acknowledgement of the various difficulties involved in separating low-income families which have many members who might attend different schools.
   e. Participation of Mexican Americans in planning.

10. The School Board will immediately begin an intensive program to include Mexican American teachers, counselors, administrative staff and other personnel with a view toward having proportionate representation within the District by January, 1971.

11. The School District will begin immediately to develop curriculum and textbook material which adequately portrays the role the Mexican American has played in this country's history.

12. Bilingual teachers using Spanish as a part of their daily work, who have a proficiency rating of at least an FS-4 (foreign service rating) will receive a 10% pay differential.

13. The School Board will insist that Mexican Americans receive more academic preparation rather than continuing the emphasis on vocational training.

14. The School Board will immediately create a career information office which will assist qualified, needy Mexican Americans to go to college.

15. The School Superintendent will use uniform regulations to each school principal, providing for the personal safety of every school child in and

around each school. Responsibility for enforcement of the regulations will not be delegated by the principal, but will be his personal responsibility. Personal safety may necessitate the use of parent hall patrols.

16. The Houston independent School District will implement recognition of the Mexican American as a separate ethnic group by insuring that a share of funds proportional to the population of Mexican Americans be allocated from funds received by H.I.S.D. under the Nixon Desegregation Bill to programs benefiting the Mexican American school children.

17. The Houston Independent School District will use the services and technical assistance provided by TED-TAC in implementing desegregation plans of the United States Circuit Court.

18. The School Board will declare the 16th of September and the Cinco de Mayo as official school holidays. This will be done with a view toward stimulating recognition and acknowledgement of the cultural heritage of the Mexican American.

19. The School Board will actively begin a program whereby minority contractors and businessmen and financial institutions will be able to participate in the business function of the District.

20. The School Board will publicly announce its support of the election of board members by district.[92]

After the meeting the superintendent publicly noted that parts of the plan to recognize Mexican Americans as an ethnic minority group could be worked out "administratively." Specifically, Garver argued that sixteen of the twenty "issues" were within the superintendent's authority. The remaining four required school board action and were to be seriously considered by the board members.[93]

Leonel Castillo stated that the meeting with Garver was a fruitful one. Although he appreciated the superintendent's favorable reaction to MAEC's plan, the crux of the problem was not an administrative matter but a policy concern. Until the matter was resolved, Castillo said, the Mexican American student boycott of the schools would continue.[94]

MAEC filed suit in federal court to intervene in the Houston school district integration case. This lawsuit, filed by MALDEF lawyers with the assistance of Abe Ramírez, Jr., alleged that pairing Mexican Americans with blacks did not achieve integration. The suit stated that the integration order failed to consider Mexican Americans as a distinct and separate identifiable minority group as required by the Fourteenth Amendment to the

Constitution and the Civil Rights Act of 1964. The parents asked that
the district integrate its black and Mexican American students with Anglo
students.[95]

Political unity of the entire Mexican American community supporting the boycott held out during the second week, but minor differences in
strategy emerged on Saturday when state representative Cruz and Ramírez
prematurely announced that the boycott might be called off if the board
continued to negotiate with the Mexican American community. At a Saturday press conference Cruz and Ramírez praised the superintendent for
his "good faith and concern" in talking with them and said that they would
reciprocate by canceling a statewide sympathy boycott of schools that had
been called for Friday, September 18.[96] They also suggested that striking
Mexican American students in Houston would "probably" return to the
public schools and end the walkout. Ramírez announced that the strike of
the schools would continue until "we are assured of justice and quality education." "At this time, however," he noted, "we have every reason to believe that if talks go on in the same vein with the school administration, all
our children will be back in Houston schools Friday."[97] Leonel Castillo
clarified later that only he and MAEC could issue such a call for ending the
boycott.[98] The apparent rift was closed almost as soon as it emerged.

WEEK THREE: MONDAY,
SEPTEMBER 14–WEDNESDAY, SEPTEMBER 16

During the beginning of the third week of the boycott a potentially dis-
tracting event occurred that almost halted the negotiations with local
school officials. This event occurred on Monday, September 14, at the regularly scheduled monthly school board meeting.[99] MAYO and the Chicano
Student Committee, a new group of high school students, engaged in militant action that led to violence and the arrest of fourteen individuals. This
"mini-riot," as the media called it, had a potentially negative impact on the
conduct of boycott activities since it undermined peaceful negotiations.[100]

To the surprise of MAEC leaders, the violent incident at the school
board meeting actually strengthened their hand by encouraging school
board members to complete the negotiations and meet their demands.[101]
The following day MAEC reported that the school board had agreed to its
central demands of identifying Mexican Americans as an ethnic group
and of appealing the pairing decision to the Supreme Court. In addition
to these two demands the board also met fifteen other demands. In total,

it agreed to meet seventeen of MAEC's original twenty demands.[102] This good-faith effort on the part of both the superintendent and the school board was sufficient for MAEC to end the boycott. On Wednesday, September 16, an important Mexican holiday, Leonel Castillo, Abe Ramírez, and others announced an end to the boycott: "We urge Mexican American parents to return their children to school on Monday peacefully."[103] The parents, students, and community members wholeheartedly supported the termination of boycott activities.

Also on that day Superintendent Garver announced the establishment of a three-member committee to implement the pairing plan and, in keeping with the spirit of the settlement, appointed a Mexican American, Ernesto Valdes, to the committee.[104] Garver also issued a policy statement directing principals to admit the formerly absent students without penalty or comment.[105]

CONCLUSIONS

The boycott that began the first day of school thus came to an end almost three weeks later. During that period MAEC brought together militant, novice, and established activists to achieve its major goal of gaining official recognition of minority group status in local school matters, especially desegregation. This was accomplished by resorting to boycotting the public schools and establishing huelga schools.

Huelga school development was extremely time-consuming, but determination on the part of MAEC eventually led to the location of over twenty schools, the selection of instructors, and the enrollment of several thousand students. Although instruction was uneven, those in charge of the huelga schools taught reading, writing, and arithmetic as well as courses on political awareness, racial identity, and cultural pride.

Boycott activities taxed the abilities of MAEC and the hundreds of individuals responsible for organizing, coordinating, and implementing them. In the first week alone over thirty-five hundred students walked out of the public schools to protest the local district's failure to recognize them as a minority group. During the second week of the boycott MAEC received support from local politicians, especially an African American state legislator and the first Mexican American state representative. The boycott expanded to the secondary grades, and plans were made to include all the schools. The expanding boycott and its increasing support by legislators encouraged the superintendent and later the local school board to officially recognize Mexican Americans as an identifiable minority group and to meet the diverse demands made by MAEC.

These significant concessions were granted despite the militant actions by MAYO and the Chicano Student Committee at the September 14, 1970, school board meeting. The "mini-riot" almost disrupted the ongoing negotiations between MAEC and the school board. It also momentarily shifted public emphasis from MAEC's demands to the militants' tactics and roused a violent reaction on the part of the community to this incident. The next chapter will explore the dynamics of violent militant involvement in the midst of peaceful negotiations and what this suggested about the limits of radicalism.

CHAPTER 7

ALL HELL BROKE LOOSE

The school board disruption of Monday, September 14, 1970, was a signifi-cant event in MAEC's struggle for recognition. It took place in the context of increasing intimidation of parents and students involved in the boy-cott and illustrated the willingness of youth to use violent tactics to effect change. Although MAEC was effectively utilizing "radical" methods to achieve its goal of board recognition, it had not resorted to violence. Vio-lence, however, was tolerated and even accepted by youth-based organiza-tions and by youths within MAEC. This became apparent at the regularly scheduled monthly school board meeting when young people from MAYO and the Chicano Student Committee (CSC) used force to get board at-tention. This disruption in the school board meeting eventually led to property destruction and the arrest of fourteen individuals, including nine MAYO members. Most members of MAEC disagreed with the youths' tac-tics but they supported them nonetheless. Many of them also blamed school board officials for this incident.

The use of violence by the young people clashed with MAEC's philoso-phy of peaceful negotiation and indicated how youths were ready and will-ing to use violence to accomplish their goals. It illustrated, in stark terms, the impatience of young Mexican Americans with established authorities. The following provides a detailed look at the events leading to what the media labeled a "mini-riot" at the school board meeting and its political consequences on MAEC's struggle for recognition and on school reform in general.

REQUESTING TIME TO SPEAK

MAEC's intention was to speak before the school board members on Monday evening and commend them for engaging in a good-faith effort to meet its demands. MAEC leaders also wanted to encourage the board to pursue an appeal of the pairing plan to the U.S. Supreme Court.

The initial preparation for this school board meeting occurred the week of September 7. During the early part of this week Abe Ramírez, legal counsel for MAEC, phoned the secretary of the school board's president and requested time on the agenda. There was no official response to his request.[1]

Over the weekend Leonel Castillo approached the superintendent about speaking at the board meeting. Garver told him that the school board normally did not honor requests from neighborhood groups because "to honor one would have meant to honor all and board meetings would be prolonged indefinitely."[2] Castillo responded that "this policy might best be changed in view of the specific problems faced by the Mexican American children and parents who were on boycott." Garver said that this matter had to be considered by the school board president and that he did not believe a change would be forthcoming.[3]

On Sunday several MAEC leaders met and voted to wire telegrams to the school board members requesting that they allow Castillo ten minutes on the agenda. Board members Mrs. H. W. Cullen and Mr. J. W. McCullough, Jr., both supported MAEC's right to be heard at the meeting. Mrs. Cullen argued that "people who have grievances should be heard."[4]

On Monday, Abe Ramírez sent a written request to the secretary of the school board president asking for time on the agenda. There was no official response to this request either.[5] Thus by Monday afternoon, when Mexican Americans began arriving for the meeting, the matter of speaking before the board was unresolved. In an effort to resolve this matter, at around 6:00 P.M., Leonel Castillo went to the superintendent's office to meet with him and to request some time on the agenda. At approximately 6:40 P.M., Gregory Salazar interrupted their meeting so that he could speak to Castillo. Outside the superintendent's meeting room he asked Castillo to look at a new list of demands drafted by junior and senior high student members of the Chicano Student Commmittee. Salazar asked him if this list could be presented as part of MAEC's agenda or separately. Castillo explained, "I indicated to Gregory that I had serious doubts about the possibility of their being allowed time and also about the possible disallowance of time for MAEC."[6] Castillo then finished the meeting with Garver. Later he reported that agreement had been reached on some matters but that there was still "no change in this regards to their policy for board meetings."[7] In other words, the school board, among other things, had agreed to appeal the pairing decision to the Supreme Court as called for by MAEC but had not agreed to MAEC's request for time on the agenda.

When school board president Robbins arrived at 7:00 P.M., Castillo briefly met with him. Dr. Robbins reiterated his stance that MAEC would not be allowed to speak to the board. Castillo then told him that if he were given some time to speak, MAEC "could probably end the boycott because it would demonstrate good faith and willingness to listen." Robbins ended the brief encounter by saying that he would think about it and later determine whether Castillo would be allowed to speak during the meeting. In the meantime, Robbins informed Castillo that it was Castillo's job to tell MAEC members that school board policy prevented the board from hearing different groups and to explain to them why they could not be heard. Thus, when the school board meeting began, the matter was still unsettled; however, there was an understanding among Chicanos that Castillo might be allowed to speak to the board either under discussion of "new business" or at the end of the meeting.[8]

THE RADICAL MEMBERS OF MAEC

MAEC members, as indicated earlier, represented a variety of activist strains. In addition to the moderate-middle-class, the lower-middle-class, and the novice activists, MAEC also included militant groups and individuals. Among the latter were Barrio-MAYO, UH-MAYO, and the CSC.

Barrio-MAYO was formed in April, 1968, and UH-MAYO was established at the University of Houston thirteen months later.[9] Both of these chapters were part of the statewide MAYO organization formed in March, 1967, in San Antonio, Texas. MAYO in general was an active and aggressive statewide organization with local chapters that offered the Chicano and Chicana youth of Texas a vehicle "with which to effect meaningful social change." It sought radical changes in the social, economic, and political structures of American society through direct action. MAYO believed that traditional approaches such as resolutions, petitions, and letters to officials were ineffective. Instead it preferred to use marches, protests, boycotts, and mass assemblies to solve the problems of institutional discrimination and inequitable treatment.[10]

The state leaders of MAYO viewed the dominant society as comprised of "gringos" and Anglos. Anglos were white individuals sympathetic to Mexican Americans and to their struggle for recognition and empowerment. Anglos, noted one of MAYO's pamphlets, "want to work with La Raza so our people can become the masters of their destiny and thereby remove the shackles of oppression that bind them."[11] The gringo, on the other hand, was defined as a racist individual or institution who oppressed Mexican Americans and who inflicted "vicious cultural genocide" on them. Gringos and gringo institutions, José Angel Gutiérrez noted in 1969, "not only severely damage our human dignity but also makes [sic] it impossible for la raza to develop its right of self-determination." MAYO's expectations were to fight the gringo society with labor strikes and boycotts and to promote barrio development. "If these tactics do not work," Gutiérrez stated, "violence may follow."[12]

The local MAYOs sought to pursue their goals in a peaceful and nonviolent manner, but if their members were attacked or abused they would "resist with equal force." In the early 1970s Barrio-MAYO elaborated on the notion of violence, stating, "Violence is not the reactions of oppressed people to their condition, but . . . the institutionalized exploitation of the people." The group then stipulated again that while the organization was nonviolent, if attacked it would defend itself with whatever means were available, including weapons. "An unarmed people," MAYO noted, "is subject to slavery at anytime [sic]."[13]

UH-MAYO had similar views to Barrio-MAYO, but it refrained from using violence. Unlike members of its barrio component, those in UH-MAYO were university students more interested in promoting an intellectual and cultural understanding of Mexican American problems than in taking direct action against institutional discrimination.[14] UH-MAYO had "revolutionary" goals as did its barrio counterpart, but UH-MAYO members did not believe in armed conflict or in using violence to achieve its goals. In the spring of 1971 Jaime De La Isla, the chair of UH-MAYO, described the organization as "on a continuum a little more conservative than Barrio MAYO—a little to the right of left."[15]

While both MAYO chapters participated in and supported MAEC, they also took independent actions. The public in general, however, tended to view their involvement as extremely controversial. Barrio-MAYO, for instance, engaged in a series of highly dramatic and controversial actions in 1970. In February, 1970, it occupied the Juan Marcos Presbyterian Church in the Northside barrio. The church building at 3600 Fulton Street belonged to the Brazos Presbytery, a regional governing body for the Presbyterian, U.S., but was vacant at the time. The Brazos Presbytery had given permission for the Juan Marcos Presbyterian Church to move into this facility with the understanding that the congregation would undertake a community center program to include a Spanish worship service, sewing and cooking classes, bilingual classes for adults, a Mexican history library, and recreational programs. MAYO members complained that the Juan Marcos program was too spiritual and did not address the full needs of the poor people in the barrio. They proposed to offer their own program of free breakfasts for neighborhood children, preschool bilingual education, job training, and community meeting rooms. For two weeks MAYO occupied the building and negotiated with the Juan Marcos ministry and the Brazos Presbytery for acceptable terms concerning a "relevant" community program. It also implemented its own programs, on a limited basis, and familiarized the community with what MAYO hoped would become a community center.[16]

The politics of protest and confrontation continued for the next several months as MAYO confronted established religious and political leaders. In late March, MAYO demonstrated at the First Presbyterian Church for several weeks to protest the lack of response by church officials to the social needs of barrio residents.[17] In April, MAYO demonstrators marched in front of the Bates College of Law at the University of Houston to protest a conference on Mexican American affairs. After a while the protesters marched inside the conference meeting hall. Although the conference was organized by Mexican Americans, MAYO members charged that it was aimed at getting support for Republican politicians, not at solving the problems of those who lived in the barrios of Houston. They also criticized the conference for being held on a weekday, "when the working people could not attend"; for being at the University of Houston instead of in the Mexican American community; and for scheduling an expensive meal at the Shamrock-Hilton Hotel. On their way out one of the MAYO members shouted at the conference participants, "you can tell President [Richard] Nixon we don't want his favors." Later that same evening MAYO members stormed into a banquet in the Shamrock Hilton Hotel; shouted verbal insults at federal officials, including U.S. senator John Tower; and occupied the banquet site for about two hours. The "invasion," Yolanda Birdwell stated, "was to express the feelings of the Mexican American community."[18]

On San Jacinto Day, Barrio-MAYO demonstrated at the speech of Gov. Preston Smith and shouted slogans questioning his account of Texas history. In late July the organization participated in sponsoring a march and rally against the war in Vietnam. On August 3 the organization supported Chicano children blocking the Eastwood Park director from entering his office.[19] The UH-MAYO chapter supported these actions and at times also participated in them.[20] These and other militant actions made them a controversial group in the Mexican American community.

The Chicano Student Committee was a fairly recent group comprised of junior and high school students. Its adviser most likely was Gregory Salazar, who had been actively organizing students in the huelga schools.[21] The CSC wanted to present its own list of demands for improving the schools, many of which promoted student empowerment. Four of them, for instance, called for the creation of student-faculty councils to handle disciplinary matters and investigate complaints, the granting of full freedom of speech and press, the right to engage in political activity on campus, and the right to speak Spanish in school at any time without intimidation. Other demands sought the immediate establishment of Chicano history courses, the declaration of September 16 and May 5 as official school holidays, and an end to corporal punishment.[22]

Both MAYOs and the CSC then attended the Monday night school board meeting to express their support for MAEC and to voice their own concerns.[23] None of the groups, however, got an opportunity to address the board due to its abrupt adjournment.

THE SCHOOL BOARD MEETING

The meeting was stormy, contentious, and confusing. For several hours school board members discussed a variety of issues pertaining to the desegregation case and proposed several recommendations for modifying the court-mandated plan. The exchange of comments and decisions on desegregation plans such as freedom-of-choice, majority to minority transfers, and pairing confused the audience. Individuals in the audience applauded, booed, or jeered comments made by the board members who opposed or supported these varied positions. Despite several requests by Castillo and others to stop the applause and noise, these continued unabated.[24]

After the last item on the agenda the audience expected Castillo to speak. Under new business, Robbins read a letter from an Anglo who on religious grounds opposed immunization shots being given to his child in school. He then gave the floor to the letter's author so that he could elaborate. After this person finished speaking, Robbins announced that there was no other new business and abruptly adjourned the meeting. This surprised and angered MAEC supporters, especially barrio youths. They, as well as many other community activists, yelled and demanded to be heard. "When we asked for time," said Alex Rodríguez, one of the youths at the meeting, "the board members got up [and] started closing the curtain." [25] Lorenzo Díaz noted, "They started shutting the door in our faces and left Leonel Castillo standing there waiting for a turn that never came." [26]

At this point Gregory Salazar ran to the board table and pleaded with Robbins to listen to the Chicanos.[27] Robbins refused. Salazar demanded the right to be heard and said, "all hell will break loose if I am not heard." [28] Before he finished speaking, a police officer tried to get him out of the room. "As soon as he put a hand on Salazar, the whole hell broke loose and the Latin temper exploded," noted Díaz.[29]

Security guards immediately rushed forward to close the sliding partition separating the board from the audience. About two dozen young Chicanas and Chicanos also rushed forward to stop them. Gregory Salazar and Yolanda Birdwell leaped onto the board table, took over the microphone (which was by then turned off), and tried to hold back the sliding panel that security guards were attempting to close. Other MAYO members also tried to hold back the sliding panel. It was then that "pigs started hassling us," said Alex Rodríguez.[30] Shoving and pushing ensued; ashtrays were overturned, papers were thrown, and drinking glasses fell off the table.

"The police hassled Walter [Birdwell] and started beating on him," said Yolanda Flores, a MAYO supporter, and "then Yolanda [his wife] jumped in." "Then everybody jumped in," added Gloria Rubeck. A police officer during this confusion hit Edgar, Yolanda Birdwell's seven-year-old son, in the eye. Yolanda Flores saw the "pig" hit Edgar. "What a brave man," she said.[31]

The police instigated some of these actions as they pushed and shoved Chicanas and Chicanos into the halls, even isolating and detaining some in other rooms.[32] During the melee militant youths chanted "Chicano, Chicano, Chicano." [33]

Robbins, who had been pleading with Salazar, and the other board members quickly left as police, several school officials, and some members in the audience began scuffling. By this time the sliding door had been knocked off the tracks. School board member J. W. McCullough remained in the boardroom for a while and tried to quiet the chanting youths who now were taunting the police. When six uniformed police, led by Sgt. A. D. Bonds, confronted the shouting militants, McCullough decided to leave the boardroom.[34]

After McCullough's departure the militants moved into the corridor that separated the back door of the school board meeting room from the board services office. They chanted, "We'll be back, we'll be back" as they started toward the front of the building. The militants smashed water coolers and overturned chairs, tables, and potted plants. When police began arresting participants, the youths changed their chant to "police brutality, police brutality."[35] Two school administrators, Joe Tusa and Les Burton, former college football players, assisted the police in subduing the youths. During this commotion an unidentified gray-haired Anglo struck Robbins on the left cheek as he talked in the board services office. Burton stopped him and hustled the man out of the building.[36]

After thirty minutes police restored order and arrested fourteen people. They were taken outside where about eight to ten police cars were ready to escort them to jail. In the meantime a police helicopter circled overhead illuminating the area. Yolanda Birdwell shouted, "Police brutality" and told the media, "We smash it [the building] because they didn't want to talk to us." "Houston is going to be sorry because we are going to stand up," she added. The youths, holding clenched fists in the air and shouting in Spanish, were searched one by one by the police and loaded into cars. Some had their hands cuffed behind them. During the loading a cry of "Chicano" could be heard from one of those arrested or from a Mexican American in the crowd. The crowd of Chicanos then shouted in chorus "Power."

Of those arrested in the melee nine were MAYO members and five were juveniles. According to one source, at least one of those arrested was nowhere near the scene of the action but "had arrived after the police had herded the arrested to police cars." Juveniles arrested included three boys, ages fourteen to sixteen, and two girls, ages fourteen and fifteen. (Due to their ages, their names were not published.) They were interrogated, and despite attempts by parents to gain custody that same night, several were held for three days. They were charged with misdemeanors and sent to the county probation department. Among the nine MAYO members arrested were Gregory Salazar, twenty, a laborer; Walter Blake Birdwell, twenty-eight, a mailman; Yolanda Garza Birdwell, twenty-nine, a community organizer; and Idelfonso "Poncho" Delgado Ruíz, twenty-six, a VISTA worker. Teams of detectives interrogated them until early Tuesday morning.[37] The "MAYO 9" were transferred to Harris County jail where they were charged with malicious mischief, a felony. Salazar was charged with two counts and the others with one each; bond was set at one thousand dollars for each count. The nine also were charged in municipal court with disorderly conduct, one charge each, and a twenty-five-dollar cash bond was posted on each count.[38]

THE AFTERMATH

On Tuesday, MAEC issued a statement apologizing for the violence and stating that "the action taken by the youth activists was not sanctioned nor condoned by the council." The prepared statement noted, "Had the council spokesman [Castillo] been allowed to speak, he would have commended the board for its decision to appeal the order of the Fifth Circuit Court of Appeals to the Supreme Court." "However," the statement continued, "it should be noted that despite written request to speak for ten minutes, the board denied the council any time at all."[39]

In addition to the violence, the media reported that MAYO was chanting statements in support of freedom of choice. Castillo noted that he was unclear why MAYO voiced its support for freedom of choice at the school board meeting. This option was not part of MAEC's demands and was voiced primarily by Anglos who opposed the "forced" integration of the school district. Prior to the melee the school board had been discussing appealing the desegregation decision and asking for a freedom-of-choice plan. Large numbers of supporters of this plan were in the audience along with MAEC supporters. Twice during the meeting the crowed either applauded loudly or booed the board members engaged in a discussion of this plan. The board defeated the motion to include freedom of choice in its appeal to the Supreme Court with four opposed and three in favor. It did, however, vote to appeal the court-ordered pairing of twenty-five elementary schools, mostly involving predominantly black and Mexican American schools.

According to Castillo, the discussion over amendments to the desegregation lawsuit probably confused many individuals in the audience, including MAYO members such as Gregory Salazar and Yolanda Birdwell. "I was somewhat confused when the group [i.e., MAYO] started clapping for freedom of choice," Castillo said. "There was some misunderstanding there." MAEC and the Mexican American community, reiterated Castillo, did not advocate freedom of choice; they supported an appeal of the pairing of the schools.[40] Castillo felt that Robbins's decision not to allow any public input at the end of the meeting may also have added to the demonstrators' sense of frustration, and he noted, "It is really unfortunate the incident occurred when it did. The board had just made a very substantial step forward by agreeing to appeal the pairings to the Supreme Court." Appeal of the pairings was one of MAEC's key demands to end the two-week boycott of the schools.[41]

Because of the possible negative effect that the violent incident could have on the agreement that had developed between MAEC and the school board officials, Castillo stated that MAEC would have to reissue the call to boycott the schools.[42] According to him, MAEC had "no alternative but to continue the boycott until the agreement is once again solidified and put into writing."[43]

MAYO issued a statement and held a press conference to condemn the board, police, and media.[44] Salazar first clarified its stand with respect to the integration case. MAYO, noted Salazar, "is totally opposed to freedom of choice" and agreed with MAEC on the position of desegregation. He added that freedom of choice was a means for excluding "Negro and Mexican American students from Anglo schools."[45] He charged the police with using excessive force and said that some of those arrested were not members of the organization but innocent bystanders. Norma Trevino, another MAYO member, supported Salazar's version and later said that police started striking members of the audience without provocation before any property in the building was destroyed.[46]

Others responded by blaming the board and the police. Yolanda Flores blamed the board for MAYO's actions: "They said they would read the telegram [requesting time to speak] at the end of the meeting under new business, but they didn't even do that." She stated that they "just ignored us completely." One of the parents who attended the meeting said, "All we wanted was ten minutes. Just ten minutes. That's all. Ten minutes"; another stated, "We sent them letters, telegrams, and earlier we even called them."[47]

Another MAEC member, Lorenzo Díaz, regretted the violence at the school board meeting and did not condone or condemn the actions taken by Chicanos. "The whole blame should fall on Dr. Robbins," he said. "If he had given us the ten minutes, none of the violence would have happened, and the school boycott would have been over sooner." He concluded, "Now we realize our fight will never be over . . . the battle has just begun, and we are confident that it will end in a victory for rights over privileges."[48]

Dolores Castillo, an MAEC supporter, succinctly expressed in poetic form the variety of responses and anger that were expressed by the Chicano community. Entitled "Chicano Power," her verse talks about the impact of this action on the struggle for equality and justice:

It's time that you people should listen to me,
I'm trying to tell you what's going on, can't you see?
Chicanos are mad and it won't be for fun,
When we take what's ours and the white will run.
We tried to be heard, but they gave us no thought,
So Chicanos took stand and the white man we fought.
We had no intentions of doing all this,
But words did no good, so we tried with our fists.
They think that it's over, and they think that they've won.
But we're gonna show them that we've just begun.
We'll get what is ours and we'll do it alright,
But if they don't listen to us,
Get ready to fight!!![49]

The mini-riot, as labeled by the media, did not have negative consequences on the group's negotiating strategy. Paradoxically, it strengthened MAEC's hand at these negotiations and led to immediate concessions by the board. Within twenty-four hours after the mini-riot school officials agreed to meet seventeen of the original twenty demands. Of primary importance to MAEC was the willingness of the board to recognize Mexican Americans as an identifiable minority group for both desegregation and educational purposes and to appeal the pairing decision to the Supreme Court. The board's agreement to meet most of MAEC's demands led to the end of the boycott. On Wednesday, September 17, MAEC officially called an end to the boycott and asked all Mexican American students to return to the public schools.[50]

AN EVALUATION OF BOYCOTT ACTIVITIES

A few weeks after the boycott ended, Leonel Castillo assessed its impact and accomplishments. He concluded that the boycott had had a significant impact on the community and the schools. As a result of the boycott and despite the existence of political and ideological differences, various sectors of the Mexican American community became united in purpose.

It was "probably more united on the issue of better education for their young people" than it had been at any time in the past, argued Castillo.[51] This unity was based in large part on the community's acceptance of a new racial identity in the struggle for equal treatment in the schools and on its willingness to use "radical" direct action such as boycotts, pickets, and marches to achieve this end.

The change in identity is crucial to an understanding of MAEC's participation in the boycott. "For years," noted Leonel Castillo, "the Mexican American thought that if we were only classified as white we would automatically be in good shape." The court decision to pair Mexican American and African American schools, however, showed "in a very personal way" how the school district was using this "white" classification to circumvent desegregation in Houston. This decision led to an awareness among Mexican Americans that, in Castillo's words, "if we and the Anglos were white then how come I'm the one whose [sic] being paired?"[52] He continued: "He [i.e., the "Mexican American"] began to realize that he must be a different kind of white. He realized that even if he was white, he wasn't Anglo. And that the mere designation of white doesn't mean the granting of equality or the elimination of any injustice. . . ."[53]

In order to obtain justice, then, the community had to abandon its identity as white and accept a new one. This new identity, however, was not fully defined, and as a result several distinct interpretations emerged among the diverse group of activists. At one extreme were those influenced by the nationalist ideals of the Chicano movement. They considered themselves members of the brown or bronze race. These were the Chicano or "brown power" advocates. Most of the MAYO and CSC members as well as some PASSO activists belonged to this group. At another extreme were those influenced by legal principles and developments. These individuals considered themselves an ethnic minority group within the white race, i.e., a distinct group of "whites." Most members of MAEC and other organizations subscribed to these sentiments, as did Abraham Ramírez, Jr., when he said: "We have fought long and hard to get legally white. I think in general, Mexican Americans do not want to be identified as brown. Legally, we are in the white race."[54]

A third but minor group simply viewed itself as "Mejicanos." This small group, comprised of barrio residents, especially women who had come from Mexico and settled in the United States, experienced institutional and personal discrimination by the dominant Anglo society on a daily basis. Their lived experiences had convinced them that they were not white nor brown nor any other term. For all intents and purposes they were merely Mejicanos living in the United States.[55] Thus, while little agreement existed on how Mexican Americans should classify themselves (were they nonwhite, brown, or minority?), most of them concurred that they were "a separate group" with a distinct point of view.[56]

Additionally, MAEC members accepted a new politics. Unlike existing organizations such as LULAC or the American G.I. Forum, MAEC and its supporters resorted to the use of "street politics," i.e., boycotts, pickets, and marches, because "it was the best way to call attention to the problem," noted Abraham Ramírez. Lacking political clout and financial resources, MAEC utilized the boycott to protest a "very unjust situation." The boycott not only called attention to the problem at hand, it also led to significant concessions from the board. "I think it was worth it," noted Castillo.[57] He added, "I wonder why it was never done before." [58]

The acceptance of a new identity and a new politics was an integral part of the Chicano ideology or what Ignacio García calls the "militant ethos" of that era. These ideals reflected the national context of protest and the Mexican American civil rights movement and became powerful motivators for increased activism and school change in Houston.[59]

The boycott and huelga activities had an extremely positive influence on the schools. The community's diverse needs were presented to HISD officials, noted one of its supporters, "in a fashion which cannot be forgotten and many people now have been discussing these problems and a possible solution." [60] This eventually led to the board recognition of Mexican American students as a distinct ethnic minority group and to inclusion of Mexican Americans and their interests in the making of school policies. For instance, Mexican Americans gained representation in court-appointed and board-appointed committees.[61] Their interests also were now represented in school policies, programs, and practices.

Recognition had an additional impact. It led to the promotion of school reforms and to programmatic changes or considerations "which probably would not have occurred to this degree had all of this not taken place." [62] Bilingual education, curriculum revision to include Mexican American contributions, sensitivity sessions for school personnel, and the hiring of Mexican American teachers and administrators, for instance, increased after the board granted recognition to Mexican American students as a distinct ethnic minority group. In total, programs and services for the

Mexican American student population that were estimated to cost at least $2 million were enacted as a result of the board's recognition of Mexican Americans as a distinct ethnic minority group.[63]

These gains were obtained after much personal and group suffering and grief. "Some of the people," noted Castillo, "had to pay heavily in the sense of their loss of freedom. . . . Others have been detained, still others will probably be expelled or suspended, and some others will suffer in their school work." Collective action on the part of the community, however, improved school conditions for Mexican American students and included them in the local desegregation efforts.[64]

MAEC promised to continue the struggle for "just" integration. "We are now at a point in which the continuation of the struggle is mandated for one primary reason and that is a sense of justice impels us to continue to fight," said Castillo. "Continuation is also demanded for strategically we cannot allow H.I.S.D. or any other school or any set of authorities to come in and undo the work which has been done," he added.[65]

MAEC proposed several future plans. These included taking legal action against the school district, filing administrative complaints against discriminatory actions toward students and parents, monitoring programs developed by HISD to meet the needs of students, developing tutoring and remedial educational programs, conducting an informative public relations campaign, and fund-raising.[66]

MAEC's optimism was premature. Five months after the boycott was terminated, the group encouraged the Mexican American community to engage in another boycott of the public schools and to send their children to huelga schools. This grassroots organization had won an important battle in September, but the war against educational inequality had yet to be won.

CHAPTER 8

Simple Justice

Despite the board's commitment to consider Mexican Americans as an identifiable minority group, it continued to view them as white. This became apparent in December, 1970, when district officials drafted a new integration plan for the spring term that failed to consider them as an identifiable minority group. Under this proposed plan predominantly Mexican American schools were paired with predominantly African American ones. MAEC members criticized the school board's action and recommended additional changes, including the inclusion of Anglos in the pairing of schools. Their pleas were ignored. Incensed with the school board's response, MAEC called on the community for further action. Realizing its organizational limits and the possible dissolution of mass support for continued protest activity, MAEC called for a policy of noncooperation that included a limited "stay-at-home" policy, selective pickets of individual huelga schools, and further negotiations with school board officials. The events that unfolded during the spring of 1971 indicate how traditional black/white racial policies of the past continued to clash with the new Chicano ideology of nonwhiteness and cultural pride. This chapter focuses on the activities associated with the politics of school desegregation from December, 1970, to February, 1971.

INITIAL RESPONSE TO HISD'S MODIFIED PAIRING PLAN

MAEC's boycott in September ended in large part after the school board agreed to most of MAEC's demands, including the decision to appeal to the U.S. Supreme Court the pairing part of the Fifth Circuit's integration order. School pairing was based on the premise that Mexican American children were white for desegregation purposes; it directed the district to pair Mexican American schools with black schools. The appeal was predicated on the belief that Mexican Americans were not white but rather a distinct ethnic minority group. Thus, more Anglo schools had to be included in the pairing of schools in order for the district to achieve equitable integration. In response to the pressure from the Mexican American community and other sources, the school district also filed a request with the Fifth Circuit to delay implementation of the pairing provisions of its August 25 mandate until the Supreme Court reached its decision.[1]

On December 12 the Fifth Circuit denied HISD's plea to delay implementation of the pairing provisions.[2] The following day the school board stated that it would appeal the pairing order to the district court. As part of its appeal, the school district submitted a modified pairing plan to Judge Connally for review.[3] This plan ignored the district's commitment to MAEC to consider Mexican Americans a distinct ethnic minority group for desegregation purposes.

The modified plan, according to Superintendent Garver, was prepared in conjunction with parents involved from all the schools to be paired. A journalist, however, described this plan as the result of closed sessions with a few select parents and principals and the three-member administrative committee of the twenty-five schools to be paired.[4] Neither MAEC nor its supporters were active participants in the plan's formulation.[5] Lorenzo Díaz, the Northside MAEC representative, also charged that this was not a community plan. "This is their [the administration's] plan," he said. "They presented it to us and said we could take it or leave it."[6]

Under the traditional pairing concept mandated by the court, grade levels were restructured in the paired schools so that kindergarten through the third grade were offered in one school and grades four through six in the other school. This type of pairing affected every neighborhood involved since all the children had to attend a school outside the community for at least three years of the elementary grades. The proposed plan retained kindergarten through the sixth grade in each school and only moved 1,876 pupils to different schools. The majority of those moved were "white" and black students residing in the north and east sides of town. Unlike the court's original plan that paired twenty-seven elementary schools, this one paired only twenty-two. Under HISD's plan two additional elementary schools were rezoned and three of them—Eliot, Easter, and Ryan—were dropped from the pairing.[7]

The result with respect to Mexican Americans, however, was the same as the court's earlier plan. Generally speaking, the new plan ignored their new identity and continued the injustice of the earlier plan by viewing them as legally white for desegregation purposes and by pairing them with blacks. Seven of the schools in the proposed pairing plan were predominantly Mexican American in student enrollment, and twelve of them were predominantly black.[8]

Despite these shortcomings, the superintendent and the board supported the plan because it was not as disruptive as the earlier plan—that is, it did not offend many Anglos.[9] It also helped to maintain the neighborhood school concept intact by limiting the number of schools involved to those in the minority communities.[10]

The modified pairing plan was approved at an emergency board meeting on December 16. A formal vote was not taken until nearly midnight. By that time the public, including about one hundred MAEC members, had gone home.[11] Lorenzo Díaz, selected to speak on behalf of MAEC, charged that Mexican Americans were excluded from commenting on the plan prior to its adoption by the board. The meeting, he stated, did not allow Mexican Americans to argue against the plan since the open session did not start until 11:55 P.M.[12] Díaz vowed to protest the pairing plan. "We'll use every means to oppose it," he said after the meeting. "If necessary, MAEC will launch another boycott of schools to protest it."[13] Díaz's four children attended Ryan, one of the excluded schools.[14]

Díaz was not the only one incensed at the board's refusal to honor its commitments. Most of MAEC's leaders and supporters voiced their strong opposition to the new plan. Several of them echoed Díaz's sentiment and threatened another boycott.[15] Leonel Castillo likewise supported those who called for a further boycott of the public schools. Ironically, the night before passage of the modified plan by the board Castillo had told the membership at a MAEC banquet that the organization did not plan any further boycotts of the public schools because of "improved situations" for Mexican Americans.[16] On Wednesday evening a reporter asked Castillo to compare the talk of a new boycott to his comment on Tuesday evening. Castillo responded, "That was 24 hours ago."[17]

Gregory Salazar, speaking on behalf of MAYO, also criticized the board's decision to implement a new pairing plan that continued to use Mexican

Americans as pawns in the district's desegregation design. Salazar noted that the plan omitted two elementary schools where the Mexican American boycott conducted in September was most effective—Eliot and Ryan. Under the original August 25 mandate Eliot was paired with Atherton and Scroggins; Ryan was paired with Ross and Looscan.[18] Similar to other MAEC members, he supported more drastic action, including a boycott of the HISD schools.[19]

On Friday, December 18, MAEC held a general meeting to discuss the pairing plan and a possible boycott of the public schools. Unlike other meetings, significant differences between many of MAEC's members and Barrio-MAYO emerged. Most members believed that the organization could still get the school board to recognize Mexican Americans as an identifiable minority group for desegregation purposes. They, in other words, still supported just integration. Barrio-MAYO members, however, opposed integration and argued that they should push for community control of the schools rather than integration.

MAYO's position had officially been voiced the day before at a press conference the group set up. At this press conference MAYO spokesperson Gregory Salazar said that the organization was not "an official part of the MAEC" anymore because of its disagreement over goals.[20] The real issue facing the schools and the education of Mexican Americans, Salazar stated, was not integration but rather "the control of the barrio schools by the people in the community." He added, "We seek the complete control of barrio schools by the community whose children attend these schools."[21]

MAYO's new position was based on the cultural nationalist ideals and social change program of El Plan Espiritual de Aztlan, a program of action developed at two National Chicano Youth Liberation Conferences held in 1969 and 1970. These conferences, hosted by Rodolfo "Corky" González's group, the Crusade for Justice, promoted a cultural nationalist ideology and action plan to "liberate" the Mexican American masses from the dominance of Anglo America. More specifically, conference participants agreed that "Chicano" nationalism would be the common denominator for mass mobilization and organization in the United States and that "social, economic, cultural and political independence" was the only road to "total liberation from oppression, exploitation and racism." In practical terms, this meant that the struggle for liberation would be based on the "control of our Barrios, campos, pueblos, lands, our economy, our culture, and our political life."[22]

MAYO's position was also probably influenced by the "peaceful revolution" taking place in Crystal City. In 1970 Chicano and Chicana activists took control of the local city council and school board and initiated a series of significant social and political reforms, i.e., the "peaceful revolution," that improved the lives of the predominantly working-class Mexican American population.[23] The realization of self-determination in Crystal City in combination with other factors encouraged Barrio-MAYO to take a position in favor of community control. This, rather than integration, held the possibility for true reform in the Mexican American community. Those in attendance probably rejected Barrio-MAYO's arguments and continued to support MAEC and its goal of equitable integration.

In addition to determining the group's major goal, those at the meeting also decided on its demands. Because the court had not yet granted them legal status as a distinct identifiable minority group, they decided to demand that Anglo schools be added to any pairing plan. This became MAEC's major demand.[24] The group also decided to continue its negotiating strategy with school officials. In addition to meeting with school board members and the superintendent, MAEC also agreed to voice its concerns before the court-appointed Bi-Racial Committee.[25]

THE POLITICS OF NEGOTIATION

On January 8, 1971, Castillo wrote a letter to the board clarifying MAEC's position on the pairing plan. He pointed out that the desegregation plan handed down by the Fifth Circuit Court allowed more flexibility than was being exercised by HISD. The section of the ruling under discussion read: "The District Court is directed to implement the forgoing modifications as to the elementary school zones or alternatively the court may adopt any other plan submitted by the School Board or other interested parties, provided, of course, that such alternate plan achieves at least the same degree of desegregation as that reached by our modifications." The modifications the court referred to in this section, Castillo argued, were those pertaining to the pairing and grouping provisions of the ruling. "We feel that this clause clearly allows you leeway to change the pairing and grouping so as to bring Anglos into a desegregation plan," he said. "It is our contention that by simply adding a few Anglo schools into the formula a greater degree of desegregation could be achieved and a greater degree of educational quality could be maintained."[26]

Castillo then suggested several additional actions that could be taken to achieve the flexibility allowed by the court. They were:

1. If we must pair and group, then the two predominantly Black elementary schools, Frost and Rhodes, should not be paired with one another.
2. If possible, why not have a larger number of minority students moving to predominantly Anglo schools than Anglo students to minority schools? This would achieve more integration statistically and also improve teacher-pupil ratios in the minority schools.
3. Convene a group of M.A.E.C. and H.I.S.D. attorneys to fully explore the flexibility allowed under the ruling.[27]

The board took no actions on Castillo's suggestions.

The second major strategy, to meet with the Bi-Racial Committee, was initiated on January 5, 1971. On this date Leonel Castillo wrote to John Wheat, chairperson of the court-appointed Bi-Racial Committee, requesting a hearing before this committee. Two days later Wheat responded that he was unsure whether the committee should hold a hearing on "the pairing and grouping provisions" of the court's August 25, 1970, judgment. He informed Castillo, nonetheless, that he would request guidance from the court "as to when and to what extent we explore the subject."[28] On the night of January 12, 1971, Superintendent Garver contacted Castillo and told him that the Bi-Racial Committee would allow MAEC to present its case at a formal hearing on Tuesday, January 19, and that comments would be heard from "no more than five individuals."

On Friday, January 15, MAEC held a strategy session and decided on the topics to present to the board. Those present agreed to discuss MAEC's philosophy, its legal perspective of desegregation, its views on grouping and pairing in the different barrios, and its ideas on some new approaches to desegregation. Leonel Castillo would discuss the organization's philosophy, Abraham Ramírez would focus on the legal issues, and three others would discuss issues and problems in several different barrios.[29]

On January 19, 1971, MAEC members spoke at the Bi-Racial Committee hearing.[30] Leonel Castillo summarized MAEC's key points. First, Castillo stated that MAEC strongly endorsed integration: "We agree with the 1954 Supreme Court Ruling, we agree with the principles which have been announced by various Presidents and by the Congress of the United States, and we are eager to see Houston become a place where all the ethnic and cultural groups can live together in harmony." "However," he added, "the present pairing and grouping plan, which has been submitted by the Houston Independent School district, is a sham of these principles which we value so highly." He explained that MAEC members did not believe that pairing Mexican Americans and blacks was sound practice. "We do not think," noted Castillo, "that it makes sense from an educational point of view, from a philosophical point of view, or from a simple justice point of view." The plan was viewed as a "sham" because it did not allow for parental involvement and because it was based on some false premises. Mexican Americans were not white, as the district court had ruled, but rather an identifiable minority group.[31]

Castillo charged that the zoning concept adopted by the school board discriminated against poor people. Furthermore, he called for the establishment of a triethnic rather than biracial committee to monitor desegregation in the city, questioned the use of federal funds for desegregation purposes, and asked for assistance in persuading Judge Connally to allow MAEC the opportunity to be heard in court. Finally, he urged the committee to impress upon the district court that the plan suggested by the Fifth Circuit was not rigid but rather allowed room for flexibility. "The most obvious need is to bring the Anglo into the desegregation formula," he concluded. The other presenters agreed with Castillo and elaborated upon these arguments and ideas.[32]

MAEC's presentations, while eloquent and articulate, had no immediate impact on the Bi-Racial Committee. The committee did not add any new members, nor did it support MAEC's or MALDEF's friend-of-the-court brief. The committee also did not seek modifications in the district's pairing plan.[33]

PLANS FOR IMPLEMENTING THE MODIFIED PAIRING PLAN

During January, MAEC continued to express disapproval of the modified pairing plan as a desegregation remedy. Most members hoped that they would gain some concessions when school started again after the holidays. They were mistaken. On Tuesday, January 26, the school board issued the new pairing plan for the remainder of the academic year. Instead of triethnic pairing, the plan continued the pairing of Mexican American and black schools.[34]

To facilitate the plan's implementation, district officials decided to phase in the school pairing. On Friday, January 29, Poe would be paired with MacGregor, Frost with Rhoads, and Dodson with Lantrip. On February 3,

Burris was to be paired with Roosevelt, Pleasantville with Port Houston, and Sanderson with Chatham. On the fifth of the month Bruce was to be paired with Anson Jones and Crawford with Sherman. On February 8, Atherton was to be paired with Scroggins, Nat Henderson with Pugh, and Ross with Looscan. In each case school officials would announce which paired elementary school each student would attend.[35]

On Thursday, January 28, MAEC met at Juan Marcos Presbyterian Church to discuss its response to the new pairing plan. Over two hundred parents, teachers, and community leaders attended the meeting. Those present voiced their anger over the pairing decision. Romualdo M. Castillo said that he and others were angry that the district failed to consider Mexican Americans a separate ethnic minority group within the white population. "We are legally white," he noted, "but we have not had all the opportunities of the whites." Others such as Maggie Landron accused HISD of using Mexican Americans for political purposes. HISD officials, she argued, could not afford to develop a "just" integration plan during an election year because it would upset Anglo voters and parents. "Politically for HISD," noted Landron, "the Anglos were more important." Leonel Castillo supported this theme of political expediency. "In other words," he said, "the Mexican American does not matter because he doesn't have very many votes." School officials, he continued, have been "playing games with us for five months, they never intended to change the pairing plan."[36]

An activist later elaborated on this theme of political expediency. When ordered to comply with federal integration laws, HISD officials designed a plan that was, by their own admission, "politically expedient and immoral, improper, and a flagrant denial of the essence of the federal law," the activist noted. Furthermore, this plan "was a deliberate attempt to circumvent the inherent justice of the integration laws by pairing a minimum number of Anglo students with the black community." Bigotry and white inconvenience were the reasons given for "this blatant disregard of our human dignity," this person continued. "The majority faction in the district are bigots, and they would vote the school board members out of office if they did not devise a plan to perpetuate white supremacy." Furthermore, mandating school pairing for white children would inconvenience board members since it would force them "to wake up earlier than they are used to."[37]

Aware of their organizational limits and the lack of resources, MAEC members decided to adopt a strategy of "non-cooperation with the pairing of schools" that would include a stay-at-home policy, selective picket-

ing of the schools and the administration, and establishment of "alternative schools."[38] Castillo noted that MAEC was in a much better position to
set up huelga schools than it had been in September, 1970: "We have a few
dollars this time. Last time we were broke." MAEC threatened to hold the
huelga schools through the end of the school year "if necessary," said Castillo, adding, "Given the attitude of this school board toward Mexican
Americans it is very possible."[39]

The struggle was on again, noted one community activist. This person
said, "Maybe this time the Anglos will get the message that the Chicanos
mean business. Just integration and quality education are two things that
the Mexican American people will not be cheated out of any longer."[40]

MAEC's plans were announced at a press conference the following day.
The stay-at-home policy, noted Leonel Castillo, was not a general boycott
but a selective one; it would affect only those children assigned to the
paired schools. MAEC recommended that parents whose children were affected by the pairings keep them home. The council was planning to set up
schools and transportation systems to aid the stay-at-home policy.[41]

MAEC also would protest the first day of pairing by holding a demonstration at Lantrip Elementary School, a predominantly Mexican American school to be paired. Lantrip was the major target for this day, and others would be focused on later. Those choosing not to send their children
to public schools could send them to huelga institutions. The new pairing
of schools necessitated these actions. "The pairing of Mexican-Americans
with blacks and the pairing of blacks with blacks cannot be construed
by any reasonable person to mean integration has occurred," Castillo said.
"The majority population, which consists of Anglos, must be brought into
any equitable just plans."[42]

THE STRATEGY OF NONCOOPERATION:
JANUARY 29–FEBRUARY 20, 1971

The stay-at-home policy was relatively successful in accomplishing its goal.
On the first day of school only Lantrip and Sherman Elementary Schools
were affected. MAEC's chairperson, Leonel Castillo, led eighteen women
in protest at Lantrip. He reiterated the reason for the protest: "In the last
four months the school board has failed to bring Anglos into the [pairing]
formula."[43] The mothers of these children marched up and down in front
of the school with their signs reading "Hell No, No Vamos" and "Education Si, Mickey Mouse Games No."[44]

Parents also boycotted buses scheduled to take the Mexican American children from Lantrip to Dobson Elementary. Although MAEC had only a few days to organize Lantrip parents, its efforts were successful. Most of the seats of the "shiny, yellow HISD school bus" were empty as the Mexican American children stayed at home to protest pairing with blacks.[45]

At Sherman Elementary in the Northside barrio Mexican American parents successfully boycotted the bus. The parents led by Lucil [sic] Rivera, Victor Bueno, Frances Jasco, Rachel Lucas, Charlotte Aguilar, Virginia Vara, Amalia Ponce de León, and Margarita Calsade effectively led a bus blockade. Only seven of eighty-five children boarded the bus. "And some of those didn't count," noted one MAEC member, because "three were anglos and the other an oriental."[46]

Throughout the week Mexican American pickets at selective sites were relatively successful in encouraging parents to keep their children at home. On February 3, for instance, more than one hundred Mexican American parents picketed in front of Port Houston Elementary School. Mrs. María Moncevais and Mrs. Morales (no first name provided) led them. Only two of the eighty students who were supposed to transfer to Pleasantville boarded the bus. At Roosevelt twenty-four parents picketed, and only seven of the ninety students boarded the buses to Burrus Elementary at this site.[47]

On a chilly Friday morning, February 5, 1971, "many Raza" showed up to picket at Anson Jones, located in El Segundo barrio. The night before the boycott started the parents used the cafeteria to plan their tactics. Much to the dismay of the principal, who thought that the parents were interested in the pairing of schools, they used this time to plan their boycott. Daniel Torres led the effort. Only 10 out of 110 students were bused that day.[48] Mexican American parents also picketed Sherman Elementary. Only 10 of 84 students from that school appeared at Crawford on Friday. Pickets continued at Port Houston, where only 7 of 80 students boarded the bus going to Pleasantville.[49]

The resistance to the district's pairing plan continued into Monday, February 8. In addition to boycotting the buses, Mexican American parents also picketed several elementary schools, including Scroggins, Pugh, and Looscan. Monday was an extremely cold day with temperatures in the low twenties, but Mexican American parents showed up to picket the schools. There were some thirty of them picketing Pugh Elementary and at least forty at Scroggins. José Padilla and Victor Bueno instructed *las madres* at Scroggins on the art of picketing. "The result," noted one MAEC member, was that only "ten out of 110 boarded the bus." At Pugh Elementary, Rumaldo Castillo, Marie Juárez, Frances Fernández, Mary Villareal, and Dolores Tamayo all stood in twenty-degree weather to picket for their cause.[50]

The largest group of protesters was at Looscan. Over sixty parents and community people picketed this school. Carmen Beltran was in charge of this large group. With her were Collie López, Bertha Ybarra, and Lucie García. Abel Alejándro and his wife reported that their family was not affected but they still supported the boycott "porque somos Chicanos [because we are Chicanos], and we need to stick together." Rosie Limón was also present although she was not affected. All carried signs with different messages. Some condemned the school board; others told the board to "learn their ABCs—Anglos, Blacks, Chicanos"; and others questioned why Anglos were not included in the pairing plan. A sixty-five-year-old woman, Victoria Hernández, told reporters that Chicanos must get it together and "que sigan adelante (keep struggling)." Only seven out of sixty-three Mexican American children boarded the bus at Looscan that chilly day in February.[51]

Denver Harbor parents helped out in other ways. Mr. Ayala, for instance, kept his children from attending Eliot Elementary to express solidarity with the striking parents of Scroggins. Mrs. Villaseñor and Dora Guerra had no children in school but still aided the cause by walking the picket lines. Amalia and Linda Ávila both had children in Eliot but were in the picket line.[52]

For the most part the strategy of noncooperation pursued by MAEC was perceived as quite successful. The boycott of the busing plan, according to MAYO member Pédro Vasquez, was about 85 percent effective. This, he noted, was in contrast to Superintendent Garver's comments that little difficulty had been experienced in pairing the elementary schools.[53] "Either Garver was ignorant of all the resistance that the Mexican American Education Council and Chicano parents put up," said Vasquez, "or he knew of these incidents but was afraid to expose the failure of the pairing plan." Notwithstanding Garver's comments, the Chicano community was optimistic of changing school desegregation policy. "If MAEC can continue this and open up the Huelga schools, then Garver will have to admit the sham of the pairing plan," stated Vasquez.[54]

MAEC had another opportunity to voice its concerns at the regular school board meeting scheduled for Monday, February 8. That day a large number of Mexican American parents marched outside the administration building for four hours. Some of "las mujeres" carried a black casket on their heads that said "Justice is Dead." "Justice from the schools," noted one observer, "died when the whites used the Mexican Americans as the only source of integration."[55]

Inside the board meeting three individuals—Mrs. María Moncevais from the Port Houston area and José Pérez and Memo de la Cerda, MAYO members—were given the opportunity to speak. MAYO members recommended that the school district be subdivided on the basis that would ensure "barrio control of barrio schools." The school board stated that it would look at the merit of the idea and then "ended the matter with a ho-hum."[56]

Mrs. Moncevais talked about Port Houston Elementary and explained that it was already integrated. According to her, the school had 515 students whose racial composition was 15 percent black, 60 percent Mexican American, and 25 percent white. She then noted how busing of the children would "put a hardship on a lot of people that live here." She explained, "We are not fighting anybody, we are not violent people, we just want our children to go to elementary school in their own neighborhood." Referring to the boycott, she stated: "And it is not the stupidity of parents that their children are not in school: it is the stupidity of other people who brought all of this upon us."[57]

Despite vocal protests by MAEC and MAYO, the school board ignored them. "Like ostriches with their heads in the sand," noted one observer, "they [board members] carried on the meeting 'business as usual' spending two minutes on the pairing plan." Superintendent Garver declined to determine the number of students who had refused to board the buses at the different schools.[58]

Official neglect of the community's interests further encouraged MAEC to continue the boycott. Although it is unclear how many participated or how long it lasted, some evidence suggests that the boycott attracted several hundred and lasted longer than a month. By late February community activists writing in *Papel Chicano* defended the ongoing boycott and criticized individuals, especially Anglo liberals, who were beginning to oppose this action. Liberals, one of the activists argued, were confused over the community's opposition to pairing and were wondering why MAEC attacked both conservative and liberal board policies, why it expressed pride in being an ethnic group, and why it displayed racism toward blacks and Anglos.[59] In general, this activist argued that these criticisms reflected the biases of white liberal middle-class individuals who did not understand minorities and who tried to "fit their pre-conceived ideas of what is best for 'our world.' " [60]

In an effort to understand MAEC's support for the boycott, this activist continued, liberals had to understand what the organization stood for and how it interpreted the "facts relative to the pairing plan and to the boycott." MAEC was a barrio or grassroots organization that sought to meet the educational needs of Mexican Americans. The council was comprised of people from the Houston barrios "who themselves are personally the daily subjects and recipients of white racism and bigotry." MAEC was formed specifically to oppose racism, prejudice, and inequality of education. The organization's philosophy was based on the notion of cultural diversity and pluralism, that is, "on the right of each group to maintain its cultural values, pride in its heritage, and respect for its historical evolution." This was in contrast to the schools that sought to "destroy this philosophy by its total insistence that all children are the same by conformity and rigidity." MAEC recognized that if the schools promoted respect and understanding of each group's contributions, integration would be beneficial to all racial and cultural groups, "including anglos." However, "the schools are unequipped to do this," the newspaper article noted.[61]

The way to judge MAEC, the author of the article further noted, was by its actions. MAEC favored the "just integration" of all children on a triethnic basis. "The only integration that has taken place in Houston," according to the article, "is with Chicanos and Blacks." Readers were reminded that MAEC and the Chicano community were not against blacks; they opposed racism in general and worked "side by side" with them for years in the civil rights struggles. Leonel Castillo, for instance, fought for integrated housing in San Antonio in 1961, and Sister Gloria Gallardo spent four years teaching in Mississippi. The article pointed out that Ben Reyes and Romualdo Castillo were also key players in the coalition between Operation Breadbasket (a black-sponsored organization) and the Denver Harbor MAEC chapter.[62]

MAEC opposed pairing of minorities because Mexican Americans had suffered "the same indignities, discriminations, and poverty as the Blacks" simply because they were brown and maintained "a Spanish-speaking culture." "Minority with minority, [and] poverty with poverty integration," the article writer noted, "is a disaster to both groups—it gives the white its token integration and also gives them the excuse needed to keep the schools educationally backward." Thus, the arguments raised by liberals that the Mexican American boycott was racist and their conclusion that

the school board's pairing decision was "appropriate" were both misleading since they were based on a misunderstanding of the Mexican American community and its responses to the pairing plan.[63]

CONCLUSION

Despite MAEC's strategy of selective boycotting and picketing, by the end
of February the community had failed to get the courts or the schools to
seriously recognize their legal status and their needs. Although concessions
had been exacted from the superintendent and the members of the board,
local officials continued to function on the basis of black-white race relations rather than on a triethnic basis. Local school officials, notwithstanding their pledges to the Mexican American community, were legally bound
to ignore this group in the development of integration plans. Failure to
consider a change in the legal status of Mexican Americans, however, did
not lead to despair; it only encouraged the community to struggle harder
for this reform. The possibility for changing a policy based on outdated
racial ideals guided MAEC's actions. Sooner or later, the organization's
members believed, the board would take them seriously and change its integration plan. But for now the school board's indifference continued to
fuel MAEC's oppositional efforts. The struggle was far from over.

CHAPTER 9

CONTINUING THE STRUGGLE

For the next several months, from March through June, 1971, MAEC as well as groups of Mexican American parents, students, and community members continued to struggle on behalf of school reforms. Setbacks in the courts and inequitable treatment in the schools fueled the growing disenchantment within the district. During this period MAEC responded to the challenges raised by the courts and the schools in diverse ways. It pursued litigation, engaged in the politics of protest and group pressure, and took steps to increase its organizational stability. More significantly, MAEC underwent a transformation from an activist group to a quasi–social service organization. This chapter discusses these developments and its impact on MAEC's school reform efforts.

LITIGATION

Although MAEC had filed a lawsuit to intervene as defendant in the local desegregation case in September, 1970, by May of 1971 the court had failed to rule on the case. On May 20, 1971, Abraham Ramírez, MAEC's legal representative, asked the district court judge for a hearing on its request for intervention since the Supreme Court had refused both the school board's stay of the pairing order and its request to intervene in the case.[1]

The court held this hearing and issued its decision on the May 24, but it was not a favorable ruling for MAEC. In his ruling Judge Connally castigated Mexican Americans for trying to intervene in the desegregation case at this late stage. He argued that HISD had always treated "Latin Americans as of the Anglo or white race." For all purposes, Mexicans were considered as whites or regarded as a race apart. There never was a "separate but equal" policy applied to them in the schools, as was the case with African Americans. "Never in the fifteen years since the initiation of this action have they [Mexican Americans] complained of this treatment [being claimed as white]," he said. That is, Mexican Americans did not complain until the court of appeals ordered the pairing of certain predominantly Mexican American schools with predominantly African American ones. The motion to intervene, he argued, was filed September 11, 1970. The pairing order of the court of appeals was dated August 25, 1970. "Content to be white for these many years," he added, "now, when the shoe begins to pinch, the would-be-intervenors wish to be treated not as whites but as an 'identifiable ethnic group.'" "In short," he concluded, "they wish to be 'integrated' with Whites, not Blacks."[2]

Even if Mexican Americans were considered an identifiable minority group, Connally noted, it did not follow that they were entitled to the relief sought. The courts, especially the *Swann* case, emphasized that it was the effects of "state-imposed segregation" that the courts were obligated to eliminate. Connally continued, "Neither Swann [*sic*] nor any other authority with which I am familiar suggests that every identifiable minority group—as Italian-American, German American, Polish American—who have been treated by the law only as white-Americans, are now entitled to escape the effects of school integration."[3] The motion to intervene was denied.

MAEC's response to Connally's ruling was predictable.[4] Leonel Castillo, chairperson of MAEC, described the decision as "disappointing" and said that he was sorry Judge Connally could not understand "the problems of Mexican Americans today." MAEC, for instance, was not trying to "escape integrating with any group," as Connally had stated; rather MAEC was calling for a triethnic desegregation plan, i.e., one that would involve all groups, not simply Mexican Americans and African Americans. Castillo charged that Connally was "simply unaware" of the history of Mexican Americans in Houston. "Fifteen years ago we were a small, almost insignificant percentage of the school population," he said. "Since then the number of Mexican Americans in the school district has almost doubled."[5] Mexican Americans had indeed become a significant part of the total population since 1950. In 1950 they comprised less than 1 percent of the total population in Houston, a mere forty thousand out of six hundred thousand residents. Their numbers increased significantly over the next two decades so that by 1970 they comprised 12 percent of the total population.[6]

As for the right to be considered an identifiable minority group, Castillo said that the judge was "distinctly at odds" with other federal agencies such as the Census Bureau; the Justice Department; the Office of Health, Education, and Welfare; and the U.S. Civil Rights Commission. Within the previous three years each of these agencies had issued policies recognizing the minority group status of Mexican Americans. For instance, in 1967 congress enacted the first bilingual education act in this country's history. This bill recognized the special needs of Mexican American school-age children and provided financial assistance to local education agencies to develop and carry out new and imaginative elementary and secondary school programs designed to meet these special education needs.[7] In 1970 the Office of Health, Education, and Welfare (HEW) issued a statement recognizing the "national origin" minority status of Mexican Americans. Known as the "May 25 Memorandum," it identified four major areas of concern relating to district compliance with title 6 of the Civil Rights Act of 1964.[8] In the areas of curriculum, placement practices, ability grouping or tracking, and informing parents about school activities, the memo forbade discrimination on the basis of national origin background.[9] Even the Census Bureau, the federal courts, and the U.S. Commission on Civil Rights recognized Mexican Americans as an identifiable minority group.[10] Castillo commented: "It's especially ironic that his [Connally's] ruling follows a monumental report by the U.S. Commission on Civil Rights which clearly documents a high degree of ethnic isolation of Mexican Americans in Texas."[11]

Abraham Ramírez, Jr., agreed with Castillo that Judge Connally had a wrong impression of Mexican Americans. "Mexican Americans don't oppose integration with Blacks," he noted; "they oppose failure to include [the] entire community, especially Anglos, in the decision."[12] Eduardo N. Lopez, writing in *Papel Chicano*, was more caustic in opposing Connally's ruling. He accused Connally of demonstrating "an extraordinary ignorance concerning the problems, character, and culture of la Raza." He further noted that the Mexican American community would not tolerate "more injustices nor their deformed opinions and interpretations over integration laws." "Forward and onwards with the struggle for a comprehensive and impartial integration," he added.[13]

Felix Ramírez, another *Papel Chicano* writer, also commented on the decision. He criticized Connally's decision that Mexican Americans wanted to be integrated with whites and not blacks, writing, "I wish to remind this ignorant human being [Judge Connally] that it was the Supreme Court of the United States of America who ordered the schools integrated[,] not the Mexican American people." "His decision," he added, "proves his and a lot of other racist people's point that the Supreme Court's decisions hold no water and that they are a farce." If Judge Connally did not want integration of races, Ramírez further noted, then he should go to some "all white" country, "because he has not noticed [that] the U.S. is a composition of many races, including the Mexican American and the Negro." Ramírez concluded, "The decision this man made is not progressive; it definitely proves his lack of respect for law, for the Constitution, and the rights of people whom he swore to serve."[14]

On May 26, MAEC filed an appeal of U.S. district judge Ben C. Connally's decision against Mexican American intervention.[15] Despite disillusionment with the decision, MAEC was not discouraged from continuing the struggle. The decision, many of its members believed, was unjust but not unalterable.

PRESSURE

MAEC's involvement was not limited to the politics of litigation during the second half of the 1970–71 academic year. The group also sought to influence school policy and practice at the school-board level. MAEC's emphasis on policy involvement was apparent in at least three types of activities.

First, MAEC inquired into the distribution of federal funds. On April 2, Castillo wrote a letter to Beatrice M. Smith, director of the Title I/Model Cities Planning and Coordination Department in HISD. He wanted to know how the district was spending its federal funds. The district had been allocated more than $1 million for a massive urban rehabilitation project entitled the "Model Cities Program." By late March approximately $180,000 had been spent to improve secondary schools in the "lower economic areas of the district." The district used these funds to establish a variety of programs in eight junior and senior high schools. These programs provided recreational and educational centers for students and adults, encouraged active participation by the community, and provided employment for some residents of the area. "Everything from table tennis to English for Mexican American adults is included in the program, which has already provided forty-six jobs for adults," noted a reporter for the *Houston Chronicle*.[16]

MAEC members, however, were not involved in this program or in distributing its funds. Castillo wrote to Director Smith in order to find out "how much of the funds are being used to increase educational benefits for Chicano students and teachers." He then requested a meeting with her and suggested that three agenda items be discussed: Chicano participation in the program, budget allocations for Chicanos, and concerns about quality. "Based on our limited information," he argued, "there is no Chicano participation in the decision-making or priority-setting processes." With respect to budget allocations Castillo asked how much money had gone for Chicano programs and who designed and administered the programs. "How effective were these programs and who evaluated them?" he further inquired.[17]

A second major area of concern for MAEC was the Bi-Racial Committee appointed by the court to monitor desegregation of the HISD schools. Judge Connally selected the ten-member committee from nominations made by the NAACP Legal Defense Fund and the Houston School Board. The committee, formed in the fall of 1970, had two Mexican American members, but neither was known to the east-side community or supported by them.[18] MAEC raised questions about the types of Mexican Americans serving on the Bi-Racial Committee. Abraham Ramírez, Jr., in a letter written on May 20, told Leonel Castillo that he had heard through the grapevine that "safe" Mexican Americans had been recommended to the committee, which probably meant individuals who were not MAEC members or who were uncritical of school district actions. He also told Castillo that one of the MAEC members, Manuel Velasco, had conferred with Gonzalo Garza, the first Mexican American area superintendent of public schools, about this issue.[19] Garza, in turn, requested from Ramírez a list of individuals whom MAEC would like to have appointed. "Gonzalo," he noted, "wants to push for Mexican Americans with guts on the bi-racial committee." Ramírez sent Garza a list of persons whom he felt "would do the Mexican American justice in the bi-racial committee."[20]

PROTEST

MAEC's strategy during the spring of 1971 also included protest and pickets, but much of this was localized—that is, it was concentrated in a few barrios and directed at specific schools. The organization's members participated in several protest actions between March and June. On Wednesday, April 17, 1971, Mexican American parents at Franklin Elementary confronted the principal and teachers about school conditions and discrimination. Franklin had been vandalized several times, and food had been thrown on the cafeteria floor, chairs, and tables. Because HISD would not send anyone to clean up the mess—it was against the "rules and regulations," noted the staff at the school—the Mexican American children were being asked to do it. Some of the teachers contended that a few parents had given permission for their children to clean. Parents responded that they were not told that the children would be responsible for cleaning the huge mess caused by vandals. Some were under the impression that the children would clean up their own messes.[21]

Parents were also upset over remarks of a substitute teacher who called the children names such as "ugly Mexicans" and "niggers." One girl was told "to go ahead and shit in her pants" when she asked permission to go to the bathroom. Parents demanded to know what disciplinary action was going to be taken to make sure that this treatment did not reoccur. The principal responded that the substitute had been reported to the administration but that she did not know what had happened to that report. She was not sure if the substitute had been permanently removed from the list of those qualified to teach.[22]

Another confrontation between parents and school officials occurred at a teacher in-service training session. Parents attended this session to raise a variety of questions about school conditions and the treatment of Mexican American children. Although some of their questions were answered, the principal complained of the inappropriateness of the occasion for hearing complaints. The teachers responded that they resented parental "interference" at their training session.[23]

Maggie Landron, one of the MAYO members and staff at *Papel Chicano*, commented on the incident. She suggested that the central issue involved was "ownership," i.e., "to whom do the schools belong?" The parents, she argued, were not wanted as problem-solvers but only as "money-makers for certain projects." Parent-teacher organizations, she argued, were boring, "gossipy," and elitist. Furthermore, the teachers in these schools were not committed to teaching. For them teaching was a job and an unsatisfying one at that. Teachers, noted Landron, "hate to go to class as much as the students and feel alienated as much as the parents." In this climate the students felt unwanted. "From about the third grade up, students begin to hate school and express their dislike by vandalism, false sickness, extreme messiness, [and] disciplinary problems," Landron commented. Franklin as well as all other schools, she argued, were no longer symbols of learning since they had become "cold, dark, dirty, and inhuman." They did not belong to anyone and had become impersonal "monsters" that aggravated and frustrated everyone stepping through their doors. For Chicanos and blacks the schools were society's effort to keep them in their place. "As long as minorities are taught from an early age how dumb and inferior they are, the less trouble society will have teaching them inferiority as adults," Landron concluded.[24]

A second set of incidents inspired by MAEC members, especially Mexican American parents and students, occurred in May, 1971. First, over fifty Chicano students, both male and female, walked out of Edison Junior High to support Cinco de Mayo activities.[25] Second, Mexican American parents filed complaints against the principal and teachers at Burnet Elementary for mishandling parents and pushing students. During the incident, which occurred in mid-May, a teacher commented that Mexican American parents did not care about their children's education. An activist questioned this comment and stated in a newspaper article that if any parent cared about his/her children, "it is the Mexican American." The article said that the entire Mexican American culture was built around children but that "La Raza parents know that the schools mistreat their children and try to destroy their culture so they allow the children to drop out to PREVENT their children from being harmed."[26] Third, MAEC members on May 20, 1971, organized a community protest of an award given to HISD for an exemplary community involvement program designed to put a desegregation plan into effect. The award, which included a trophy and a one-thousand-dollar prize, was given to HISD by the Association of Classroom Teachers of the National Education Association (NEA). The Houston Teacher Association, a group of local teachers, nominated the district for this award. The HISD school board was judged as having made greater educational achievements during 1970 than any district in the nation with seventy thousand or more students. It was especially cited for the Volunteers in Public Schools (VIPS) program of preschool screening as well as for the appointment of a citizens' advisory committee to define educational goals, expansion of vocational education programs, and the addition of more than fifty special education classes. Emphasis was placed on the district's efforts to achieve a smooth desegregation of schools under a plan set down by the federal courts.[27]

MAEC members did not believe that HISD deserved this award. While Houston Teacher Association officials formally presented the HISD board with the NEA award, about fifty MAEC members picketed outside. A spokesperson for MAEC told the board at its Wednesday afternoon meeting that the members of the organization were protesting the award for a good reason. "I think it is unusual that this district, with so many problems and trouble, should receive such a national award," said Leonel Castillo. He criticized the board's attitude toward Mexican Americans and cautioned that if the board did not act to improve the Chicanos' plight, "more trouble will occur next year." Castillo noted that the district's court-ordered Bi-Racial Committee had no Mexican American members and neither did the school board. He urged the board to form a committee with which Mexican Americans could more easily communicate to get answers.[28]

The third set of protests occurred in mid-June and in July. During the middle part of June, Mexican American students presented several demands to the school board aimed at resolving the inequalities that existed between Chicano and Anglo schools. This set of demands emerged out of an exchange program between Jefferson Davis and Westbury High Schools that HISD arranged in the spring of 1971. Davis was a predominantly minority school, while Westbury was predominantly Anglo. Chicanos noticed the vast differences between these schools. The curriculum, physical maintenance, and equipment were all vastly inferior at Davis (see table 5).

Moved by their discovery, they drafted a list of demands, which they presented to the school board on June 14, 1971. Louis Tellez, father of one of the students and an MAEC officer, presented the list and asked for a meeting to discuss a new principal and "hopefully some new teachers." The board made no comment on the demands or on the request for a meeting to discuss the principalship.[29]

One final protest action occurred in midsummer and was aimed at criticizing one of HISD's summer tutorial programs seeking to improve language and reading achievement. The new summer program, called the Project to Assist Mexican Americans (PAMA), was based at Sidney Sherman Elementary. Its purpose was to help Mexican American students enrolled in grades one through six who had language "disabilities" and other academic weaknesses. Forty-five students were enrolled in this program taught by three Mexican American tutors from Jefferson Davis High. Although the program was beneficial to Chicanos, one activist argued that it was a "band-aid" program.[30]

Table 5. Result of Student Exchange between Jefferson Davis and Westbury High Schools, May, 1971

Jefferson Davis (Mexican American)	*Westbury (Anglo)*
1. One of oldest buildings in HISD	One of newest buildings in HISD
2. Almost all minority	All Anglo
3. Poor economic community	Economically well-off
4. Many dropouts	98 percent graduate
5. Curriculum: get students out	Curriculum: college-bound
6. Inferior facilities, halls not clean, "toilet odor," PTA has to buy visual aids and P.E. equipment	Excellent facilities, "no toilet odor," science, laboratory, and P.E. equipment
7. One art class for 1,600 students, little encouragement to attend college, few advanced courses	Advanced math course
8. Poor library	Excellent library

Source: "Students Protest Conditions in Jeff Davis," *Papel Chicano* 1, no. 18 (July, 1971): 5.

Chicano and Chicana activists not only protested existing policies, they also sought to develop innovative proposals for improving the schools. In one particular case they sought the creation of an independent school district in the East End barrio. Mario Quiñones, owner of Houston Tile Sales, importers of building tile, originated this idea and organized a steering committee of fifteen businesspersons to create the new district.[31] The group proposed to carve a new twenty-square-mile school district out of the western section of the HISD and a portion of the Spring Branch Independent School District. The area would include twelve thousand students from nine schools. The proposed school district would be comprised primarily of Mexican American students, but black students would make up approximately 10 percent of the student body.[32]

The reasons for creating a predominantly Chicano school district were stated by Quiñones: "The Houston School Board has always neglected the East End. . . . our schools are always the worst and no attempt is made to improve them." The creation of a new school district in the East End would pump in much-needed resources to improve the schools since the biggest taxpayers were industries along the Ship Channel. "We have to put up with their pollution and noises and the majority of the [Mexican American] people employed by them live in the East End," Quiñones said, adding, "It's time that we see some improvements in our area from [industries'] tax dollars. We want the best for our children and believe we can get it by forming our own school district."[33]

Quiñones's steering committee was supposed to meet later in the week to define the boundaries of the proposed school district and then hold a press conference. No further evidence has been found on this group, so it is likely that the committee's efforts were unsuccessful.[34] Despite this failure, here was another indicator of the increased sense of political efficacy that guided the Mexican American community during these years.

ORGANIZATIONAL TRANSFORMATION

While MAEC continued to struggle against discrimination and for changes in the schools, the group also took steps to ensure its survival as an organization. From the beginning MAEC was a volunteer organization with limited financial resources. Its program of school change was based on community fund-raising efforts, and its staff was based on the labor and time of volunteers who came from existing organizations or from the community. Between October, 1970, and January, 1971, for instance, MAEC "through its own sweat" raised over nine thousand dollars through tamale sales, dances, raffles, and other fund-raising projects.[35] This money was used to operate a variety of educational services that MAEC developed after the fall boycott.[36] However, MAEC leaders felt that in order to sustain protest and social activism they had to create a more enduring organizational structure. The organization, in other words, had to raise funds from a variety of sources outside the community. In order to apply for these types of funds, MAEC had to become a legally chartered nonprofit corporation.[37] It did so on January 22, 1971.[38] Afterward MAEC began to apply for and receive federal and state funds.[39] Between November and February of the 1970–71 academic year MAEC submitted several proposals to the federal and local governments. In March, 1971, the organization was awarded a grant of $65,000 dollars from the Department of Health, Education, and Welfare for the establishment of programs geared toward facilitating desegregation in Houston. The MAEC proposal requested

$165,000 and was submitted to the Emergency School Assistance Program (ESAP), a federal desegregation program. The funds were to hire tutors and counselors to inform students about scholarships and to assist them in career planning.[40]

Once word of these funds was received, Leonel Castillo called a meeting of MAEC officers to "assure that the money is spent in the best possible way." The group named an advisory board to administer this project and then began to hire personnel, establish office procedures, and set up a budget. Castillo noted that the grant helped to reduce the financial strain on MAEC by enabling the organization to pay for rent, office equipment, supplies, telephones, bonding, accounting services, travel, and salaries. "However," he noted, "this grant cannot by itself relieve us of all our fundraising. Much of what we do cannot be paid for with ESAP funds. This is simply the start."[41]

The acceptance of federal funds and the trend toward social services led to increasing criticism from the more militant and generally younger activists within MAEC. They questioned MAEC's commitment to *la causa* because of the group's acceptance of federal funds and called MAEC's grant "hush money" or "tokenism" to keep the community organization busy. They asked if MAEC was "selling out." If MAEC got too militant, would HEW withdraw the grant? According to Enrique Pérez, a MAYO member, withdrawal of federal funds could well "dampen the spirit of active organizations to the point that they become just another service group but not bring about any changes in the institutions." MAEC leaders assured him that this would not happen to them.[42] The possibility for co-optation, however, was implanted in some MAEC members even as the organization began to strengthen its capability for providing increased services to the Mexican American community.

CONCLUSION

The continuing protest and lobbying activities of MAEC members as well as the increasing frustration of the more militant factions within the organization worried MAEC's leaders, who believed that the situation was becoming "much worse." "What can be done to avert a massive disruption?" Leonel Castillo asked a federal agency. His solution to this potentially explosive situation was the development of an action-research project aimed at "marshalling proof, statistical and narrative, regarding the educational plight of Mexican Americans in the District." This type of research, Castillo argued, might thwart possible "militant activities" by Mexican Americans.[43] However, no funds or additional studies were forthcoming. The school board's response to the court's pairing order in the summer of 1971 ensured that the only option available for the organization and its supporters was another round of boycotts of the public schools. The feared "massive disruption" was being realized.

CHAPTER 10

THE MOST RACIST PLAN YET

Prior to the start of the 1971–72 school year MAEC assessed the impact it had had on school officials since its founding and the challenges it faced in the coming year. The organization had exacted certain concessions from the school superintendent and the school board. The former, for instance, had agreed in principle on viewing Mexican Americans as an identifiable minority group. This recognition, in turn, had led to the expansion of bilingual education programs, the development of ethnic studies curricula, and the hiring of more Mexican American administrators, faculty, and staff. Because of MAEC's involvement, local officials had begun to address the special linguistic and cultural needs of the Mexican American population in the schools.

The district's efforts to meet the Mexican American children's special needs were reflected in its proposed budget for the coming school year, in proposals for federal funding developed by school officials, and in the staffing and curricular decisions made by the board. A proposal to the Emergency School Assistance Program (ESAP) for federal funding in 1971–72 asked for $9.5 million, of which $4.9 million was to be applied directly to the needs of Mexican Americans. This money would fund four new school programs benefiting Mexican-origin children. A significant amount of monies, approximately $1.6 million, was used to establish the 3-4-5 Club, a bilingual program for preschool children. The rest of the funds covered operating expenses for a variety of other programs, including a Spanish-language program for teachers ($70,000), the Mexican-American Student and Parent Involvement Project ($291,229), and a credit course in Mexican American history in grades ten through twelve ($33,000).[1]

Because of MAEC's involvement, the district also expanded and strengthened a staff recruitment program and increased the number of Mexican American teachers and administrators. In the year before the boycott the district had four Mexican American principals and assistant principals. This number increased to six in 1970–71 and to thirteen the following year. The number of Mexican American teachers also increased from 1969 to 1971. The district had 181 Mexican American teachers in 1969–70, 260 in 1970–71, and 308 in 1971–72. The number of teachers was still small because of a limited supply of Mexican American teachers and competition between school districts.[2] Finally, in January, 1971, the superintendent hired Gonzalo Garza as one of six area superintendents. Garza was the first Mexican American in an important administrative position.[3]

MAEC had less success with the school board. Although some concessions were exacted from the board—e.g., MAEC encouraged the board to appeal the pairing decision to the courts and to include a few Mexican Americans in at least one desegregation committee—the board continued to operate on the basis of traditional black-white race relations. For integration purposes Mexican Americans were still viewed as members of the white race. Board members argued that they were legally bound to ignore Mexican Americans in the development of integration plans because of the court rulings. MAEC was convinced that the district could develop a more comprehensive desegregation plan that included Anglos.

In late June of 1971 MAEC's anxieties and frustrations increased when the HISD school board issued a new pairing plan and initiated busing for minority students but not Anglos. Although busing was needed and desired by Mexican American parents who could not afford to take their children to the new paired schools, many of them viewed it as another example of educational discrimination since the burden of desegregation and of busing was being borne solely by minorities. Failure to act equitably ushered in yet another round of militant activities. This chapter describes MAEC's responses to the new pairing plan issued during the summer of 1971.

HISD'S NEW PAIRING ORDER

On June 25, 1971, the HISD school board issued a desegregation plan that paired Mexican American children with blacks; no Anglos were included.[4]

Table 6. List of Paired Schools by Grades and Student Enrollment, 1971–72 School Year

Schools Paired	Grades Covered	Black Enrollment	White Enrollment
1. Atherton	1–2	304	609
Eliot	3–4	343	722
Scroggins	5–6	302	612
2. Nat Q. Henderson	1–3	273	390
Pugh	4–6	278	323
3. Pleasantville	4–6	400	151
Port Houston	1–3	355	227
4. Bruce	3–6	663	261
Anson Jones	1–2	106	488
5. Crawford	3–6	532	50
Sherman	1–2	370	432
6. Dodson	1–3	763	494
Lantrip	4–6	486	465
7. Ryan	1–2	460	341
Ross	5–6	610	254
Looscan	3–4	333	337
8. Chatham	4–6	940	100
Sanderson	1–3	976	109
9. Burrus	3–6	766	145
Roosevelt	1–2	390	131
10. Frost	4–6	1207	129
Rhoads	1–3	1040	116

Sources: Frank Davis, "HSD [sic] Elementary Pairing Plan Revealed," Houston Post, June 25, 1971, n.pag.; "Garver Gives Details for Pairings of 22 Elementary Schools," Houston Chronicle, June 25, 1971, sec. 1, p. 1.

This plan was in response to the district court's May 24, 1971, ruling ordering HISD to implement desegregation based on school pairing. Under this plan twenty-two elementary schools would be paired. Approximately 19,448 out of an anticipated elementary school enrollment of 142,481 for the entire district would be involved in the pairing plans. The schools paired, the grades covered in each school, and the number of black and white (mostly Mexican American) students are listed in table 6.

The school district also called for busing of minority children to achieve integration. In July the superintendent presented several transportation plans to the board. According to him, no federal funds were provided for transportation, and the U.S. court order was also silent on the issue. He estimated that between sixty thousand and ninety thousand dollars was needed for busing. His office, he noted, was in the process of developing proposals to fund the expanded desegregation program.

One of the proposals was to be sent to the Emergency School Assistance Program (ESAP) under the Office of Education.[5] ESAP funds were available to school districts moving ahead with plans for court-ordered integration. Most of the funds would go to the twenty-two paired schools. Ironically, in order to receive federal monies the school district had to meet the federal government's requirements. One of these was that the district name a triethnic advisory committee to provide advice on the distribution of funds. Consequently, on August 6, HISD named a fifteen-member triethnic committee.[6] The district called this group the Multi-Racial Advisory Committee (MRAC). An equal number of Anglo, black, and Mexican American individuals were appointed to the MRAC.[7]

MRAC reviewed over forty-one applications for federal grants totaling over $9.4 million.[8] The applications included a $325,000 request for busing. All of the applications were approved and sent to the respective federal agencies for further action.[9]

The superintendent was not optimistic about receiving these funds. President Richard M. Nixon's plan to prohibit the use of federal monies for desegregation purposes in the latter part of July strengthened Superintendent Garver's argument.[10] Busing funds thus would have to come from the school district. Board members asked the superintendent to draft a list of alternatives to cover these transportation costs, and he presented this list to them on July 13 at the board's regular meeting.[11] Opposition to the plans emerged, and no decision was made.[12] On August 7 the board voted to support the plan that bused students in paired schools if they resided more than one mile from school.[13]

MAEC RESPONDS

The school board's pairing and busing decisions upset many MAEC members and supporters. An activist member of the organization noted that the new pairing plan "is obviously the most racist yet, and totally destroys the 'neighborhood schools' concept, and will absolutely ruin the few existing bilingual programs." This person added, "Its effect on the Chicano communities will be drastic."[14]

A *Papel Chicano* writer noted the plan's failure to recognize Mexican

Americans as a distinct minority group and to include Anglos. The writer stated, "There is not even one predominantly Anglo school included in the pairing plan," and further charged that the only "all white" school included in the original pairing plan—Poe Elementary—had been removed from the new list. Even the children of the black elite attending "all-black" MacGregor Elementary would not be involved in the pairing of the schools. The writer argued, "Only the Blacks and Chicanos in the poverty neighborhoods are the victims of the racist plans," and concluded with a plea for just integration: "The entire community, not just one segment of it, must bear the burden of integration." [15]

Abel Álvarez, an active MAEC member, called it the "worst blunder that the Administration of the HISD has to date made." He argued that the cumulative impact of the varied rulings by the court and the new pairing plan by HISD could be the main cause of turmoil in Houston. "It is never too late to correct a wrong," he further added. Álvarez also noted that while the "people of the Barrios" would have their day in court, Chicanos would resist the pairing plan. "We, the Mexican Americans, will no longer tolerate this double standard form of educational guide as set by a few individuals who care not one iota about the ethnic minorities, other than to throw them together and isolate them from the mainstream of life." [16]

One of the more vociferous voices was Tomás García, a staff member of *Papel Chicano*. He argued that Connally's ruling was "the Great Insult to the dignity of both minority cultures in Houston." He asked, "Are we supposed to ignore the ignorance of bigotry and intolerance simply because the 'great sage' and 'racist fool' like Connally tells us that we don't exist?" He explained that it was the Chicano community's moral responsibility to resist and added: "If we fail our moral responsibilities, we are the fools. History will call us fools; our own children will call us that, and more." [17]

MAEC's official response reflected the sentiments of its members. The new chair, Romualdo M. Castillo, noted that the pairing plan was unjust because it only paired minority groups and did not include Anglos. [18] He stated that MAEC would oppose the pairing decision "to the bitter end." [19]

MAEC's determination to fight the pairing plan was supplemented by the efforts of two relatively new youth-based organizations that had joined the group, the Association for the Advancement of Mexican Americans (AAMA) and the Chicano Youth Council (CYC). MAEC continued to be comprised primarily of neighborhood representatives and a few barrio organizations. By the summer of 1971, however, Barrio-MAYO and UH-MAYO had both become relatively inactive. Barrio-MAYO had disbanded in March, 1971, and UH-MAYO's activism declined because its membership, comprised primarily of university students, was on summer vacation.[20] AAMA and CYC replaced these two groups and continued the tradition of youth-based activism within MAEC. Both groups organized rallies, spoke before the board, and actively participated in additional MAEC activities.

The CYC was initially founded in the fall of 1970 during the boycott but had not been active since then. It resurfaced as a viable organization in January, 1971. Its purpose was to inform students of their rights in school and to promote curricular changes in education. "We need to know what kinds of courses . . . should be offered in the Mexican American high schools, what are offered and what are not offered and why," one of its members wrote. CYC was also engaged in organizing and recruitment activities as well as in writing a student rights manual.[21]

AAMA was founded in September, 1970, by a group of fifteen young, educated individuals who felt that few organizations were doing anything about community services and especially about the problems encountered by youths. These individuals decided to "do something." They bought an old, run-down house in the east side of town to use as a neighborhood center. They then repaired and renovated the house with funds collected through dances and the traditional *tamaladas* (tamale sales).[22] In September, 1970, during the height of the boycott, AAMA opened the neighborhood center and developed a variety of recreational and cultural awareness activities for young people. The group was legally incorporated on November 23, 1970.[23]

These organizations, then, had been involved in different types of community issues prior to the announcement of the pairing plan in late June. CYC, for the most part, focused its efforts on organizing in the secondary grades and on recruitment of new members. During its first year of existence AAMA provided community services. Both, however, increased their involvement in protest activity during the summer of 1971. On July 11, for instance, AAMA organized a unity rally at Settegast Park to expose the hypocrisy of the local school district. About three hundred Chicanos attended the Sunday rally as two of its spokespersons—Luis Cano and Ed López—spoke on racism and HISD. Two short plays were presented, and music was provided by a group called Santa Fe.[24]

On July 15 AAMA and CYC made presentations before the school board. Carmen Medina, AAMA spokesperson, exposed the continued abuses of Mexican Americans in the present school system. Over thirty

Chicanos and Chicanas applauded her presentation, but board members failed to comment because, as one activist noted, they were "stunned." Raymond Valdez, speaking on behalf of the CYC, accused HISD of "stagnancy" in failing to recognize Chicanos as a separate ethnic group with regard to the "racist pairing issue." The board was suffering from a case of "extreme naiveté or convenient oversight," he said. The school board ignored their concerns.[25]

Although these new activist groups at times took action on their own, they were active members of MAEC. This organization, still comprised of various groups and individuals with different ideological orientations, continued to be the most important group directing protest activities against the local school district. In the summer of 1971 MAEC proposed a twofold strategy to deal with the discriminatory pairing and busing decisions: plan for another boycott and expand the base of support.

PLANNING THE BOYCOTT

During most of July, MAEC conducted a campaign to inform the Mexican American community about the unfair pairing plan. MAEC utilized the media—especially *Papel Chicano*—small meetings, rallies, dances, and fiestas to explain to residents of the barrios what HISD "was doing to them." HISD, MAEC argued, continued to provide Chicanos with an unfair education. The federal district judge continued to rule that Mexican Americans were "non-existent." An MAEC leader stated, "We must stand up and show these bigots that their comfort and convenience comes second to our children's welfare." This person continued: "If we sit and do nothing, as before, there is no chance of changing the infamous pairing plan before August 26. The due process of Judge Connally's and the school board's law has not given us justice in Houston as in the nation. The only solution now is to show solidarity in our case, to band together and to demand that we be given our rights under our federal Constitution."[26]

On July 30 MAEC called a general meeting to make final plans for the coming school year. The meeting was held at the Juan Marcos Presbyterian Church in the Northside barrio and was attended by representatives of ten barrios. At this meeting the general assembly voted to ask for yet another boycott. Unlike the previous year, the group elected to extend the boycott to all grades, not merely those schools that were being paired. The editor of *El Papel Chicano* supported the need to boycott the schools since they were being "ruled by men who sought their own gains."[27] The decision to boycott the schools, however, was not unanimous; seven barrios favored the action, and three abstained. It is unclear who actually abstained or why, but it is possible that some questioned a boycott's usefulness.

Despite this vote, Romualdo Castillo, the chair, said that sentiments against the "black-brown" pairing were running high in the Mexican American neighborhoods. "We've met with the school board, with [Superintendent] Garver, with the biracial committee [appointed by Judge Connally to report on the progress of integration here]," he said. "People have taken more than they can take, and some have even reached the point of violence." [28]

Castillo reported that boycott leaders were aiming at keeping six thousand students out of school. Abel Álvarez said that the boycott would continue all year if Anglos were not added to the pairing plan. He added that MAEC was planning huelga schools similar to those established in September. A rally to build support for the boycott was called for Sunday, August 15, at 2:30 P.M. at Moody Park.[29]

Although the membership was ready and willing to boycott, Castillo stated that the action could be stopped if the district included Anglos with Mexican Americans and blacks in a triethnic pairing plan.[30] Inclusion of Anglos in the plan would send a message to Mexican Americans in the barrios that they were not being "used" when they were classified as whites in the pairing plan. Superintendent Garver responded later that there was no chance of adding Anglos to the pairing formula, although he acknowledged that the school board had the power under the court-ordered plan to add them "if it wants to." "All school board members have opposed all pairing and have fought it all the way to the U.S. Supreme Court to no avail," Garver said. "They can't very well enlarge the pairing [at the twenty-two schools to include whites] and be consistent with their opposition to pairing," he added, further noting that "the fact of the matter is, in this city and state, Mexican-Americans are white." [31]

In the latter statement the superintendent erred. U.S. district judge Jack Roberts of Austin, for instance, ruled in late June that Mexican Americans constituted a separate ethnic group and appointed a triethnic advisory committee to replace the previously biracial committee of Anglos and blacks in the Austin school district. This ruling followed a similar decision made in June, 1970, by U.S. district judge Woodrow Seals recognizing Mexican Americans as an "identifiable ethnic minority" in Corpus Christi and ordering triethnic integration. These as well as other federal decisions in the area of jury discrimination proved that in Texas, Mexican Americans had been recognized as an identifiable group for some time. Only in Houston did the judge refuse to acknowledge the special status of Mexican Americans.[32]

During the first two weeks of August, MAEC focused on establishing huelga schools and on preparing parents for the boycott. Efforts to organize huelga schools were initiated by a special MAEC Huelga School Committee (HSC) headed by Froilan Hernández. He explained that committee members were soliciting sites, teachers, and community help for the schools. He obtained commitments from Mexican American teachers in the district and from students at several universities. "We already have commitments from the MAYO chapters at the University of Texas who will send students to help teach at the beginning of the boycott and from students in San Antonio who have agreed to teach the first three weeks of the boycott to get things started," he reported in early August. He further stated that the committee had obtained three sites and was working on five more for the huelga schools. In addition committee members were planning on approaching the Catholic schools for use of their facilities for evening classes. "We can't anticipate how many students will walk out and want to enroll in the schools, so we will just come up with as many sites as we can," he explained.[33]

Mexican American parents prepared themselves for the boycott in various ways. The experiences of Justine Villaseñor and Mrs. Antonio Gonzáles, both PTA leaders in their schools, represented those who heeded MAEC's call for militant action. Villaseñor had three children enrolled in Scroggins Elementary.[34] She served on the Scroggins PTA executive board but had plans to resign to support the strike. She believed that the pairing plan was unfair to the poor since it left most schools in the more affluent areas unaffected and because it failed to include Anglos. "We feel that we are being used to 'integrate' Houston schools since they classify us as whites instead of as the ethnic minority which we are," she said. Despite the unjust nature of the desegregation plan, she was confident that the court order would be overruled. If not, then she thought it would be "only fair to have a triethnic pairing plan where each school would have a percentage of Anglos, Negroes and Mexican-Americans."[35] Mrs. Gonzáles also served on the executive board of the PTA at Pugh School. She supported the strike plans because of the unfairness of pairing. "I am sure there are black parents who will join us on this. Many live in my neighborhood and they don't want their children bused away either," she stated.[36]

The planning for the boycott occurred in the midst of rumors about an empty treasury and dissension among MAEC members. Unlike the previous year, this time differences over strategy and goals emerged. These differences were apparent at a meeting held on August 13.

Two key positions were expressed at this meeting: those who supported integration and those who favored community control of schools. Gregory Salazar, former MAYO chair, at earlier community meetings had opposed the boycott and proposed community control as the solution to the problem of underachievement and as a road to empowerment. Most of MAEC's leaders now were receptive to the ideas of community control. Romualdo Castillo, MAEC chair, wanted further discussion of the issue of community control. He told the members that the subject of community control "hadn't been adequately discussed and wasn't understood by the membership." Otto Landron, first vice chair, agreed that as an alternative to integration community control was "a very good idea." He said, "I don't see where integration is going to help our children." [37]

In addition to questioning the goal of integration, Landron was skeptical of the boycott. He was not alone in expressing this sentiment. Leonel Castillo, for instance, had publicly stated on August 6 that while supportive of the council's decision against HISD, he preferred to "avoid the boycott because of the tremendous costs involved." "I am very concerned with getting negotiations started with HISD," he added. [38]

Romualdo Castillo, MAEC's chair, was opposed to the boycott but felt that "if it's the only way to bring some justice to our students and our people—it's what we have to do." Castillo, although expressing support for another boycott, hoped to avert the action. [39] In early August he met with school board president Dr. George Oser and area superintendent Gonzalo Garza, the highest-ranking Mexican American administrator in the district. The meeting failed to produce an agreement because of the district's failure to negotiate with MAEC. [40] The position of the district was firm that no changes would be made to the pairing plan. Superintendent Garver reported that he was not worried about a "massive" boycott by Mexican Americans, since even if all the Chicano students walked out, they would still be only a fraction of the total school-age population. More specifically, he said: "At the height of the boycott last year there were only 2,000 to 3,000 students out. Percentage-wise, the boycott was just a fraction. If the total Mexican American population stayed out, that would be only about 36,000 students." According to Garver, a boycott would merely be a minor inconvenience. However, he discouraged parents, whether Mexican Americans, blacks, or Anglos, from using their children as "pawns," stating, "We don't like pairing either, but we recommend that people who don't like it should go to court and test it—not use their children."[41]

In some respects the consideration of community control as an alternative to integration was based on the community's increasing disillusionment with the idea that schools would improve if Anglo students enrolled in them. Many people did not want Anglos in the Chicano schools, and many, especially former MAYO members and those in AAMA and CYC, felt that Chicanos and Chicanas should take control of those institutions that affected them the most. Community control of the schools, not integration, was the road to empowerment.[42]

Most MAEC members rejected the community control arguments and supported the council's original stand in favor of triethnic integration. A few of them even criticized the leadership for being receptive to the issue of community control. Abel Álvarez, in particular, charged that failure to dismiss the notion of community control of schools outright implied opposition to integration. Álvarez then added that he would leave the council and form a rival group to conduct the boycott if MAEC leaders canceled it. Chairman Castillo replied that only the membership, not the leaders, could call off the boycott. He also said that any member who wanted to had the right to leave the organization.[43]

Differences of opinion over finances also emerged. This is especially true with respect to the huelga schools. Romualdo Castillo estimated that it would cost approximately two thousand dollars per week to maintain the eight to ten huelga schools. When he raised the issue of costs, some MAEC members argued that he was making a case against the boycott. "I'm not against it [the boycott]. "I'm just looking at both sides of the coin," he explained.[44]

Despite these differences, the council voted unanimously to call for a "total Chicano boycott" of the public schools. All fourteen barrio delegations attending the meeting voted in favor of the boycott. Many parents said that they would keep their children out of school even if there were no huelga schools, though Castillo stated that he expected to raise the necessary funds to operate the huelga schools. Although it was a unanimous vote, the organization was internally divided since a good portion of them questioned the goals or eventual success of the boycott.[45]

On Sunday, August 15, MAEC held a rally at Moody Park; over two thousand individuals attended. Those at the afternoon event listened to speakers and were entertained by a play and a variety of singers. The key speakers included Romualdo Castillo, chair of MAEC, and the Reverend C. Anderson Davis, chair of the local NAACP.[46] Davis was invited to the rally as part of MAEC's plan to broaden its support among African Americans, an issue that will be discussed further in the next section.

Castillo discussed the boycott's purpose. First, Chicanos were being considered "white" by the court and federal district judge Ben Connally had refused to recognize that Chicanos "exist except for the purpose that HISD has in mind." Second, HISD was pairing two "disadvantaged" minority groups. He criticized the idea that the pairing of blacks with Mexican Americans was called integration and reported that the district was prepared to spend $325,000 to bus Chicanos and blacks into each other's schools. MAEC, he further argued, was not against integration if it included Anglos; HISD, however, "is using the Chicano and Black to keep from adding any gavacho [Anglo] schools to the pairing plan." He felt that the Chicano community must not allow school officials to get away with the "plot against la Raza." MAEC was willing to do anything, including calling for the firing of the superintendent, that would lead to fair integration. MAEC, however, had not been successful in getting justice. "We have met, we have bent over backwards with the school board, and its been to no avail," lamented Castillo. Although MAEC's stand from the start had been to avoid a boycott, there was no other choice now. The only option left was a full-scale boycott on the opening day of school.[47]

Reverend Davis was extremely supportive of the boycott. He accused board members of using "brown people" to suit their case. He also proposed the formation of a coalition, stating, "To make sure this white man doesn't keep you divided there should be a black-brown coalition that should get rid of Garver if necessary and get rid of the school board if necessary." He hinted that if no accord could be reached between MAEC and the school board, blacks, if asked, might join the boycott.[48] The exuberant crowd enthusiastically received his comments.

EXPANDING BASE OF SUPPORT

In addition to informing and uniting the Mexican American community, MAEC sought to expand its base of support by cultivating the interest of federal officials, LULAC, and African Americans. MAEC leaders contacted and sought the support of federal officials, especially Martin G. Castillo and Armando Rodríguez. Castillo was chair of the Cabinet Committee on Opportunity for the Spanish-speaking, whereas Rodríguez was chief of the

Office for Spanish-speaking Affairs in the Department of Health, Education, and Welfare. MAEC requested financial and technical assistance in
the preparation of a triethnic desegregation plan from the former and suggestions on school reforms from the latter. MAEC leaders occasionally met
with other federal officials to explain and garner support for the boycott
and the local community's struggle for legal recognition. Sometime in the
summer of 1971 MAEC got a promise of support from the U.S. Commission on Civil Rights.[49]

MAEC also sought LULAC's support. Several of MAEC's leaders, including Abraham Ramírez, Jr., and William Gutiérrez, were members of
local LULAC chapter 60. During the previous year Gutiérrez had requested
the support of the national LULAC for MAEC's struggle. The governing
board of the national office agreed to support the organization's efforts
to gain legal recognition as a minority and representation on the court-
appointed biracial advisory committee but did not take a formal stand on
the boycott.[50] Most state and local chapters, similar to the national office,
did not take a formal stand on the boycott. In many ways LULAC was still
committed to the ideology and tactics of the Mexican American Generation and shied away from direct action and mass mobilization. The only
exception to this general practice was LULAC Council 60, one of Houston's strongest chapters, which grudgingly supported MAEC but only because Abraham Ramírez, Jr., was the organization's president.[51] In early
August, MAEC also got a pledge of support from Tony Bonilla, state president of LULAC, but did not obtain the official support of the statewide
LULAC organization.[52]

MAEC leaders likewise sought support from the African American
community. Although blacks had initiated the integration lawsuit and opposed the district's actions, including the pairing plan, most of them were
unaware of the Mexican American community's plight and its civil rights
struggle. In mid-July, MAEC met with black educators to discuss common concerns. The meeting was sponsored by Texas Southern University's
teacher training program. Dr. J. B. Jones, program director, and Mrs. Bob-
bie Rose, assistant director, acted as cochairs and discussed the purpose
for calling the meeting: to gain an understanding of each other and to
work together to improve the schools.[53]

MAEC members Eduardo López, Leonel Castillo, Tomás García, Sister
Gloria Gallardo, Mario Quiñones, and others explained the importance of
the pairing plan to the African American educators. They pointed out that
blacks had never included Chicanos and Chicanas in the integration plans

and that they had raised few objections to the school board. African American educators responded that they knew "little about them [Mexican Americans]." Most contended that they had never heard of Mexican Americans or Chicanos until the previous year. They also charged that blacks had started the movement for civil rights and that Chicanos were "Johnny or Poncho come lately." Because of poor history books, blacks had not learned that for the past one hundred years Chicanos had been fighting for their rights.[54]

In their assessment of the meeting MAEC leaders noted that understanding between both groups would take a lot of effort. At this meeting, one activist noted, blacks did not even admit that the pairing plan was unjust, though the plan was "just as unjust to the concept of integration that they [blacks] have fought so long and so hard for." MAEC also reached another conclusion about the meeting: "The Chicanos were there ready to talk seriously but one must wonder whether these educators were or not actually serious in their attempts to communicate or whether they are just fulfilling federal regulations because they have been told they must." Most felt that it was not a fruitful meeting and that "the teachers, principals, and administrators in schools . . . are far too 'brainwashed' into supporting the past methods of education to change much."[55]

MAEC was more successful with civil rights leaders. In that same month MAEC leaders met with Rev. C. Anderson Davis, the chairperson of the local NAACP chapter, and state representative Curtis Graves. Both of these individuals pledged their support for the boycott and promised to work more closely together on this issue.[56]

During the month of August, Davis took a more active role in MAEC's activities. In early August, MAEC asked Davis to attend a meeting with Houston school district officials several days before school began to discuss ways of resolving the controversy over the school pairing of two minority groups. In the meantime MAEC made final plans to boycott the schools.[57] In mid-August, MAEC invited Davis to be a speaker at its August 15 rally; after the rally and as a follow-up to his comments, MAEC leaders asked Davis to work with them on the boycott.[58] Davis agreed to a closed-door meeting to discuss the nature of his support. At this meeting, held on Saturday, August 21, 1971, Davis and Castillo agreed to issue a statement to the press seeking a joint meeting with school officials "to see if some kind of agreement can be worked out to avoid a boycott."[59] MAEC repeated its support for a boycott when school began on Thursday, and the NAACP threatened to join. Their joint statement accused local officials of "sticking with the pairing minimum handed down by the federal court." Davis said, "The school district has not gone as far as it can go. The court only said they couldn't go below this pairing in its ruling but you can go above it." Davis also reported that the two groups had decided "to cooperate not only in the boycott, should it come off, but also in other endeavors." He did not elaborate on what the other endeavors might be.[60]

The statements of support from the NAACP, however, were only rhetorical. Once the boycott began, neither the NAACP nor any other black group provided material or financial assistance. The political crisis over the firing of Superintendent Garver by the board probably contributed to the lack of support.[61]

CONCLUSION

During the summer of 1971 local officials continued to view Mexican Americans as white. This was reflected in the new integration plan they developed in June of that year. Under this plan predominantly Mexican American schools would be paired with predominantly African American schools. MAEC committed itself to opposing this latest pairing plan and to increasing its base of support. Of particular importance was the support of African American political leaders, especially Reverend Davis, the chair of the local NAACP. Davis threatened to join the boycott if no progress was made in developing a just integration plan that included Anglos. The talk of a possible and massive boycott of the schools by two minority groups, however, had no significant impact on HISD. During the two weeks prior to the opening of school in late August, the board made plans to conduct an orderly and efficient desegregation of the schools based on the pairing of schools. When the schools opened on August 26, MAEC once again took to the streets and boycotted them, the third time in a span of two years.

CHAPTER 11

A Racist Bunch of Anglos

For the first several weeks in the fall of 1971 MAEC conducted another boycott. Unlike the one the previous year, the 1971 boycott included all public schools rather than only those affected by the pairing plan. This boycott was not as successful as expected, although MAEC encouraged between two thousand and six thousand students to boycott the schools. A significantly smaller number attended the huelga schools.

Local school officials, downplaying the number of students out of school, argued that most Mexican Americans failed to heed MAEC's call for a public school boycott. Interim superintendent J. Don Boney stated that the enrollment figures for the first day of school were within the normal range at 199,664.[1] According to him, the district expected 20,752 students to be enrolled at the paired schools. However, only 14,141 students enrolled in them on the first day of school. In other words, about 25 percent, or 5,611, of those expected to enroll in the paired schools failed to show up. It is unclear how many other students in those schools not included in the pairing plan failed to attend. But even without the exact figures, the number of students who failed to enroll in the paired schools suggested that absenteeism was much more serious than officially reported to the public.[2]

The local mainstream media also reported that the "threatened boycott failed to materialize." A *Houston Chronicle* article noted that "Only a scattering of Mexican American students failed to attend school." These reports did not consider the large numbers of students who failed to enroll in the paired schools. As late as October, HISD reported that it could not account for several thousand students.[3] Most of these "missing" students were from the paired schools.[4] This chapter documents MAEC's involvement in protest activities during the 1971–72 school year and the impact of increasing disunity and fragmentation within the Mexican American community on the struggle for recognition.

RAPID EROSION OF SUPPORT FOR BOYCOTT

The strong support for the boycott rapidly eroded within the first week. By the middle of the first week of the boycott more than 2,722 of the students out of school enrolled in the paired schools. By Friday of that week approximately 17,098 of the estimated 20,752 who were supposed to be attending the paired schools were enrolled in them. By the second week enrollment stabilized and a constant number of children were reported not showing up at their assigned schools.[5] Several factors probably account for this rapid erosion of support for the boycott, including lack of support from African Americans and middle-class Mexican-origin organizations, growing disenchantment, disunity within MAEC, and growing concerns with the education provided at the huelga schools.[6]

The rapid erosion of support for the boycott led to two unexpected political developments: the organization of Mexican American parents within the paired schools and the leveling of racial bias charges by Chicanos against the local school district. Increased enrollment in the public schools quickly led to the formation of a new group of parents called The Paired Parents (TPP). This loosely organized group was not associated with MAEC since it accepted the pairing decision and sought to improve its implementation. Once formed, probably during the middle of the first week of school, TPP called for a meeting with local administrators to discuss problems involving Mexican American children attending paired schools. At their meeting with local school officials held at the end of the first week of school, parents raised three major concerns: danger at bus stops and on the buses, poor schedules, and lack of student discipline in the vehicles. They charged that serious problems concerning busing were making "instant dropouts" of their children. One woman predicted "a disaster" at one of the bus stops due to narrow streets, unsupervised children, or rapidly moving buses. She also noted that since school had begun, her eight-year-old child had not returned home until after five P.M., two hours after school dismissal time.[7]

For two hours TPP, comprised of over two hundred parents, complained to local administrators. TPP parents also protested the transfer from neighborhood schools and the lack of free breakfasts. Likewise they cited nonsupervision by adults at school-designated bus stops and urged officials to have someone ensure that the children got on the right buses going home. Ray Westmoreland, the district's assistant director of transportation, told the parents that his department was swelled with calls. He explained that bus stops had been designated so as to minimize the number of stops and meet scheduling timetables. With only eighty buses accommodating sixty-six passengers each and eleven buses holding thirty-six passengers each, the vehicles often had to make two to four trips to and from schools daily. He added that thirty additional buses had been ordered at a cost of nine thousand dollars each. Once these buses arrived, probably by mid-December, the problem would be alleviated.[8]

Westmoreland's response did not quiet down the group. Mrs. Rachel Lucas, for instance, argued that because of busing problems the Mexican American dropout rate, which was 89 percent, would soon increase to "99 percent." She asked if the teachers and teachers' aides were putting the children on the right buses to return home. "I feel that is the schools' responsibility," she said. Another Mexican American parent said that she was not sending her children to school "because when the court took away the right to go to the school of their choice, I have the right not to send them to the court's choice."[9]

Administrators listened to their complaints and tried to respond. Larry Marshall, moderator at the meeting and area superintendent of one of HISD's zones, told the group that their grievances and recommendations would be heard at the school board meeting scheduled for Monday, September 13. With this comment the group left the meeting.[10] No further evidence has been found on this group, but one possibility is that the group disbanded shortly after meeting with district officials.

The erosion of support for the boycott as well as the inability to impact local desegregation policy led to increased criticism of educational authorities and to charges of racial bias. In early September an MAEC supporter charged that racism was responsible for the oppression of Mexican Americans.[11] Two months later Charles Guerrero, another activist, blamed the "racist bunch of Anglos" on the school board and in the courts for the problems confronting the district. They had "turned a deaf ear to our plea for justice and fair treatment" and abused Chicanos for too long, he charged, adding, "We are tired of all their bull."[12]

In mid-September, William D. Broyles, Jr., director of community relations for HISD, wrote a letter to the editor of *Papel Chicano* to refute these charges. School pairing, he noted, was not "nor has it ever been" a plan of HISD. The school board, he argued, submitted two plans for desegregation to the courts. One of these was known as the equidistant plan for the elementary schools and the other was the geographic capacity plan for the secondary schools. Neither plan called for the pairing of schools. The pairing was a requirement of the Fifth Circuit Court of Appeals. The school board had appealed this provision to U.S. district judge Ben Connally, but the appeal had been denied. The school board then appealed the pairing plan "all the way to the U.S. Supreme Court." "The basis for the appeal," he stated, "was the very objections you mentioned in your article: such pairings 'integrated' Mexican American with Blacks and resulted in no more than 'statistical integration.'" Broyles then reiterated HISD's position: "In summary, HISD shares your concern for the possible consequences of this pairing plan and has consistently opposed this pairing in the courts with the legal means available to us. Pairing is not an HISD plan. It is a court-ordered plan. We will, however, carry out the court decision to the best of our ability in an effort to provide the best education possible under the circumstances ordered by the courts." [13]

The editors of *Papel Chicano* fired back at Broyles's argument. "Like most Anglos, you must think we Chicanos are stupid," they responded. They argued that members of the Mexican American community were quite aware of Connally's decision and of the school board's stand on this issue. The problem was that the school board was not listening to Chicanos since it did have the power to change the integration plan. What the Chicano community wanted was "just integration," i.e., integration that would include all ethnic groups, not simply blacks and Mexican Americans. "If Anglos were included in the pairing plan," the editors stated, "then the quality of the schools would improve rapidly since the mostly white school board are [sic] not going to let the 'little white kids suffer.'" They concluded, "This is why *Papel* [*Chicano*] is calling, and will continue to call, the school board and Connally a racist bunch of Anglos until justice is done." [14]

DISUNITY AND FRAGMENTATION

The "Anglo establishment" was not the only one attacked. Militants vented their anger on other groups within the community, including professional and business persons, MAEC leaders, barrio residents, and staff members of *Papel Chicano*. Increased criticism of middle-class leaders, activists, and journalists by militants initiated a process of political fragmentation and disunity that complicated MAEC's role in carrying out its activities.

Disunity within the Mexican American community was not a new phenomenon. It was, as noted Arnoldo De León, a prominent historian of Mexican American history in Texas, an aspect of this community's complex political and ideological evolution. In the most recent period this diversity was reflected in the increased criticism of moderate Mexican American groups by more radical activists. This type of conflict emerged in the late 1960s as young militant members of MAYO and La Raza Unida mounted political attacks on the older and more established middle-class groups and individuals throughout the state.[15]

This process of political fragmentation and ideological differentiation also occurred in Houston as MAYO and other militants criticized established leaders and organizations. Officially MAYO had a policy against fighting other Mexican Americans. "We need to spend less time fighting, physically or verbally, other Chicanos who are weak before the gringo, and to spend more time building a Raza Unida to combat the gringo and his methods," MAYO's platform stated.[16] Despite this policy, MAYO militants in Houston still denounced Mexican-origin businessmen and professionals in the community and portrayed them as complacent and opportunistic. They viewed middle-class individuals as being aloof from the working class except when it served their own particular economic or professional interests. LULAC especially was denounced for failure to speak on behalf of the Mexican American working-class community. Instead of working on behalf of the collective good, LULAC only assisted individual families or offered a few scholarships for college-bound Chicano and Chicana students, these militants argued. PASO, on the other hand, was criticized for focusing more on political maneuvering and individual gains than on the "collective needs" of barrio residents. In general, then, political differences based on varied ideological perspectives were common and integral parts of Mexican Americans' political development.[17]

Political differences and disunity, however, were rare in the politics of school reform. As LULAC, the American G. I. Forum, and MALDEF had demonstrated, unity in support of the campaign for educational equality in general and for the desegregation of the schools in particular was strong and unwavering during the entire twentieth century.[18]

Unity in support of the struggle for equity and justice was also strong in Houston, especially in the fall of 1970.[19] But in 1971 the apparent unity seen in the desegregation arena broke down as the younger and more militant activists attacked all segments of the Mexican American community, especially the middle class. Eduardo López, a *Papel Chicano* columnist, began this trend in mid-September in an article he wrote decrying the lack of support for the boycott among the Mexican American community:

Up to the present there has been little publicity of our struggle. There have been no protests, there have been no pickets in the schools or in the school administration. In summary, the energy, the anger, and the valor of our Raza appears to be asleep. Wake up Raza. Do not allow "los gringos" to laugh at us due to lack of determination or laziness. We need to scream, to march, and to create such a scandal that the school authorities and the courts will understand that we, los mejicanos, do not support any more injustices.[20]

López further argued that much more needed to be done if Chicanos expected to achieve their goal of reforming the schools. "All struggles on behalf of reforms require tremendous sacrifices," he warned.[21] The entire community needed to contribute in some way, whether it be in publicity, protests, supplies, or money. "It is our civil and religious duty," he added, "to fight for our brothers."[22]

Other activists charged that the more successful Mexican Americans were oblivious to the needs and problems of the less fortunate. "How about our people who have made it, the Mexican American Doctors, Politicians, Lawyers, Grocers and others who have used La Raza as a stepping stone for their own personal gain?" inquired one activist. "Does money or position make a person change color? Or have they simply assumed the characteristics of the coconut? Brown on the outside but white on the inside?"[23]

The comments about apathy in the professional and business sectors of the Mexican American community also applied to the working classes. The lack of strong support for militant actions by barrio residents became apparent at a rally held on Saturday evening, September 25, 1971. Earlier that day a group of youths held a march that began at Hidalgo Park in the Magnolia Park barrio and ended at Eastwood Park in the East End. The march began with twenty-five individuals and increased as it continued through the barrio. But by the time the group reached Eastwood Park, only twenty-five bikes and six cars had joined in. Although the march served its purpose—to inform the community of the unfairness of the pairing plan—few barrio residents showed up to support it.[24] The reasons for the low turnout are unknown but may have been apathy, inadequate planning and organization, a combination of both, or other factors.

The criticism of Mexican Americans, especially of the middle-class professionals and the business community, increased during the next several months. In late October, López criticized awards for "Most Distinguished Mexican American" presented at one of the fiestas patrias. These fiestas were sponsored by middle-class Mexican nationals and attended by thousands of people from the community. The award, given to an individual involved in what López called "middle class" activities, was inappropriate because it was not presented to a working-class activist. López proposed broadening the criteria for these awards to include individuals involved in community organizations serving the barrio. Individuals who deserved these awards were those working with senior citizens or involved in providing health services or "educational problem solving."[25] One such individual deserving such an award was Martin Cavian, owner of Martin's Café. He gave strong support to the *movimiento* and contributed to the success of the boycott.[26]

In November an activist writing in *Papel Chicano* criticized LULAC for its empty "promises" of support for the boycott. His comments were directly aimed at Tony Bonilla, state LULAC president, and at the state organization in general. In August, Bonilla had pledged his personal support for the boycott. His pledge also implied organizational commitment to MAEC.[27] Bonilla, however, failed to honor his pledge. The state organization also failed to provide any financial support. In the meantime Chicanos had to conduct the boycott and huelga schools on a shoestring budget. According to this activist, nobody but "the people in the barrio" were contributing to the effort. The weekly expenses were being paid through the nickel and dime contributions of the community. It was not an easy task. "As a matter of fact, it has been quite a struggle, for thirteen weeks, we have fought," the *Papel Chicano* writer stated. The struggle became more difficult because of the expected support of LULAC and other established organizations. The article continued: "Organizations of so-called intellectuals and[/]or the affluent such as yourselfs [*sic*] are probably worse than the most biased and bigoted gringo, for we know what to expect from them. But you, our brothers, who could do so much, are content to just sit back and bask in the conformity of social and economic gains. What have you contributed to La Causa—nothing but promises."[28]

Militants continued their attack on Mexican American leaders who failed to support the boycott. In late February, López wrote an article criticizing the Mexican American business, professional, and working-class communities for not supporting "equity struggles." "La Raza," he argued, "must bring pressure on these 'coconuts' to change their ways."[29]

The diversity and disunity among activists was quite apparent in November during the school board elections as several Mexican Americans with different political persuasions ran for the same position and lost. Prior to the mid-1960s only one Mexican American individual, Felix Tijerina, had run for a school board position. In 1969 four Mexican Americans ran against each other for two positions, although none won.[30] In 1971 the number of Mexican Americans running for school board positions increased to five. Three of these individuals—Gregory Salazar, Rev. James Novarro, and Manuel "Tank" Barrera—ran against each other for position number seven. David López, a lawyer, ran for position number five while Abel Álvarez, one of the boycott's leaders, ran for position number six.[31]

Those running for position number seven were quite distinct from each other. Reverend Novarro was a conservative Protestant minister who had been instrumental in the farm workers' struggle in Texas. Tank Barrera was a University of Houston student and a member of the Young Socialist Alliance. Salazar was the former MAYO spokesperson and an avowed Marxist. Both Salazar and Barrera supported community control of the schools and opposed racism, but they were opposed to each other's ideological stance and so were ideological and political enemies. Salazar was ostracized by *Papel Chicano* for his Marxist views. This position led to charges of right-wing tendencies of *Papel Chicano* by Salazar and his supporters. Gloria Guardiola, a former MAYO member, specifically charged that *Papel Chicano* was shifting to the right of the political spectrum because the paper refused to place an ad for Salazar's campaign.[32] Reverend Novarro, on the other hand, was the publisher of the community newspaper *El Sol.* He advocated equality in the schools but failed to publicly support the boycott. Barrera and Salazar argued that he was "irrelevant to the community."[33]

The other two Mexican Americans running for the school board were not as controversial or as diverse in their ideological perspectives as Novarro, Barrera, or Salazar. David López was a well-known lawyer supported by an alliance of liberal Anglos and Mexican Americans. Abel Álvarez filed at the last moment. He opposed the pairing plan and supported MAEC's boycott, and he wrote for *Papel Chicano*.[34]

Only David López won election to the school board. Whether the differences among the candidates and the disunity among the different factions kept the others from winning is unclear. What is clear is that the solidarity apparent during the summer of 1970 was diminishing as further ideological divisions surfaced.[35]

MAEC was not immune to criticism. In July, 1971, an activist criticized the organization for focusing too much on "internal struggles" and for forgetting who was the "real enemy—the federal Judge Connally and his decision."[36] In February of 1972 another *Papel Chicano* writer accused MAEC's advisory board of developing a "superiority complex" in its relationship to the community. This person also charged that "unscrupulous" individuals in MAEC were placing their own personal needs above those of the community. "The advisory board's duty is to advise," this person admonished. "If they are not willing to abide by this then the community will have to replace the members before they bring down the only organization which at this time represents La Raza in Los Barrios."[37]

Despite this criticism, *Papel Chicano* chronicled the important role MAEC was playing in bringing unity and direction to "la Causa." The paper also publicized MAEC's success in raising funds and in promoting community activities. In October, for instance, MAEC sponsored a successful raffle and barbecue at Moody Park, a softball game between the Looscan Elementary School kids and some of the huelga school kids, and a huelga school Halloween carnival. In December and January the organization sponsored a well-attended boxing match in the community and a fund-raiser at the Salvation Army gym.[38]

The ideological and political fragmentation within the community touched all groups, including *Papel Chicano*. In late May the editors expelled one of its members for using the newspaper to promote another organization's activities. Pedro Vásquez was expelled for using the newspaper's name to collect money for the Youth Socialist Alliance (YSA). The YSA, a Trotskyite organization, was distrusted in the Mexican American activist community. "He has now joined this group [YSA] and is no longer welcomed in the barrio," noted a *Papel Chicano* editor.[39]

Surprisingly, MAEC continued to be the key organization and the only visible actor in the struggle for educational equality during this period of increasing fragmentation and disunity.[40] One primary reason for MAEC's continuing influence was the lack of active opposition to its actions from Anglos or from other more conservative groups. Another possible reason is that MAEC had an activist liberal stance. Although radical members of the Mexican American community criticized it, MAEC maintained its presence and continued the struggle under trying circumstances.

LEGAL SUCCESS IN THE CONTEXT OF DECLINING ACTIVISM

After September, MAEC did not engage in any significant protest activity during the 1971–72 school year. Although the organization continued to monitor the desegregation of the schools during the year, increasingly more time was spent developing new educational programs for Mexican American students or ensuring the continuity of existing schooling opportunities provided by the huelga schools. During the fall, for instance, MAEC sought funding to develop tutorial and cultural programs, dropout prevention and career orientation, and parental involvement programs in the schools.[41] In the spring of 1972 the remnants of the huelga schools were incorporated under the name Centro-Escolar Mexico-Americano.[42] Many of MAEC's members became involved in electoral politics and worked to elect David López to the school board and Leonel Castillo to the city controller position.[43]

While MAEC's involvement in protest actions decreased, it continued to support the struggle for recognition in the courts. The organization's involvement in litigation, as noted earlier, began in early August, 1970, when Ramírez encouraged MALDEF to submit a friend of the court brief to the Fifth Circuit Court asking the court to consider Mexican Americans as intervenors and to declare them as an identifiable minority group for desegregation purposes. The court denied MALDEF's request but argued that the organization could seek redress in the district court. In early September, 1970, during the height of the boycott, MALDEF filed a motion to intervene in the local desegregation case with the district court. It also filed a complaint alleging discrimination against Mexican Americans as a class and in the pairing of elementary schools.[44] MAEC argued that the pairing was unjust because it involved predominantly Mexican American and African American schools.[45]

On May 24, 1971, U.S. district judge Ben C. Connally denied MAEC's intervention request. Connally ruled that Mexican Americans had been treated historically and in the contemporary period as white by the courts and were never considered or treated as a separate race or group in the schools. Additionally, he speculated that while Mexican Americans might be a minority, they were not entitled to relief. In other words, there were no constitutional grounds for intervention. He also severely castigated MAEC for the timing of its suit and noted that Mexican Americans had not raised any objections to segregation in the fifteen years since the *Ross* case was initiated.[46] MAEC appealed this decision to the Fifth Circuit Court in New Orleans.[47]

The Fifth Circuit Court responded to MAEC's appeal in the early days of the 1972–73 school year. On September 6, 1972, the court ruled that the district court had to reconsider its earlier decision not to allow Mexican Americans to intervene in the desegregation case. It noted that in denying Mexican Americans the right to intervene the district court had argued that this group was and had been considered part of the white race.[48] The premise for this ruling, however, was no longer legally accurate in light of two recent Fifth Circuit Court decisions. In these two decisions, one pertaining to a desegregation case in Austin and the other to a case in Corpus Christi, the court ruled that Mexican Americans were an identifiable minority group and had to be included in integration plans.[49] In the Austin case, for instance, the court ruled that

> No remedy for the dual system can be acceptable if it operates to deprive members of a third ethnic group of the benefits of equal educational opportunity. To dismantle the black-white segregation system without including the third ethnic group in the desegregation process would be to deny to that group all of the benefits of integrated schooling which the courts of this nation have been protecting for twenty years. To exclude Mexican-Americans from the benefits of tri-partite integration in the very act of effecting a unitary system would be to provide blacks with the benefit of integration while denying it to another (and larger) group on the basis of ethnic origin. This in itself is a denial of equal protection of the laws.[50]

This ruling was an important one for MAEC.[51] Although the decision did not yet, as Abraham Ramírez, Jr., noted, "put us in the case," its implications for Houston were "quite clear."[52] More specifically, as noted a journalist, it could influence Connally to officially declare Mexican Americans a separate ethnic group and impel him to end the unpopular court-ordered pairing of twenty-two mostly minority elementary schools.[53]

Local officials, however, did not want the courts to issue such a ruling and believed that they could "handle it administratively without formally reopening the desegregation case." On September 9, 1972, the school board voted to recognize Mexican Americans as an ethnic minority but only for student transfer purposes.[54]

The intent of this policy change was to broaden the existing court-ordered majority-to-minority transfer rule whereby a black or a white student assigned to a school where his/her race was in the majority could transfer to any school where his/her race was in the minority. This policy was based on the notion that Mexican Americans were white and could only transfer to schools where they were in the minority. In other words, Mexican Americans could only transfer to predominantly African American, not Anglo, schools. The new policy viewed Mexican Americans as a minority group and allowed them to transfer to either a black or an Anglo school. It expanded the provisions of the existing policy and allowed for triethnic transfers.[55]

Local officials believed that this plan "would go a long way towards putting the Houston district in compliance with the latest Fifth Circuit decision" and, as district lawyer Harry Patterson said, "might put us in full compliance." But this proposal fell short of what Ramírez and new Mexican American school board member David López sought. They believed that the court should end the school pairing and require increased hiring of Mexican American teachers, who comprised only 3 percent of the district's instructional staff. In order to move the district beyond simply a broadened school transfer policy López proposed the establishment of a fifteen-member committee to review the district's entire desegregation plan. The committee would present its recommendations for a new desegregation plan to the school board and request the board to pass them to Connally as a response to the recent Fifth Circuit Court ruling. The board took no immediate action on this proposal or any other that significantly impacted the education of Mexican American students.[56]

As these actions indicate, Mexican Americans were far from reaching their goal of equitable and quality education. But unlike in previous years, they now had a foot in the door. Although the local court had not and would not officially rule on their legal status, by the beginning of the 1972–73 school year the Fifth Circuit Court of Appeals decision legitimized Mexican Americans' interests in the politics of local school reform. In 1973 the U.S. Supreme Court ruled, in a different case, that for desegregation purposes Mexican Americans were an identifiable minority group.[57]

POST-1972 DEVELOPMENTS

For all intents and purposes, then, and with the exception of the district court, by the fall of 1972 MAEC had accomplished its most important goal of formal recognition by the superintendent, the school board, and the federal courts. For two years and in the face of innumerable obstacles, both internally and externally, MAEC had engaged in a struggle to correct an institutional wrong by mobilizing thousands of community people and by successfully convincing them to accept a new ethnic identity and a new politics. Mexican Americans, the organization had argued, were not white; they were brown. MAEC members were not afraid to use militant tactics to reach their objectives. The combination of this new identity and new politics eventually contributed to success. MAEC had shown local and federal officials that Mexican Americans had officially arrived.

Despite MAEC's accomplishment, Mexican Americans still faced many obstacles in their quest for recognition and inclusion. For the next decade a variety of organizations and community activists continued to struggle on behalf of Mexican American political and cultural interests. The nature of the struggle as well as the context in which Mexican Americans struggled, however, changed. The struggle for recognition, for instance, was transformed from a mass-based movement to a more limited one based on interest groups and individual activists. The major activist groups leading the quest for recognition in the early 1970s—MAEC, MAYO, and AMAE—either disbanded or assumed new roles. MAEC, for instance, abandoned the advocacy role it had played and became a federally sponsored social service organization. In 1973 MAEC formally changed its name to the Educational Association of Mexican Americans (EAMA), although it continued to go by MAEC for several more months.[58] MAYO and other radical youth groups became inactive during these years or else disbanded and, like much of the Chicano movement, became part of history. Other groups such as AMAE continued their involvement but not in challenging HISD's policies and practices.[59] The only group that continued to thrive and to have an impact on local politics during the post-1972 years was MALDEF. In most cases David López, the new Chicano school board member; a few activist lawyers; and the sporadic actions of a few ad-hoc community groups supported this organization. For the next decade and, in the context of a disappearing Chicano movement, these community activists undertook three major strategies to continue the struggle for legal recognition and board inclusion: a residual form of protest, a continuing one of litigation, and an emergent one of participation in school board decision making and in court-appointed committees.

Protests

Mexican American parents and community groups protested to HISD officials, but this type of strategy became nonexistent by the mid-1970s. During the 1973–74 school year a group of Mexican American parents from the Magnolia Park barrio became embroiled in a clash with school officials. In November, 1973, these parents, with the support of the remnants of MAEC, asked the Department of Justice to investigate discriminatory conditions at Edison Junior High School. The following month Sam Saenz, director of the United States office of Health, Education, and Welfare (HEW) in Dallas, advised De Anda, director of MAEC, to "quit trying to solve Edison's educational problems," although without much success.[60] On January 25, 1974, the organization filed a complaint with the Office of Civil Rights (OCR) against HISD. It charged HISD with denying Mexican American parents their civil rights and MAEC its legal rights. No evidence has been found indicating that the OCR office in Dallas investigated.[61] The complaint had no impact on HISD but served to increase the community's disenchantment with the school district in general and with the current desegregation policy in particular. In some respects this was the last gasp of community protest in the 1970s.[62]

Litigation

The litigation strategy, as noted above, was always in the background of Mexican American activism. Although the Fifth Circuit Court in 1972 and the Supreme Court in 1973 ruled that Mexican Americans were an identifiable minority group, the district court in Houston did not. MALDEF's intervention lawsuit was aimed at getting this legal recognition at the local level and ensuring that Mexican American interests would be considered in all future educational matters. For an additional nine years after the 1972 Fifth Circuit Court decision, or until the district court declared HISD a unitary district, MALDEF sought to gain legal recognition.

This effort picked up soon after the Fifth Circuit Court issued its decision in September. In fact, a week after this ruling MALDEF inquired about its intervention suit. The district court told MALDEF to wait until the court had an opportunity to review HISD's new "majority-to-minority" transfer plan aimed at achieving triethnic desegregation.[63] Although MALDEF did not know it then, this was the last time the court would formally address the organization on its intervention lawsuit.

The following year MALDEF, going on the assumption that the court would soon hear its intervention case, began to make plans for going to trial. However, organization members found out that the Mexican American community in Houston now had serious doubts about this strategy. Awareness of decreasing support for desegregation in general and for the group's intervention suit in particular came in July, 1973, when Guadalupe Salinas, MALDEF's lawyer, met with several community leaders from Houston to hear their concerns. Among those he met were Abe Ramírez, MALDEF's referral lawyer; several Chicano lawyers; a former boycott leader; and the executive committee of MAEC. Salinas wanted to meet with the plaintiffs too, but they were not available. All of them informed him that many parents and community leaders preferred their own community schools, opposed busing per se, and supported quality education. Most, however, were unclear on how quality education could be achieved.[64]

Despite these concerns, Ramírez told MALDEF that it should proceed with its intervention case. MALDEF, however, wanted greater assurance of community support for the lawsuit.[65] The organization specifically asked Ramírez and others to educate the community about the benefits of desegregation and the detrimental consequences of segregated schools.

In the next several months Salinas met with several other community leaders. On November 20, 1973, for instance, he met with José Pérez, Leonel Castillo, José Torres, and Alfredo Saenz. In late February he met with still others. None of these leaders expressed support for desegregation. Salinas reported to MALDEF that it was unclear what the Chicano community in Houston wanted to do with respect to desegregation.[66]

In March several Mexican American activists, including Raul De Anda, director of MAEC, and several African American groups publicly voiced their opposition to desegregation. These activists not only voiced their opposition to elementary school pairings but they also argued for developing an alternative to pairing that did not include desegregation. They, in other words, voiced their support for quality neighborhood schools. In order to accomplish their goals, these activists made plans for the establishment of a new organization called the Black-Brown Coalition to oppose the district's pairing plan.[67]

Despite this opposition, MALDEF continued to hold firm to its belief that desegregation was the most effective strategy to pursue. Plans for the intervention hearing proceeded, and by late March one of MALDEF's lawyers reported that the organization was ready to proceed with the hearing. This momentum, however, was derailed by the Mexican American Service Organization's (MASO) filing of its own desegregation case. MASO, as will be noted below, was a new community organization opposed to HISD's pairing plan.[68] By the spring of 1975, then, two different groups had two distinct lawsuits before the district court. Neither would officially get its day in court, although the judiciary did informally recognize MALDEF as the representative of Mexican Americans on this case.

Although derailed for a few years, MALDEF as late as 1978 was hopeful that the court would hold a hearing on its request for intervention and for declaring Mexican Americans a minority group. The court, however, stalled on the issue and instead focused on other, more-pressing legal concerns, including challenging the legality of establishing a breakaway school district known as the Westheimer Independent School District, replacing the pairing desegregation order with an alternative magnet school program, and reconstituting the Bi-Racial Committee.[69] Despite motions by plaintiffs and intervenors to implement metropolitan desegregation and without deciding on the legal status of Mexican Americans, the district court in 1981 ruled that HISD had become a unitary district. This formal acknowledgment indicated to the court that "HISD had made every attempt to desegregate and that the racial composition of its schools now was a result of housing patterns, increasing minority population, and decreasing white population." The plaintiffs and intervenors signed a formal agreement ending all claims in the summer of 1984.[70] The era of federal overview of HISD thus came to an end by the early 1980s. Much to the dismay of activists, the federal district court did not formally rule on Mexican Americans' legal status, although it did informally recognize them as an important force to be reckoned with in all school matters.

Board Involvement
The participation of Mexican Americans in board policy making emerged as the most important strategy for legal recognition and board inclusion. Their participation was diverse and at different levels. Mexican American leaders participated as school board members, as members of board-appointed task forces, as members of court-appointed task forces, and as independent voices.

Their participation as insiders began in 1972 when David López was sworn in as the first Mexican American school board member and lasted until 1975, when he failed to be reelected. As a school board member, Ló-pez pushed for the recognition of Mexican Americans as an identifiable minority group, for their inclusion on board committees, for the additional hiring of Mexican American teachers and principals, for the expansion of academic programs aimed at meeting the needs of Mexican American children, and for replacing the pairing plan and the Bi-Racial Committee with triethnic desegregation. The request for this recognition and inclusion was usually done with the advice and support of Ramírez and MALDEF.[71]

During the 1973–74 school year a larger number of Chicanos became involved in the politics of desegregation as a result of their appointment to a task force formed by the board in November. The school board appointed the Task Force on Quality Integration to halt white flight, promote integration, develop alternative plans for pairing, and provide more opportunities for students. Gonzalo Garza, deputy superintendent, was appointed chairperson. After a long series of closed meetings the task force issued a report with twenty-five recommendations. Three minority members of the task force opposed the report and were critical of support for magnet schools. Two minority board members, Leon Everett and David López, also opposed it. López called the report "sugarcoated freedom of choice." Because of this criticism the board decided only to "accept" the report.[72]

Ben Canales, a Mexican American task force member, later said that the group he belonged to, the Mexican American Service Organization (MASO), would ask the U.S. Civil Rights Commission to investigate desegregation in HISD and the workings of the task force. MASO, however, only asked the commission to investigate charges of discrimination against parents and against MAEC.[73]

During the following school year Mexican American activists increased their participation in HISD desegregation efforts and their criticism of HISD's commitment to replace the mandatory pairings with a voluntary magnet school program. MALDEF continued to prepare for a possible intervention hearing.[74] In the meantime the school board, on November 25, 1974, moved to establish a twenty-two-member task force to explore alternatives to school pairing and ways to combat white flight.[75] Six of the members were Mexican Americans. For the next several months several Mexican Americans on the task force and the lone school board member voiced criticism of its intentions. They charged that the real intent of the task force was to substitute the magnet school program for the pairing plan without significantly increasing the scope of desegregation.[76]

On February 21, 1975, the task force completed its work by approving recommendations that called for the elimination of pairing and the establishment of a voluntary magnet school plan. On this day some members of the task force who belonged to MASO filed a lawsuit to prevent the pairing of schools. This lawsuit alleged that the current desegregation plan was unconstitutional because it excluded Anglos.[77] MASO recommended more extensive desegregation.[78] The lawsuit had no impact on the task force's deliberations.

At its March meeting the school board adopted the report seeking court approval for replacing the pairing of schools with alternative education.[79] Both minority board members opposed its adoption. Everett charged that the board was breaking its promises to achieve equitable desegregation. López called the members racist in their support for the magnet program.[80]

Three of the six Mexican American members on the task force also opposed this report and refused to sign it. These individuals submitted a minority report critical of the magnet school concept as a primary means of desegregation.[81] Instead of magnet schools, they recommended metropolitan desegregation.[82] School board members ignored the minority report and accepted it without any comments.

Participation in Court-Appointed Committee, 1975–76

Although absent from school board decision making after 1975, Mexican American activists became active participants in a few court-appointed committees during the second half of the 1970s. Their involvement indicated that the district court informally recognized Mexican Americans as an identifiable minority group even though not formally making such a ruling. The informal recognition of Mexican Americans occurred on February 24, 1976, when the district court issued an order reconstituting the Bi-Racial Committee to include Mexican Americans, although it had not yet heard MALDEF's complaint on intervention.[83]

Despite this ruling, no formal action was taken to appoint members to this committee or to reactivate it. This changed on August 5, 1977, when the new district judge, Finis E. Cowan, issued several decisions pertaining to the desegregation of HISD. One of these was an order to reactivate and reconstitute the Bi-Racial Committee. Unlike the 1976 order, this time Judge

Cowan asked MALDEF and HISD to come up with several names. Two months later, on December 2, he appointed the eleven-member Tri-ethnic Committee. Three appointees were Mexican Americans: José Adan Trevino, James Novarro, and Mario Quiñones. He also made several assignments and hinted at the possibility of having metropolitan desegregation.[84]

Although Mexican Americans felt welcome, on April of the same year Judge Cowan held a hearing on achieving unitary status and did not invite MALDEF. Only the official parties to the suit were invited, and since MALDEF was not one, the judge did not feel compelled to invite the group.[85]

On October 3, 1978, Judge Cowan established a schedule for achieving unitary status. For the next three academic years the NAACP and the federal government proposed that because of changing demographic considerations the district court consider metropolitan plans for desegregating HISD. Judge Cowan asked the Tri-ethnic Committee to look into this possibility and encouraged members to explore the options for metropolitan desegregation. The NAACP and the Justice Department also submitted motions for metropolitan desegregation. The district judge, however, denied these motions and ruled on June 17, 1981, that HISD was a unitary system.[86]

CONCLUSION

The struggle for legal recognition and board inclusion thus continued for over a decade. It did not end in 1972 when the Fifth Circuit Court ruled that Mexican Americans were a minority group; it assumed a new form. Unlike the first two years of the 1970s, the struggle lost its mass-based constituency and was carried forward by a group of dedicated community activists determined to win their rightful place in education. This struggle was initiated by MAEC, an organization of diverse political and philosophical orientations that for a brief moment in history mobilized thousands of parents, students, and community activists and utilized radical means to fight for recognition of Mexican Americans' new identity. MAEC, as noted Richard Vara, a *Houston Post* reporter in the mid-1970s, encouraged parents to become more involved with the schools, established communication within and between diverse barrios, promoted significant changes in public education that benefited Mexican Americans, and produced the first generation of Mexican American politicians.[87]

MAEC also led the fight for the acquisition of a new ethnic identity based on the ethos of the Chicano Generation—i.e., on nonwhiteness, on Mexican nationalism, and on militancy. MAEC, in other words, initiated the contemporary struggle for mainstream acceptance of Mexican Americans on their own terms and for inclusion in all decisions impacting their lives.

CONCLUSION

Reflections on Identity, School Reform, and the Chicano Movement

This study documents and explores the origins, evolution, and transformation of a local struggle for educational equality in Houston during the late 1960s and early 1970s. In the latter part of the 1960s the struggle for equality was focused on improving the quality of education for Mexican-origin children. A variety of new and old groups—students, middle-class activists, and grassroots organizers—independently protested inferior school conditions, a subtractive or assimilationist curriculum, and the structural exclusion of the Mexican-origin community. In 1970 the emphasis of the struggle shifted toward desegregation. This shift occurred as a result of the local school district's misuse of Mexican Americans' racial classification as white to circumvent desegregation mandates. Gaining legal recognition as a minority group became the primary strategy for fighting this particular act of discrimination.

The school board's misuse of the white racial identity of the Mexican-origin population also led to increased unity of the independent activist groups. Youth, students, middle-class activists, and grassroots individuals now joined forces with parents and others to form a new grassroots organization, the Mexican American Education Council (MAEC), and to struggle for legal recognition by the courts and the school district. Because of persistent resistance to MAEC's demands, the struggle lasted for two years.

This struggle is extremely important because of its impact on Mexican Americans and on public education. First, it underscored the emergence of a new type of grassroots ethnic leadership during the era of protest. Second, it signaled a shift in the activist community's identity. Finally, it introduced Mexican American interests into educational policy making in general and into the national desegregation struggles in particular.

EMERGENCE OF A NEW TYPE OF ETHNIC LEADERSHIP

The two-year struggle for recognition underscored the emergence of a new type of grassroots ethnic leadership characterized by a commitment to community empowerment in general and to a recognition of differences between Mexican American individuals. MAEC leaders, generally speaking, recognized the worth and potential of all activists, especially women and youths, and sought to empower them through the organization. In this sense, then, the organization was extremely inclusive.

MAEC's leaders, for instance, were extremely instrumental in ensuring the participation of large numbers of Mexican-origin activists in the maintenance of the organization and in the development of its goals and strategies. These leaders, especially Leonel Castillo, its first chair during the 1970–71 school year, welcomed all types of individuals—militants and moderates, young and old, men and women, middle class and working class, and seasoned and novice—into the organization.

Additionally, they provided members with a variety of opportunities for the development of collective decisions. Two decisions made collectively determined the goals of the organization and the strategies used. The members collectively decided at various meetings to pursue legal recognition as the primary goal of the organization. The emphasis on one central goal provided focus to the struggle and ensured that the organizational leaders could not be co-opted. The members also collectively decided to utilize a variety of traditional and nontraditional methods for reaching their goal. More specifically, they agreed to pursue litigation, negotiation, and militant methods such as school boycotts, picketing, and demonstrations. These methods were not viewed as contradictory but as supplementary to each other. Adoption of multiple strategies, in turn, significantly increased the chances for success.

This distinct type of leadership was quite different from that offered by older community organizations or by some of the new ones that emerged during the Chicano-movement era. For instance, the two largest Mexican American civil rights organizations in Texas—the League of United Latin American Citizens (LULAC) and the American G. I. Forum—were not inclusive, nor did they seek to empower all of their members. Their organizational structures were hierarchical and their memberships selective. Both of these organizations allowed individuals to join only if they met a specific set of criteria. They also limited the participation of women and youths to auxiliary branches of the organization.[1]

Some of the new Chicano-movement organizations also discouraged a commitment to community empowerment and were characterized by hierarchical leadership limited primarily to male-based elites or to particular sectors within the community, such as youths or students. Among these types of organizations were the Crusade for Justice and the Movimiento Estudiantil Chicano de Aztlan (MeCha).[2] Other Chicano-movement organizations such as La Raza Unida Party in Texas, El Centro de Acción Autonoma-Hermandad General de Trabajadores (CASA), and Chicana feminists in general, however, promoted varying degrees of community empowerment.[3] These groups sought the participation of all their members and encouraged their empowerment. MAEC fell into this latter category of organization and ethnic leadership. MAEC leaders likewise were extremely flexible, and they were able to overcome four major obstacles confronting the organization: persistent resistance from the school board, the judiciary, and the general public; lack of support from the African American community; youth violence; and internal factionalism.

Unlike other community organizations during the Chicano-movement era, MAEC did not experience overt resistance to its demands for legal recognition.[4] However, the organization did encounter subtle and persistent opposition. For instance, for two years the local and appellate courts consistently refused to honor the community's nonwhite racial identity despite legal trends acknowledging Mexican Americans as an identifiable minority group. The local school board also failed to consider Mexican Americans as a distinct minority group despite MAEC's protests. Between 1970 and 1972 only the superintendent, not the board, formally recognized Mexican American children's academic and linguistic needs.[5] Even after the courts ruled on their legal status, the local school board refused to officially acknowledge Mexican Americans as an identifiable minority group for desegregation purposes. The legal ruling, then, did not guarantee equitable treatment of Mexican American children or of the community's political interests. It was still up to Mexican-origin activists to ensure that their interests were adequately incorporated into school policies and practices.[6]

In addition to resistance, MAEC also faced the harsh reality of nonsupport from the liberal, Anglo population and of inadequate support from African Americans. Liberal Anglos in general did not support the legal struggle for recognition, nor did the African American community. Although a few leaders pledged their support, the majority of the African American community remained indifferent, as will be shown later, because of economic competition and interethnic rivalry and distrust.

Another potentially disrupting incident MAEC faced was violence on the part of MAYO, the militant faction within the organization. MAYO's disruption at the school board meeting of September, 1970, jeopardized MAEC's efforts at negotiating a final settlement. MAYO's militancy in actuality clashed with MAEC's philosophy of peaceful but assertive negotiations and indicated how some militant youths were ready and willing to use any means available to accomplish their goals. This clash with school officials also suggested that while the community supported the utilization of nonconventional methods to achieve its goal of board recognition, it did not tolerate or accept violence. This incident, however, did not negatively impact MAEC's negotiating strategy. The MAEC leadership used it to their advantage and threatened further action unless the board negotiated with them. This threat paid off, and a day after the disruptions school officials agreed to meet most of the organization's demands.

Finally, MAEC faced internal factionalism, especially during the second year. Activists within the organization turned against different sectors of the community and began to attack them politically and through the media. Middle-class organizations and working-class residents were also targeted for criticism by these activists during the early months of the struggle's second year. In the latter part of the 1971–72 school year, the attacks against moderate members of MAEC and against left-leaning members of the organization increased. Many of the activists engaged in milder versions of what Armando Navarro called the "politics of self-destruction."[7]

This finding of tensions and conflicts in the struggle for recognition contradicts the popular belief among many activists, and to some extent social scientists, that education was the one area in which the entire community could unite without any major differences.[8] This belief is inaccurate because it ignores the differentiation of the Mexican-origin community in general and of the Chicano movement in particular.[9] As reflected in the community's quest for recognition and educational justice in Houston, this struggle was a complex political process comprised of males and females from different social classes and with varied ideological persuasions.[10] As a result of this diversity, there were significant differences in community members' perspectives on education, especially in the goals of activism and in the strategies and tactics activists were willing to support. Some, for instance, believed that the goal of activism was to integrate Mexican Americans into the schools or to influence the structure and content of public education so that it would reflect the experiences and desires of this group. Others felt that the goal of activism was to gain community control of this public institution or to develop alternative educational institutions that would meet the specific needs of the Mexican American community. Many in the community also had different views as to who should run for the school board or who should represent them in this endeavor. This diversity of perspectives was vividly reflected in the school board elections of 1969 and 1971 as well as in the rallies and meetings held and the periodical articles appearing during the two-year struggle for recognition.

MAEC leaders, however, made sure that these differences did not deter them from their goal of gaining legal recognition. In many cases they ignored, dismissed, or deemphasized these criticisms and continued to press for a favorable resolution to the problem of nonrecognition.

MAEC, then, was able to respond to each and every one of these major obstacles and to develop appropriate responses. The organization encouraged a variety of additional political and legal responses to these challenges and did not give in to the forces of opposition or of factionalism. MAEC had too much at stake and strongly believed that the school board's unjust act was subject to change through group action. Its leadership and persistence eventually forced the schools and courts to acknowledge Mexican Americans as a distinct minority group and to include their interests in the formulation and implementation of school policies and practices.

SHIFT IN IDENTITY

The struggle for recognition was also important because it signaled a shift in the identity of the school activists from "Mexican Americanist" to "Chicano." Without exception Houston activists were significantly affected by the swirl of old and new political, racial, and cultural ideas common during the era of protest. Most of them, however, to varying degrees embraced the new ideas espoused by the Chicano movement and rejected, questioned, or contested the dominant ideas of the Mexican American Generation. These ideals, in turn, were then redefined and selectively incorporated into the struggle.

Those who believed in the Mexican Americanist identity were members of the Mexican American Generation. These activists were born or raised in the United States and became involved in civil rights, labor organizing, and electoral activities from the 1930s to the early 1960s. For the most part the majority of these activists believed in gendered notions of cultural pluralism, in structural integration, in moderate reforms of the existing social order, and in the politics of accommodation, that is, in the use of conventional means to realize social reform.[11]

The activists of the 1960s responded in various ways to the political thoughts and actions of the Mexican American Generation. Some of them seriously contested or questioned selective aspects of this older generation's identity. Others simply rejected what Ignacio García called the "liberal agenda" of the Mexican American Generation and accepted their own.[12]

The contestation of or break with the politics, culture, and social change strategies of the older activist generation as well as the acceptance of the Chicano identity did not occur all at once, nor was it as dramatic as several authors have suggested.[13] It was an evolutionary and uneven process. Some activists did so gradually, others quickly.

This dialectical process of uneven contestation, rejection, acceptance, and redefinition was part of the Chicano-movement era and was reflected in the diverse types of actions taken by Mexican-origin activists during these years. Chicano and Chicana activists, for instance, were skeptical of the Mexican American Generation's dependence on the politics of accommodation or the use of traditional methods of struggle such as litigation, lobbying, and persuasion. Many believed that conventional strategies of struggle were relatively ineffective. Instead of the politics of accommodation, these activists, including a few older members from established organizations such as LULAC or the American G. I. Forum, advocated the use of oppositional politics or direct action tactics such as marches, walkouts, confrontations, and civil disobedience.[14] In advocating these new methods of struggle, the activists of this period broke with the politics and social-change tactics of the Mexican American Generation.

Those who subscribed to the Chicano identity also rejected the Mexican American Generation's belief in cultural pluralism, in whiteness, and in middle-class life. The Chicano identity replaced these ideals with gendered notions of cultural nationalism, a complex concept that included several dimensions, including that of male-based indigenismo, cultural pride, and reaffirmation of working-class life.[15] Unlike members of the Mexican American Generation who viewed themselves as white and as sharing many similarities with Anglos, the Chicano Generation viewed itself as being different from Anglos.[16] They were of indigenous—i.e., non-white—origins, extremely proud of their Mexican cultural heritage, and devoted to their working-class barrios.[17]

Cultural nationalism also included an added dimension based on the reinvention of the collective self, or what Ignacio García referred to as the reinterpretation of the Mexican experience in this country. Unlike existing views of Mexican Americans as passive historical figures with a traditional and stagnant homogenous culture, cultural nationalism viewed this group as active agents of the historical process. More specifically, this concept viewed Mexicans as both victims and agents of history; they were oppressed by the larger society but also resisted all forms of exploitation.[18] All of these elements, then—gendered indigenismo, pride in their working-class status, strong belief in the richness of their cultural heritage, victimization, and resistance—were integral aspects of the developing nationalist identity.[19]

In addition to the rejection of the liberal agenda and the reinvention of their collective image in the United States, the Chicano identity also challenged, but did not reject, the Mexican American Generation's beliefs in moderate social reform. These activists criticized the older generation's belief in moderate social reform and initially argued for more rapid social change. By the late 1960s and early 1970s, however, an increasing number of activists argued for a new type of social change.[20]

Finally, the Chicano identity criticized but did not reject the older generation's ideals and methods of integration. Although the Chicano identity sought integration into the established social, economic, and political structures, it embraced the concept of self-determination. Chicanos and Chicanas, in other words, would determine whether and how they would integrate into society. In most cases, as stipulated in the Plan de Aztlán,

Chicanos and Chicanas would seek control of existing institutions or else they would establish their own parallel ones to accomplish the goal of social justice and equality for the working-class community. The Chicano identity thus favored integration into the existing system but on the basis of self-determination. La Raza Unida Party (LRUP) is an example of the relationship between self-determination and integration. Although the organization appeared to be separatist in its orientation, LRUP sought integration into American political life but on its own terms.[21]

The legal struggle for recognition in Houston from 1970 to 1972 shows this shift in identity and the rejection of Mexican Americanist ideals. Three specific aspects of the latter identity were rejected or contested in this struggle: its white racial status, its belief in gradual social change, and its dependence on conventional methods of struggle. In turn, the Houston activists accepted a nonwhite racial identity, mobilization and protest as a legitimate form of struggle, and militancy in social change.

Rejection of White Status

The overwhelming majority of activists involved in the struggle for legal recognition rejected the white racial status of the past for several important reasons. The primary one was political. Local school officials were abusing the classification of Mexicans as white and using it to limit the participation of Anglos in desegregation. In the past the classification of white was used as a means for eliminating discrimination against Mexican Americans, but this time around it was being used for discriminatory purposes. Thus, in order to prohibit discrimination against Mexican Americans, the community rejected its historically based white racial status.

In the place of a white racial identity, activists adopted a new identity that was influenced by personal experience, legal developments, and the Chicano movement. Ambiguity and lack of consensus accompanied the adoption of this new identity. In many ways those who looked to the Chicano movement for inspiration viewed their identity as brown, those who focused on legal developments argued that they were an identifiable minority group, and those who looked to their heritage chose Chicano or Mexicano.[22]

Legal developments influenced the emerging racial identity in Houston. The U.S. courts, for instance, argued that Chicanos and Chicanas were an identifiable minority group on the basis of cultural characteristics, political powerlessness, and economic deprivation. This implied that Mexican Americans were both an exploited ethnic group, with distinct cultural and linguistic traits and common historical backgrounds, and a racial group, one that shared a history of exploitation with African Americans.[23]

The other branches of the federal government also viewed Mexican Americans as a distinct group. These policy rulings were based on the notion of "national origin," not on the more legalistic concept of "identifiable minority group" used by the courts. According to these policies, as expressed through executive rulings, national surveys, and legislation, Mexican Americans were members of a distinct social group that was discriminated against on the basis of national origin, particularly language and culture.[24]

Personal experience guided some MAEC members in determining their collective identity. Many activists, especially mothers and community elders, were not aware of these legal developments or of the Chicano movement. From experience, however, they realized that they were racially and culturally different from the Anglos. Despite Mexican Americans' willingness to work hard and to be accepted, Anglos tended to view them as racial inferiors and as merely laborers, not equals. They were not white, as noted Lucy Moreno, one of the female leaders of MAEC; they were "brown."[25]

For many activists, especially the youth, students, and even some middle-class individuals, identity was based on cultural nationalist ideals developed by the Chicano movement leaders. Luis Valdez was one of the first to suggest an alternative view of identity at the national level. He argued that there was only one identity appropriate to the oppressed Mexican American and that identity was rooted in the nonwhite indigenous past and in the working-class history of the people.[26] In March, 1969, this emerging nationalist consciousness with its two key dimensions of acceptance of an indigenous racial identity and pride in a working-class Mexican cultural heritage was legitimized at the Chicano Liberation Youth Conference held in Denver, Colorado.

The thousands of youths attending this conference issued a document, El Plan Espiritual de Aztlan, that reflected this new racial identity. In a certain respect this Denver conference signaled the break at a national level from the assimilationist ideology of the Mexican American Generation. El Plan Espiritual de Aztlán was a national plan of liberation that viewed nationalism as the instrument and self-determination as its goal. In the plan's preamble was a call for liberation through solidarity based on culture and nationality. More specifically, it identified Chicanos as members of a nonwhite indigenous group, i.e., as "the inhabitant[s] and civilizers of the northern land of Aztlán, from whence came our forefathers."[27]

El Plan also promoted social change, or what it called "Chicano liberation." More specifically, it called for political unity among all Mexican Americans, economic control of Mexican communities, community control of schools and teachers, self-defense, political liberation through independent action, and cultural action.[28] The latter was especially appealing to many of the activists in the movimiento who viewed culture as part of the plan for "total liberation from oppression, exploitation, and racism."[29]

Most of the activist youths in Houston supported the premises and promises of El Plan de Aztlan and its promotion of indigenous ancestry, cultural pride, and struggle.[30] Other, older activists in the struggle for legal recognition also supported various aspects of El Plan, especially its emphasis on using culture as part of the strategy for "total liberation." This sentiment was reflected in the demands for recognizing Spanish as a language of instruction in the schools, for incorporating Mexican history and culture into the curriculum, and for declaring September 16 and Cinco de Mayo official school holidays. The latter, noted one of MAEC's demands to the school board, "will be done with a view toward stimulating recognition and acknowledgement of the cultural heritage of the Mexican American."[31]

Acceptance of Mobilization

The second major indication of a new identity among activists was their acceptance of mobilization and protest as legitimate forms of struggle. Conventional strategies of litigation, negotiation, and lobbying, however, were not totally abandoned. For the most part they continued to be used but in conjunction with the more nontraditional ones. Paradoxically, it was the conventional strategy of litigation, not the nontraditional one of mobilization, that was directly responsible for the community's success in getting the local board to recognize its distinct identity and to include Mexican Americans in the desegregation of the schools. This finding substantiates several scholars' generalization that protest indeed was not enough to achieve the goals of equality.[32]

Despite the acceptance of the politics of protest, most activists rejected violence as part of their social change methods. Generally speaking, they appreciated and understood the reasons for violent methods, as indicated by the community's response to MAYO's disruption of the local school board meeting in September, 1970, but they did not embrace these tactics. Peaceful, nonviolent, and militant protest was their credo. Violence was not.

Houston activists also accepted mass mobilization, especially the participation of large numbers of youths and women, as a means for promoting change. Historically, both women and young people have been welcomed as members of Mexican-origin organizations. Women, for instance, were the sole members of Club Chapultepec in the 1930s, and groups such as LULAC and the American G. I. Forum had both "ladies" and youth auxiliary chapters.[33] But in the late 1960s and early 1970s youths and women with little experience in political issues were encouraged to participate in organizations alongside the men.[34] Their participation fueled and energized the struggle against discrimination in the schools.

Evidence presented in this study suggests that both young people and women played essential roles in the struggle for legal recognition in general and in MAEC in particular. Youths from the community, the university, and the public schools were integral to this struggle and played important roles. They picketed the public schools, mobilized students against discrimination, taught some of the classes in the huelga schools, wrote articles in support of these actions, and served in leadership positions during this struggle.[35] Although the youths played an important role, they were not the central characters in this struggle; the adults were.[36] This finding contradicts Carlos Muñoz's argument that students were central to the Chicano movement in general. This study suggests that Muñoz's argument is only applicable to California and not reflective of the experiences of Chicanos and Chicanas in other parts of the country.

Women were also essential to the mobilization process and played a variety of roles during the years from 1970 to 1972. As members of MAEC and other organizations they formally helped determine the direction and dynamics of the struggle for recognition. More specifically, las mujeres organized and participated in pickets and protest marches, taught in huelga schools, provided food and housing for movement leaders and volunteers, pressured male leaders not to accept halfway measures toward ending the boycotts, and generated popular support for the movement among barrio residents. They also assumed important leadership positions in organizational and political activities. During the 1971–72 school year, for instance, women comprised 50 percent of MAEC leadership.[37] A year earlier they assumed important leadership roles in the huelga schools and in the organization of pickets or demonstrations in specific schools throughout the Houston barrios. Women, as noted Mrs. Celine Ramírez, one of the activists, were "right in the middle of it [i.e., the struggle for recognition]." "Como unas gallinas culecas [Like fighting chickens]," she added, "women were fighting for better schools for their children." [38]

Las mujeres involved in this struggle did not experience or express dissatisfaction with the rhetoric or praxis of their *compañeros* as did women in other Chicano-movement organizations. Women in the Chicano student movement, for instance, questioned the double standard in sexual activity and in political activism, the sexist attitudes of males, and the traditional gender roles assigned to them by Mexican culture.[39] Some of them also suffered politically and professionally for being too outspoken on gender issues.[40]

Women activists in Houston did not have these types of experiences. Theirs was a positive one of active inclusion in MAEC's decision making and in the organization's implementation of decisions. Even in those cases when males led, women still played key roles in shaping their decisions. Mrs. Ramírez, for instance, noted that while their husbands were the leaders of MAEC, "the men rarely were by themselves, they were usually with their wives." She also noted that the men did not make any major decisions without their input and did not take any actions unless the women agreed to them. Mr. Abe Ramírez and Mr. Mario Quiñones, two prominent leaders of MAEC, agreed with her assessment. "We wouldn't do anything without them," stated Mr. Ramírez.[41] Some of the interviewees even argued that while men led, they did so only because women allowed them to lead.[42] Mrs. Ramírez, for instance, argued that the men, especially those who were married, could not do anything, including assuming leadership positions, unless they got their wives' approval.[43]

Women activists in Houston, then, were not explicitly feminist in orientation, nor were they "loyalists." The former challenged male authority within the Chicano movement, made decisions independent of men, and emphasized issues that were pertinent to women. The latter supported Chicano leaders and argued that "the gavacho [the Anglo], not the macho," was the central issue in the Chicano movement. Las mujeres in Houston were in a third category of feminism that historian Vicki Ruíz called the "Adelitas" or the "soldadera" perspective. The historical view of Adelita, an image born during the Mexican Revolution of 1910, was of a strong, courageous woman fighting beside her man and caring for his needs. This image, argued Ruíz, embodied a conflicted middle ground be-tween the two major factions of Chicana activists during the early 1970s—the feminists and the loyalists. Those with an Adelita mentality "could be fiercely independent, yet strongly male-identified."[44] Las mujeres involved in the struggle for recognition in general and in MAEC in particular dis-played these characteristics. They identified with the male leaders, yet they took independent action in conjunction with other activists.

Acceptance of Militancy
The third indication of a new identity among activists was the rejection of the Mexican American Generation's belief in gradual reform and the ac-ceptance of militancy. MAEC activists, for the most part, did not reject the Mexican American Generation's goal of moderate social change, only its pace. Social change was never clearly defined by members of this earlier generation, but it implied minor reform of mainstream political, eco-nomic, and social institutions. In the case of education it usually meant in-stitutional reform—i.e., efforts to change the structure, content, or oper-ations of the schools to reflect the society's ethnic and racial diversity as well as to improve the scholastic performance of Mexican American stu-dents. These types of changes were aimed at improving a system of school-ing that was viewed as basically in order.

The majority of MAEC activists supported these reformist goals. A few, however, questioned them and promoted radical reform. This was espe-cially the case with Barrio-MAYO, whose members viewed the existing public schools and all other institutions as part of an "evil" capitalist sys-tem that had to be replaced with a more equitable and equalitarian one. They sought major reforms of American economic, political, and educa-tional institutions, including the replacement of capitalist schools with so-cialist ones. Few people in the community, however, listened, accepted, or even understood Barrio-MAYO's ideology and its call for the replacement of capitalism with socialism. Some MAYO members also did not fully em-brace these radical ideas.[45]

Most community activists, then, were not opposed to the goal of mod-erate social change but to the slow pace of reform in general. These indi-viduals wanted immediate changes in the schools and were unwilling to accept the traditional reasons given for the this lack. MAEC's members, for instance, wanted the immediate hiring of Mexican American teachers and administrators, the establishment of bilingual and dropout programs, changes in the curriculum to reflect the community's experiences, and the channeling of additional resources to the minority schools. Most important, these activists wanted immediate recognition of their newly found ethnic minority identity.

A Note on Integration

Although most members were in agreement with the acquisition of a new racial identity, the use of protest, and the rejection of gradualism in social change, they became increasingly divided over the goal of integration. As late as 1971 most activists were in favor of integrating into the existing educational structure. Their participation in the boycotts and the struggles to gain full but equal access to one of the most important mainstream institutions in the United States—the public school system—indicated approval of the goal of structural integration as espoused by members of the Mexican American Generation decades earlier. By the second year of the struggle for recognition, however, a significant number, including members of MAYO and some of MAEC's leadership, began to raise questions about integration and embraced separatism or community control of mainstream institutions. This position soon clashed with the dominant one of support for integration and led to increasing conflict within MAEC.

The Chicano identity, then, was not monolithic nor was it limited only to students and the youth. It comprised a set of complex and at times contradictory and evolving ideas, perspectives, and outlooks shared by a collective group of men and women of different ages and classes. Discussions about the specific nature of the nonwhite racial identity or over the use of tactics illustrated the politics of difference embodied in these ideals. Despite these tensions and differences, it could be argued that the adoption of a new racial identity, of militant reform, and of mass mobilization and protest as legitimate means of struggle signaled the emergence of the Chicano identity in Houston school politics.

AFRICAN AMERICANS AND THE CHICANO STRUGGLE

Although most Mexican Americans living in the barrios supported the struggle for recognition, this cause had mixed support from the African American community. A few prominent African American leaders supported Chicanos in their efforts to expand the desegregation plan to include Anglos, but others were suspicious about the motivations for the boycott. Some believed that the boycott was a racist reaction to integration; others did not trust the Mexican American community and believed that they were "Johnny-come-latelies." [46]

The lack of support for MAEC's militant actions was the result of an emerging manifestation of underlying social and political tensions between blacks and Mexican Americans in the Houston metropolitan area that had their origins in the early decades of the 1900s. Prior to the 1930s Houston was a typical southern town comprised of two large racial groups, a dominant white population and a subordinate African American population. During the next several decades the racial character of the city changed as a result of the rapid growth of the Mexican-origin population. By 1970 the ethnic character of Houston changed so that it was now a tri-ethnic city. This changed character implied that blacks, who were beginning to make economic, social, and political gains as a result of the civil rights movement, had to compete for public awareness of their needs with a group of "newcomers."

A movement for political empowerment also accompanied this demographic shift. This effort, in turn, complicated the history of black-white relations in Houston by increasing competition between blacks and browns over government services. [47] The struggle for recognition of Mexican Americans as an identifiable minority group was an indication of this new ethnic reality.

This competition was not limited to the political arena but also extended to housing and jobs. Mexican Americans tended to live in neighborhoods adjacent to African American ghettos or in neighborhoods that overlapped with historically black wards. They also were employed in low-wage jobs and competed for similar types of occupations in the various industries throughout the city. [48]

The African American responses to the Mexican American struggle for recognition reflected this potential clash between the growth of Mexican American influence and black civil rights and the potential threat to the economic and political gains blacks were making in the area. The success of Mexican American recognition by the courts, for instance, meant that after nearly fifteen years of waiting for desegregation, African Americans would have to wait longer. [49]

THE IMPACT OF THE STRUGGLE FOR RECOGNITION

The struggle for legal recognition did not end institutional discrimination, but it did have significant consequences for education and for the community in general. In education it led to increased resources and programs for Mexican American children. Resources for barrio schools and funds for special programs such as bilingual education, compensatory programs, and migrant education increased significantly after 1972 as a result of the struggle for legal recognition. The success of this particular struggle also led to the increased hiring of Mexican American administrators and teachers and to their presence in HISD as a force for change in the schools.

More generally speaking, the struggle for legal recognition led to the emergence of a new generation of political leadership within the Mexican American community that remained in existence for the next two and a half decades.[50] Although MAEC eventually disbanded, it launched the political careers of important leaders such as Leonel Castillo, Ben Reyes, John Castillo, David López, and Felix Fraga. It also encouraged many others to run for elective office at all levels of government.[51] This new leadership maintained and enhanced the further empowerment of the Mexican-origin community that had begun with the struggle for legal recognition in 1970.

CONCLUSION

The history of Mexican American activism in education, as this case study shows, was complex, contradictory, and contested. It was continually impacted by a variety of external factors and by its own internal contradictions. Federal, state, and local actions as well as varying acculturation rates, ideological differences, and political motivations combined to affect the form and content of Mexican American activism in the area of education in Houston. In the two-year struggle for recognition, for instance, clashing federal desegregation rulings and school board intransigence played key roles in encouraging the diverse Mexican American groups to unite around the issue of desegregation. Ethnic leadership, Mexican American willingness to subsume ideological differences temporarily, and a generalized belief among community leaders and followers that they could effectively remedy the social wrong committed by the courts and the schools also played key roles in the success of this struggle. Of particular importance was the role that the new ethnic leadership played in encouraging participation from all sectors of the Mexican American community—young and old, male and female, radical and moderate, and novice and experienced—and in keeping them united throughout this period. The ability to articulate the community's evolving identity collectively and then develop subsequent strategy also became an important element of MAEC's success in gaining legal recognition.

The Chicano movement in particular and the civil rights movement in general likewise played important parts. They provided alternative approaches and ideologies to social change that Houston activists selectively utilized to forge an evolving identity and praxis. In this sense, then, the development and implementation of strategies, tactics, and ideologies constituted a contested process involving many individuals of different genders, ages, statuses, and political ideologies.

Activism was not only a contested process; it was also a protracted one that assumed different forms over time. In the first half of the twentieth century activism was sporadic in nature because of the size, nativity, and status of the Mexican-origin population. Although no concerted effort to improve the schools was made, Mexican Americans, whenever they could, mobilized to criticize the schools or, at times, to support the feeble efforts made by local officials to accommodate poor, Spanish-speaking children and their parents. Activism increased in the post-1960 period and assumed a more definite form. Prior to 1970 it was focused on improving the quality of education for Mexican American children. During the 1970s its primary focus shifted to desegregation—that is, the majority of organizational efforts were aimed at gaining legal recognition as a minority group and inclusion in the development of an equitable triethnic desegregation plan. In the 1980s and 1990s, as several authors have noted, activism once again shifted, this time toward issues of quality education and governance, especially the selection of superintendents and the appointments of Mexican Americans to the school board.[52]

The importance of this study is not that it documents the complexity and contested nature of Mexican American activism in education over time. Its importance is that it documents this activism at a particular point in time in which the Mexican American community made a conscious decision to replace its existing identity in order to challenge a particular form of institutional discrimination. This study describes and explains, in rich detail, how at a historic moment in time during the early 1970s Mexican Americans became militant and "brown" in their quest for educational justice in the United States.

Notes

PREFACE

1. In this study three basic labels will be used to identify the community being studied: Mexican-origin, Mexican American, and Chicano. The first term will be used to describe the community in general. The second label will be used to describe those individuals who shared many, if not most, characteristics of the Mexican American Generation to be discussed later and who were active in community struggles in Houston during the period after 1960. The term "Chicano" will be used primarily in reference to youth and to those activists who shared some elements of the ideology of racial awareness and commitment to social change. For a brief history of the manifestations of this ideology in California during the 1960s and 1970s see Carlos Muñoz, Jr., *Youth, Identity, Power: The Chicano Movement* (New York: Verso, 1989). See also Juan Gómez-Quiñones, *Chicano Politics: Reality and Promise, 1940–1990* (Albuquerque: University of New Mexico Press, 1990), especially pp. 101–154.
2. Thomas H. Kreneck, *Del Pueblo: A Pictorial History of Houston's Hispanic Community* (Houston: Houston International University, 1989), p. 159.

CHAPTER 1. DIVERSIFICATION AND DIFFERENTIATION IN THE HISTORY OF THE MEXICAN-ORIGIN COMMUNITY IN HOUSTON

1. For two different examples of the diversity of the historical experiences of Mexicans see Mario García, *Desert Immigrants* (New Haven, Conn.: Yale University Press, 1979); and Michael M. Smith, *The Mexicans in Oklahoma* (Norman: University of Oklahoma Press, 1980).
2. This region was not without a Spanish or Mexican presence. During the Spanish era the Spanish explorer Alvar Nuñez Cabeza de Vaca passed through the vicinity of Houston, a presidio was established on the lower Trinity River in the mid 1700s, and in the 1810s the Galveston Bay was the scene of minor Spanish/Mexican activity. During the Mexican era the major episodes of the Texas Revolution, save for the Battle of the Alamo, occurred around the Houston area. After Texas independence, some Mexican individuals began to settle in Houston or its surroundings. Lorenzo de Zavala, the federalist liberal from Yucatán, who fled to Texas to escape the Centralists in Mexico and became vice president of the first government in an independent Texas, settled in the Houston area. Some of Santa Anna's defeated

army became servants for Texians living in Galveston. In Houston proper, Mexicans helped develop the city by clearing the swampy grounds around the city in the 1830s or acted as servants in the young town during the early years of the republic. No evidence is available on the period from the late 1830s to the 1840s. In the years from 1850 to 1880 only a handful were living in the city. Between 1880 and 1900 the number of Mexican-origin individuals increased from seventy-five to five hundred. See Arnoldo De León, *Ethnicity in the Sunbelt: A History of Mexican Americans in Houston* (Houston: Mexican American Studies Program, 1989), pp. 5–6.

3. The size of the Mexican population was seventy-five in 1880, five hundred in 1900, fifteen thousand in 1930, and seventy-five thousand in 1960. During the thirty-year period from 1960 to 1990 the population grew to over three hundred thousand. See De León, *Ethnicity in the Sunbelt,* p. 98.

4. Between 1930 and 1940 the population experienced only a five-thousand-person increase. The Mexican population was 19 percent of the total Houston population in 1980. See ibid., p. xviii.

5. During the 1920s religious exiles left Mexico and immigrated to the United States. The immigrants came largely from the central and western parts of Mexico. After 1940 most of the immigrants came from the central and eastern parts of Mexico. See ibid., pp. 98–99.

6. One example of this type of migration was the family of Mary Villagómez, a lifelong resident of Houston. Her family came to Houston by way of the East Texas lumber mills. The family had worked briefly in these lumber mills before settling in Magnolia in the late 1910s. See Mary C. Villagómez, interview by Roberto R. Treviño, Oct. 25, 1990, Houston, Tex., in Roberto R. Treviño, "La Fe: Catholicism and Mexican Americans in Houston, 1911–1972" (Ph.D. diss., Stanford University, 1993), p. 61.

7. Few studies have been done on the urbanization process among Mexicans in general. For one excellent overview of this urbanization process in the Southwest for the period from 1900 to 1930 see Ricardo Romo, "The Urbanization of Southwestern Chicanos in the Early Twentieth Century," in *New Directions in Chicano Scholarship,* ed. Ricardo Romo and Raymund Paredes (Santa Barbara: Center for Chicano Studies, University of California, Santa Barbara, 1984), pp. 183–207.

8. For a better understanding of the process of chain migration and its impact on family cohesion and cultural adaptation see Roberto Alvarez, *Familia: Migration and Adaptation in Baja and Alta California, 1880–1975* (Berkeley: University of California Press, 1989).

9. Petra Guillén, interview, Oct. 25, 1990; Petra R. Guillén, interview, Oct. 22, 1990. Both of these interviews were conducted by Roberto R. Treviño in Houston, Tex., and are found in Treviño, "La Fe," pp. 61–62.

10. De León, *Ethnicity in the Sunbelt,* p. 8.

11. F. Arturo Rosales, "Mexicans in Houston: The Struggle to Survive, 1908–1975," *Houston Review* (summer, 1981): 224–48.

12. De León, *Ethnicity in the Sunbelt,* p. 26. Some of the streets grew slowly. This is

true of Canal Street, one of the most important streets in the barrio. Few Mexican-origin individuals settled on this street. By 1920 approximately 5 percent of all the residents of Canal Street in el Segundo Barrio were of Mexican descent. These individuals lived close to downtown in the 2100, 2300, and 3300 block of Canal Street. See *Directory of the City of Houston* for 1920 (Houston: Morrison and Fourmy, 1920), p. 1435.

13. Margarita B. Melville, "Mexicans," in *The Ethnic Groups of Houston*, ed. Fred R. von der Mehden (Houston: Rice University Studies, 1984), pp. 41–62.

14. Rosales, "Mexicans in Houston," p. 232.

15. De León, *Ethnicity in the Sunbelt*, pp. 12–14; Melville, "Mexicans," p. 44.

16. The expansion of both barrios was a gradual process reflected in the changing composition of the residents on different streets. One of the most important streets that began in el Segundo Barrio and ended in Magnolia Park was Canal Street. Over time this street became increasingly Mexican American. In 1920, for instance, only 5 percent of the residents on this street were Mexican American. The vast majority of them lived in el Segundo Barrio, a few blocks from the downtown area. None lived on the part of Canal Street that ended in Magnolia Park. Over the years the percentage of Mexican-origin individuals living on Canal Street increased. In 1926, 9 percent of the residents were Mexicans. This percentage increased to 12 percent in 1936, 16 percent in 1946, and 33 percent in 1956. By 1956 about half of the Mexican-origin population living on Canal Street were on the east end of el Segundo Barrio and the other half were on the west end of Magnolia Park. See *Directory of the City of Houston* for the years 1920, 1936, 1946, and 1956.

17. De León, *Ethnicity in the Sunbelt*, p. 155.

18. De León provides evidence indicating the establishment of at least nine mutual aid organizations and seven cultural/recreational clubs with a "Mexicanist" orientation between 1908 and the early 1930s. See De León, *Ethnicity in the Sunbelt*, pp. 13–69.

19. De León, *Ethnicity in the Sunbelt*, pp. 32–33; "50th Anniversary Program," Houston Metropolitan Research Center, Houston, Tex. (hereinafter referred to as HMRC), Club México Bello Collection; "Estatutos Club Cultural Recreativo México Bello," HMRC, Carmen Cortéz Collection; HMRC Oral History Collection; *Houston Chronicle*, Jan. 21, 1979, p. 8D. De León also provides evidence indicating the establishment of at least seven cultural/recreative clubs with a "Mexicanist" orientation during these years. See De León, *Ethnicity in the Sunbelt*, pp. 13–69.

20. Kreneck, *Del Pueblo*, pp. 42–43.

21. Thomas H. Kreneck, "The Letter from Chapultepec," *Houston Review* 3 (summer, 1981): 268–69.

22. De León, *Ethnicity in the Sunbelt*, pp. 71–73.

23. This organization had several chapters and auxiliary groups. The most well-known is Council 60. For a brief history of this group see De León, *Ethnicity in the Sunbelt*, pp. 12–13, 66–68. For a general history of the parent organization see Benjamin Márquez, *LULAC: The Evolution of a Mexican American Political Organization* (Austin: University of Texas Press, 1993).

24. De León, *Ethnicity in the Sunbelt,* p. 82.
25. For a history of the struggle for independence and the defeat of the French oc-
    cupation forces see Michael C. Meyer and William L. Sherman, *The Course of
    Mexican History,* 5th ed. (New York: Oxford University Press, 1995), pp. 285–98,
    388–91.
26. For information on these celebrations see *Houston Chronicle,* Sept. 17, 1907,
    p. 11; Sept. 16, 1980, p. 3; Sept. 17, 1908, p. 5. Several newspapers reported that over
    four thousand individuals celebrated el Diez Y Seis in 1925. See *Houston Chronicle,*
    Sept. 17, 1925, p. 13; and *La Gaceta Mexicana,* Sept. 15, 1928, p. 15.
27. For evidence of the origins of Cinco de Mayo celebrations in the community see
    Houston Chronicle, May 5, 1932, p. 16; May 6, 1935, p. 7.
28. *Houston Chronicle,* Nov. 9, 1930, p. 1 ("Editorials and Features" section).
29. This newspaper, which contained literary essays and social news, was founded by
    José Sarabia, a well-known businessman. Only one issue of *La Gaceta Mexicana*
    has been located. See *La Gaceta Mexicana,* Sept. 15, 1928, HMRC; De León, *Ethnic-
    ity in the Sunbelt,* p. 34; Rosales, "Mexicans in Houston," p. 234.
30. The other four newspapers during the 1920s were: *La Tribuna, El Anúnciador,
    El Tecolote,* and *La Prensa.* See Herminio Ríos and Guadalupe Castillo, "Toward
    a True Chicano Bibliography: Mexican American Newspapers, 1862–1942," *El
    Grito* 3 (winter, 1969): 22–36.
31. This newspaper was founded on December 24, 1924, and lasted until the late 1930s.
    See De León, *Ethnicity in the Sunbelt,* pp. 37, 63.
32. De León, *Ethnicity in the Sunbelt,* p. 66.
33. De Tejada was a musician and orchestra leader who enjoyed official favor during
    the regime of Porfirio Díaz. He moved to San Antonio after Díaz's overthrow in
    1910. De Tejeda's group played for the first time during a Cinco de Mayo celebra-
    tion in 1920. See *Houston Chronicle,* May 7, 1920; Rosales, "Mexicans in Houston,"
    p. 237.
34. For a history of how Our Lady of Guadalupe was established and the role played
    by the Mexican-origin community in the growth of the institutional church in
    Houston see Treviño, "La Fe," especially chapter 3.
35. De León, *Ethnicity in the Sunbelt,* p. 28.
36. Our Lady of Sorrows was established in 1934. See Melville, "Mexicans," p. 45.
37. El Crisol, as noted earlier, was an area just east of downtown Houston. Just south
    of this barrio and across the railroad tracks and west of Lockwood Drive was an-
    other barrio called Las Lechusas, so named because of the abundance of night owls
    in a nearby wooded area. See ibid.
38. Ibid.
39. They were: Mexican Baptist Church, 2505 Canal; Mexican Methodist Episcopal
    Church, 1110 McKee; Mexican Presbyterian Church, 7535 Ave. L; Mexican Holy
    Roller Church (Pentecostal), no address; and Mexican Presbyterian Church, 915
    Houston. See De León, *Ethnicity in the Sunbelt,* p. 28.
40. Primera Iglesia Bautista Mexicana, 2720 Bering; Iglesia Pentecostal, 2706 Fox; Igle-
    sia Cristiana Pentecostal, 2332 Ann. See De León, *Ethnicity in the Sunbelt,* p. 57.

41. Treviño, "La Fe," pp. 62–66. See also Sister Mary Paul Valdez, *The History of the Missionary Cathecists of Divine Providence* (N.p., 1978).

42. The two-room structure of white stucco was built at 700 75th Street. It belonged to the Harrisburg School District until 1926 when this area was annexed to the Houston Independent School District. See De León, *Ethnicity in the Sunbelt,* pp. 16, 24.

43. The addresses of these schools were as follows: Hawthorne Elementary School, 1417 Houston; Dow Elementary School, 1912 Lubbock; Elysian Street School, no address; Jones Elementary, 914 Elysian; and Lubbock School, 412 Sampson.

44. The schools and their enrollment in 1940 were as follows: Rusk, 787; De Zavala, 623; Jones, 666; Dow, 1207; and Hawthorne, 396. No enrollment is provided for Lubbock Elementary School. For a list of these schools see the city directories for 1915, 1930, and 1951. See also De León, *Ethnicity in the Sunbelt,* p. 27.

45. In 1942 two Mexican-origin students graduated from this school, Carlos Gutiérrez and Lola Mae Márquez. See Claudia Cardenas, Oscar Cardenas, Aileen Hernández, and Veronica Madrigal, "The History of Milby High School," history paper, May 17, 1994, p. 7 (in author's possession).

46. Wendy Campos, Cecilia Cruz, Stephen Martin, and Xochitl Vandiver-Rodríguez, "Jefferson Davis High School: The Past and the Present," history paper, for History 3394, May 17, 1994, pp. 2–3; Mario Villarreal and Claudia Macias, "A Historical Outlook of the Mexican American Population Growth at Reagan High School," history paper, fall, 1994, pp. 5–6. In 1948 there were 1,230 students at Milby. See Cardenas et al., "History of Milby High School," pp. 7–8. (All are in author's possession.)

47. De León, *Ethnicity in the Sunbelt,* p. 27; Corinne S. Tsanoff, *Neighborhood Doorways* (Houston: Neighborhood Centers Association of Houston and Harris County, 1958), p. 17; *Houston Chronicle,* Nov. 9, 1930, p. 1.

48. By 1945 only one of the proposed slum clearance projects was still in the planning stages. See De León, *Ethnicity in the Sunbelt,* p. 53.

49. "To the Honorable Grand Jury of Harris County, Texas," HMRC, Mexican American Small Collection; De León, *Ethnicity in the Sunbelt,* pp. 53–54.

50. *Houston Chronicle,* Oct. 19, 1945, p. 5B (discusses blighted conditions along Navigation Boulevard); *The People of Houston vs. Slums,* 1947, Annual Report (Houston: Houston Authority of the City of Houston, 1947), p. 3 (discusses diseases in blighted area in the Second Ward). See also De León, *Ethnicity in the Sunbelt,* pp. 99–101, for a summary of these conditions.

51. *Houston Chronicle,* Dec. 11, 1958, p. 1A (describes deplorable social conditions and focuses on the lingering of tuberculosis and inadequate health services).

52. William L. Clayton, a cotton magnate and former U.S. undersecretary of state, and his wife Susan, who had long been interested in housing projects as a means of slum clearance, bought a large tract of land and offered it to the Houston Housing Authority for a low-cost housing project. See Tsanoff, *Neighborhood Doorways,* p. 85; *Houston Post,* July 27, 1961, sec. 8, p. 1; De León, *Ethnicity in the Sunbelt,* p. 101.

53. Rosales, "Mexicans in Houston," pp. 230–31, 239–40, 242, 246.

54. Other mainstream institutions such as law enforcement also mistreated Mexican-origin individuals and failed to provide them with equal treatment. For an overview of police-community relations in Houston see De León, *Ethnicity in the Sunbelt.*

55. The view differs significantly from the one offered by Richard Garcia. He argues that community institutions such as the schools were instruments of biculturation. See Richard Garcia, *The Rise of the Middle Class* (College Station: Texas A&M University Press, 1991).

56. Richard Garcia argues that in San Antonio the process of class differentiation in the Mexican-origin community occurred during the first four decades of the twentieth century. See ibid.

57. De León, *Ethnicity in the Sunbelt,* p. 56.

58. Kreneck, *Del Pueblo,* p. 28.

59. The following are examples of this small business class that provided services or goods for the Houston community by 1910: Joseph M. Gómez had a sign-painting company in Houston; Eciquia Castro owned a café on San Felipe Street; and John J. Mercado, Sr., was a Spanish-language teacher at Houston High School. See ibid., pp. 29, 35–39.

60. De León, *Ethnicity in the Sunbelt,* p. 17.

61. Kreneck, *Del Pueblo,* pp. 43–45.

62. Ibid., p. 44.

63. De León, *Ethnicity in the Sunbelt,* p. 105, argues that between 25 and 35 percent of the total Mexican-origin population was middle class. But he overestimates this figure by including the craftsmen category in the middle-class occupations. I view this occupation as part of the skilled working class, not the middle class.

64. Of these working-class occupations, 14 percent of the males were employed in skilled occupations and over 62 percent worked in unskilled or manual labor. Thirty-one percent of the females, in turn, were employed in skilled occupations, and over 53 percent were working in unskilled occupations. For further data see table 3.1 in De León, *Ethnicity in the Sunbelt,* pp. 52–53.

65. Ibid., p. 100.

66. Kreneck, *Del Pueblo,* p. 122.

67. Ibid.

CHAPTER 2. PROVIDING FOR
THE SCHOOLING OF MEXICAN CHILDREN

1. As early as 1924, for instance, Mexican children began to receive parochial school instruction provided by the Catholic sisters at Our Lady of Guadalupe Church. For a brief history of this church and the parochial school see Sachie Canales, Noe García III, and Joan Menotti, "A Historical Trace [*sic*] of Our Lady of Guadalupe," history paper, for History 3394, fall, 1994, University of Houston, Houston, Tex.

2. For several histories of the origins of school segregation in the Mexican community during the nineteenth and early twentieth centuries see Guadalupe San Miguel, Jr., "The Origins, Development, and Consequences of the Educational Segre-

gation of Mexicans in the Southwest," in *Chicano Studies: A Multidisciplinary Approach,* ed. Eugene E. García, Francisco Lomelí, and Isidro Ortíz (New York: Teachers College Press, 1984), pp. 195–208; Gilbert G. González, "Segregation of Mexican Children in a Southern California City: The Legacy of Expansionism and the American Southwest," *Western Historical Quarterly* 16 (1985): 55–76; Gilbert G. González, *Chicano Education in the Era of Segregation* (Philadelphia: The Balch Institute, 1990).

3. Evidence indicates that several hundred Mexican-origin individuals came to Houston between 1890 and 1900 due to the expansion of the railroads. It is possible that up to one-fourth of the total Mexican population was comprised of school-age children, i.e., those between the ages of six and fifteen years. However, there is no concrete evidence indicating the possible size of this school-age population or whether they were enrolled in any of the city's public schools. See Luís Cano, "Illegal Discrimination and Segregation of Chicano Students in the Houston Independent School District," unpub. MS., n.d., pp. 2–3, in the Luís Cano Collection, Box A, unfoldered materials, HMRC.

4. This school burned down in 1910. See Cano, "Illegal Discrimination," p. 3.

5. De León, *Ethnicity in the Sunbelt,* p. 27.

6. Ironically, property owners in the neighborhood threatened to bring injunction proceedings against the school board's actions to build the school. Most of these individuals residing close to the proposed new school did not want the district to build the school for Mexican children because of possible negative effects on the community. See *Houston Chronicle,* Mar. 1, 1920, p. 2.

7. De Zavala was part of the Harrisburg Independent School District. In 1926 the entire Magnolia Park subdivision was incorporated into Houston and into the city's school district. See De León, *Ethnicity in the Sunbelt,* p. 24.

8. Lynne W. Denison and L. L. Pugh, *Houston Public School Buildings: Their History and Location* (Houston, 1936),p. 87; L. H. Weir, *Public Recreation in Houston* (Houston: Houston Recreation Department, 1927), p. 3 (lists school enrollment in 1927).

9. Ibid., pp. 34, 87, 99, 111, 122; *Houston Chronicle,* May 2, 1923, p. 14; Weir, *Public Recreation in Houston,* p. 3.

10. San Miguel, Jr., "Origins, Development, and Consequences," pp. 195–208.

11. For a general overview of the development of school segregation in the Southwest see ibid.; and G. González, "Segregation of Mexican Children," pp. 55–76.

12. Mexican immigrants settled in areas outside the Southwest as early as 1917. For a brief view of Mexican immigration and settlement in Oklahoma see Smith, *The Mexicans in Oklahoma.* On Mexican immigrant settlement in the Midwest see Zaragosa Vargas, *Proletarians of the North* (Berkeley: University of California Press, 1993); *Mexicans in the Midwest,* vol. 2 of *Perspectives in Mexican American Studies,* ed. Juan García (Tucson: University of Arizona, Mexican American Studies and Research Center, 1990); and Juan R. García, *Mexicans in the Midwest, 1900–1932* (Tucson: University of Arizona Press, 1996).

13. See, for instance, the list of school board members from 1905 to 1965 provided in William A. Young, *A History of Houston Public Schools, 1836–1965* (Houston:

Gulf School Research Development Assoc., Inc., 1968), pp. 97–100. Not one of these members had a Spanish surname.

14. Mercado originally was assigned to teach Spanish at the high school in 1906. In 1915 he was teaching Spanish at South End Junior High School. Tafolla was hired to teach Spanish at the high school in 1915. Ten years later Mercado was teaching at the Heights Senior High School. He also was the director of La Tolteca, a high school Spanish club. No mention is made of Tafolla. See *Houston Chronicle,* Sept. 9, 1906, p. 16; Aug. 29, 1915, p. 14; Mar. 19, 1925, p. 18.

15. Cano, "Illegal Discrimination," p. 7.

16. Ibid., p. 2.

17. Ibid., pp. 2, 4.

18. For a history of this campaign against linguistic and cultural diversity see Shirley Brice Heath, "Language and Politics in the United States," in *Georgetown University Round Table on Languages and Linguistics—Linguistics and Anthropology,* ed. Muriel Saville-Troike (Washington, D.C.: Georgetown University Press, 1977), pp. 267–96; and Shirley Brice Heath, "Our Language Heritage: A Historical Perspective," in *The Language Connection: From the Classroom to the World,* ed. June K. Phillips (Skokie, Ill.: National Textbook Company, 1977), pp. 22–51.

19. For a brief history of the campaign to remove Spanish from the public schools in the Southwest in the nineteenth century, see Guadalupe San Miguel, Jr., "The Schooling of Mexicanos in the Southwest, 1848–1891," in *The Elusive Quest for Equality: 150 Years of Chicano/Chicana Education* (Cambridge, Mass.: Harvard Educational Review, 1999), pp. 43–44.

20. Arnold Leibowitz, "Language and the Law—The Exercise of Power through Official Designation of Language," in *Language and Politics,* ed. W. O'Barr and J. O'Barr (The Hague: Mouton, 1976), pp. 449–66.

21. Section 2 of the bill states: "Any such teacher, principal, superintendent, trustee or other school official having responsibility in the conduct of the work of such schools who fails to comply with the provisions of this article shall be fined not less than $25 and not more than $100, cancellation of certificate or removal from office, or both fine and such cancellation, or fine and removal from office" (Texas, *General Law,* 36th Leg., reg. sess., 1919).

22. For a general history of the efforts to enact English-only laws for the public and private schools in Texas see Guadalupe San Miguel, Jr., *Let All of Them Take Heed: Mexican Americans and the Campaign for Educational Equality in Texas, 1910–1981* (Austin: University of Texas Press, 1987), especially pp. 32–63.

23. San Miguel, Jr., "Schooling of Mexicanos," pp. 31–51.

24. The removal of Mexican cultural heritage courses in California occurred between 1850 and the 1860s. In New Mexico, however, school officials encountered significant opposition from Catholic officials and Mexican Americans, due largely to the combined efforts of the politically influential Catholic Church and the numerically large Mexican American leadership. Both groups fought to have Catholic topics in general and Mexican history courses in particular taught in the public schools until the 1890s. For a brief history of the campaign to remove the Mexican cultural

heritage from the public schools in the Southwest in the nineteenth century, see San Miguel, Jr., "Schooling of Mexicanos," pp. 44–45.

25. Carl F. Kaestle, *Pillars of the Republic* (New York: Hill and Wang, 1983).

26. M. García, *Desert Immigrants*, pp. 110–26; J. W. Cameron, "The History of Mexican Public Education in Los Angeles, 1910–30" (Ph.D. diss., University of California, Los Angeles, 1976), pp. 60–91.

27. See Carlos E. Castañeda, "The Broadening Concept of History Teaching in Texas," in *Proceedings of the Inter American Conference on Intellectual InterChange*, June 16–17, 1943, Institute of Latin American Studies, University of Texas, Austin, 1943, pp. 99–103.

28. See ibid.

29. G. P. Quackenbow, *Illustrated School History of the United States of America* (New York: D. Appleton and Company, 1879), p. 421.

30. Anna J. H. Pennybacker, *A New History of Texas for Schools* (Palestine, Tex.: Palestine Publishing Company, 1895), p. 229.

31. *Jefferson Davis High School Annual*, 1928; *Sam Houston High School Annual*, 1929, both of which are located in the Local History Room, Houston Public Library, Houston, Tex.

32. Kreneck, *Del Pueblo*, pp. 42–44.

33. The school district reported extremely crowded conditions in most of the schools, especially the minority ones, during the 1920s and began an ambitious program to build new schools or to expand and improve existing ones. This building program was based on the passage of several bonds in 1924, 1926, and 1928. See Young, *History of Houston Public Schools*, p. 38.

34. Although the "browning" of the schools was initiated during the 1930s and 1940s, the majority of secondary schools did not become primarily Mexican institutions until the post-1960 period. In 1937, for instance, only five Mexican-origin students were enrolled at San Jacinto High School. Less than 1 percent of the student population at Austin High School was of Mexican origin in 1940. As late as 1960 even Milby High School was predominantly Anglo, with less than 9 percent of the total student population comprised of Mexican-origin children. Marshall Junior High became predominantly minority in the early 1960s, Hogg Junior High in the late 1970s, and Deady Middle School in the early 1980s. See, for instance, *San Jacinto High School Annual*, 1937; *Stephen F. Austin High School Annual*, 1940, 1945; *Milby High School Annual*, 1961—all in the Local History Room, Houston Public Library, Houston, Tex. See also data provided in the following studies: Camille García, Yvette Gonzáles, and Alan Muñoz, "Las Escuelas del Barrio: A Cooperative Research Project: The Magnolia Barrio," history paper, for History 3394, May 9, 1996, University of Houston; Charlene Dunn, Craig Randle, Greg Govender, and Robert Kief, "The Heights Barrio," history paper, for History 3394, May 9, 1996, University of Houston; and Henry Cash, Ileana Cedillo, Martin Cortés, Virginia Peterson, David Reyna, Ilenia Solís, Wadey Y. Yaya III, and Juanita Zamarripa, "Escuelas del Barrio Research Project Northside District, Jefferson Davis High School," history paper, for History 3394, Apr. 9, 1996, University of Houston.

35. For a list of these schools see *Directory of the City of Houston* for 1930, 1940, 1951, and 1960.

36. See Tsanoff, *Neighborhood Doorways,* pp. 29–30, for a description of the incident. A similar protest was made by the Anglo community to the construction of De Zavala in 1920. See *Houston Chronicle,* Mar. 1, 1920, p. 2. Denison notes that a protest was lodged against constructing additions to a school in this area, but it was in reference to the old Fullerton School located in the 5800 block of Harrisburg. No date is provided by the authors. See Denison and Pugh, *Houston Public School Buildings,* n.pag.

37. Tsanoff, *Neighborhood Doorways,* p. 26.

38. Cano, "Illegal Discrimination."

39. *Houston Chronicle,* Dec. 3, 1958, pp. 1A, 19A; Kreneck, *Del Pueblo,* p. 121.

40. Gonzalo Campos, for instance, was hired as the first Mexican American principal at Burnet Elementary School in the mid 1960s (Gonzalo Campos, interview by author, June 15, 1992, Houston, Tex.).

41. Mr. Gonzalo Garza was hired in January, 1971, as one of six "area instructional officers" for the school districts. Prior to serving in this position he was the administrator for the Language Development and Reading Program of the Southwest Educational Development Laboratory in Austin, Tex. (Regular Board Meetings, Meeting Folders 1970, Board Services, Roll No. A51, Jan. 11, 1971, p. 7, Houston Independent School District, Houston, Tex.).

42. Cano, "Illegal Discrimination."

43. They also took other actions that negatively impacted the Mexican population. For example, the local school board members terminated the use of Rusk Elementary as a community school unless the Mexican-origin population paid a fee for its use. It also eliminated free public baths offered at this school. These types of actions affected not only Mexican-origin individuals but also the general population, but because of the Mexican community's citizenship status, its precarious economic status, and its relative powerlessness, it was more deeply affected. See Cano, "Illegal Discrimination."

44. The federal government sanctioned this type of institutional discrimination and helped finance it. For a general history of these efforts in California see Abraham Hoffman, *Unwanted Mexican Americans in the Great Depression* (Tucson: University of Arizona Press, 1974).

45. *Houston Chronicle,* Dec. 6, 1958, p. 1A; De León, *Ethnicity in the Sunbelt,* pp. 101–102.

46. For further elaboration on this process in general see Gilbert G. González, "Educational Reform in Los Angeles and Its Effects upon the Mexican Community, 1900–1930," *Explorations in Ethnic Studies* 1 (1978): 526; and González, *Chicano Education.*

47. For an excellent history of this movement see Lawrence Cremin, *The Transformation of the School: Progressivism in American Education, 1876–1957* (New York: Knopf, 1961).

48. See Young, *History of Houston Public Schools.*

49. For further elaboration on this process in general see González, "Educational Reform"; and González, *Chicano Education.*

50. Young, *History of Houston Public Schools,* p. 31. An example of the expansion occurred in 1940 when the local school board members adopted a new Distributive Education Program as part of the vocational department of the Texas Department of Education. The program was begun at Sam Houston High School and by 1943 extended to Reagan and Milby High Schools. See Young, *History of Houston Public Schools,* p. 49.

51. Denison and Pugh, *Houston Public School Buildings,* n.pag. For evidence of the growth of vocational classes with the increased presence of Mexican-origin students see *Milby High School Annuals,* 1951, 1955, and 1960 (Mexican-origin children comprised between 6 and 10 percent of the entire student population). See also the *Davis High School Annual* for 1945, when Mexican-origin individuals comprised slightly over 3 percent, and for 1951, when they comprised approximately 9 percent. In all of these cases new vocational classes in the skilled trades such as auto mechanics and sheet metal were added to the curriculum by the 1950s. All annuals are located in the Local History Room, Houston Public Library, Houston, Tex.

52. See, for instance, M. García, *Desert Immigrants.*

53. Berniece M. Fisher, *Industrial Education: American Ideas and Institutions* (Madison: University of Wisconsin Press, 1967).

54. Further research into this area, however, is needed before any generalization can be adequately developed on the consequences of vocational education in the Mexican community. For one study on the impact of progressive reforms on the education of Mexican-origin children see González, *Chicano Education.*

55. Judge Alfred J. Hernández, Oral History Collection, HMRC, Jan. 15, 1979. Some parents reported that while the public schools promoted English, only Spanish was spoken there. Ironically, the Catholic School at Our Lady of Guadalupe used Spanish in the schools during this period. See *Houston Chronicle,* Jan. 23, 1948, p. 21A; De León, *Ethnicity in the Sunbelt,* p. 113.

56. Many of these practices were documented in the U.S. Commission on Civil Rights, *Mexican American Education Study,* vols. 1–4 (Washington, D.C.: Government Printing Office, 1970–74).

57. González, "Educational Reform," p. 526; González, *Chicano Education.*

58. Tsanoff, *Neighborhood Doorways,* pp. 113–14, 119.

59. The gap between Mexicans and Anglos decreased from 6.2 in 1950 to 5.7 a decade later. The gap between Mexicans and blacks remained constant at 2.4. See Mary Ellen Goodman and Don des Jarlais, *The Spanish Surname Population of Houston: A Demographic Sketch* (Houston: N.p., 1968), p. 2.; De León, *Ethnicity in the Sunbelt,* p. 102. See also U.S. Census of Population: 1950, *Special Reports, Persons of Spanish Surname,* Census Report P-E No. 3C, rpt. of vol. 4, pt. 3, chap. C, table 8, p. 3C54; U.S. Census of Population: 1960, *Persons of Spanish Surname,* final report PC(2)-1B, table 10.

60. Only a handful of Mexican Americans attended Austin between 1938 and 1960. In the latter year less than 4 percent of the total student population at Austin

was Mexican American. See *Austin High School Annuals* for 1938, 1945, 1955, and 1960.

61. *Davis High School Annuals,* 1945, 1949, and 1951. See also Joseph Dishron, *A Population Study of Houston and the Houston Area* (Houston: University of Houston, 1949); and Campos, Cruz, Martin, and Vandiver-Rodríguez, "Jefferson Davis High School."

62. *Milby High School Annual,* 1951, 1955, 1960; *Reagan High School Annual,* 1951, 1956—both in the Local History Room, Houston Public Library, Houston, Tex.

63. Goodman and des Jarlais, *Spanish Surname Population,* p. 2.; De León, *Ethnicity in the Sunbelt,* p. 102. See U.S. Census of Population: 1950, *Special Reports, Persons of Spanish Surname,* Census Report P-E No. 3C, rpt. of vol. 4. part 3, chap. C, table 8, p. 3C54; U.S. Census of Population: 1960, *Persons of Spanish Surname,* final report PC(2)-1B, table 10.

64. For a general overview of Mexican American responses to educational discrimination in Texas see Guadalupe San Miguel, Jr., *Let All Take Heed.* For California see Ruben Donato, *The Other Struggle for Equal Schools* (Albany: State University of New York Press, 1997).

CHAPTER 3. COMMUNITY ACTIVISM AND IDENTITY IN HOUSTON

1. My concept of political activity is broadly conceived and focuses on involvement in three major areas of community life: economic, electoral, and social. Economic activism focuses primarily on organizing in the workplace, whereas electoral activism emphasizes participation in elections and in party politics. Social activism includes involvement in civic matters, in cultural work, and in all social issues impacting the Mexican community. For this broad view of political activity and for a history of Mexican-origin political involvement from the 1500s to the 1970s see Juan Gómez-Quiñones, *The Roots of Chicano Politics* (Albuquerque: University of New Mexico Press, 1994); and Gómez-Quiñones, *Chicano Politics.*

2. Gómez-Quiñones, *Roots of Chicano Politics,* suggests that it was continuous.

3. On Tejano electoral activity in Texas during the latter part of the 1800s and early 1900s see Arnoldo De León, *The Tejano Community, 1836–1900* (Albuquerque: University of New Mexico Press, 1982), pp. 23–49; and Arnoldo De León, *Mexican Americans in Texas: A Brief History* (Arlington Heights, Ill.: Harlan Davidson, Inc., 1993), pp. 56–58. On electoral activity in the El Paso area see M. García, *Desert Immigrants,* pp. 155–71.

4. For an overview of the means used to limit Mexican American involvement in the electoral arena during these years in general see De León, *Mexican Americans in Texas,* pp. 34–77.

5. Historians have disagreed whether the Mexican workers, comprised primarily of immigrants, accommodated to or resisted their oppression. Mario García has argued that because the workers were immigrants who expected eventually to return to Mexico, they took an accommodative stance. Emilio Zamora and others argue that Mexican-origin people resisted their oppressive working conditions. I would

argue that while many workers did accommodate, a significant proportion of the Mexican immigrant working-class community, in connection with the native-born, resisted their oppression. See M. García, *Desert Immigrants;* and Emilio Zamora, *The World of the Mexican Worker in Texas* (College Station: Texas A&M University Press, 1993).

6. For an example of the use of casual and more collective means of resisting oppressive working conditions in south Texas see Zamora, *World of the Mexican Worker.*

7. See Mario T. García, *Mexican Americans: Leadership, Ideology, and Identity* (New Haven: Yale University Press, 1989), pp. 13–16.

8. Arnoldo De León, *Mexican Americans in Texas: A Brief History,* 2d ed. (Wheeling, Ill.: Harlan Davidson, Inc., 1999), pp. 71–72; F. Arturo Rosales, *Chicano: The History of the Mexican American Civil Rights Movement* (Houston: Arte Público Press, 1996), pp. 56–86. See also more generally Matt S. Meier and Feliciano Ribera, *Mexican Americans/American Mexicans: From Conquistadores to Chicanos* (New York: Hill and Wang, 1993), pp. 103–130.

9. Historians use various terms to designate the complex set of ideas shared by the predominantly immigrant population living in the United States during the years from 1890 to 1930. Mario García calls it the "Immigrant" identity, Emilio Zamora calls it the "Mexicanist" identity, and Rosales refers to this as the "Mexico Lindo" identity. I prefer Zamora's term. See M. García, *Mexican Americans;* Zamora, *World of the Mexican Worker;* Rosales, *Chicano,* pp. 55–88, and F. Arturo Rosales, *¡Pobre Raza!: Violence, Justice, and Mobilization among Mexico Lindo Immigrants, 1900–1936* (Austin: University of Texas Press, 1999).

10. On the rise of this type of nationalism see Rosales, *¡Pobre Raza!* For its manifestations in the Midwest see J. García, *Mexicans in the Midwest,* especially pp. 158–22. For efforts to transform the nationalist consciousness of Mexican immigrants in Los Angeles see George J. Sánchez, *Becoming Mexican American* (Oxford: Oxford University Press, 1993), pp. 87–125.

11. Most of these were male-only organizations. Many of them, especially in the Midwest, also restricted their membership to either middle-class or working-class Mexican nationals. In Texas mutual aid societies were less restrictive and allowed U.S.-born Mexicans to join. On immigrant organizations in the Midwest see J. García, *Mexicans in the Midwest,* pp. 159–89. For information on immigrant organizations in Texas see De León, *Mexican Americans in Texas,* 2d ed., p. 76.

12. De León, *Mexican Americans in Texas,* 2d ed., p. 76. Some immigrant organizations occasionally promoted "lo americano" or American customs. For two examples of immigrant organizations involved in perpetuating both Mexican and American ways see Heather Hatch, "Fiestas Patrias and Uncle Sam: A Photographic Glimpse of Arizona Patriotism," *Journal of Arizona History* 3 (1994): 427–28; and Nina Nixon, "Mexican American Voluntary Associations in Omaha, Nebraska," *Journal of the West* 28, no. 3 (1989): 73–85.

13. Sánchez, for instance, notes that Mexican immigrants in California had the lowest rate of naturalization of any immigrant group in the state in 1920. See Sánchez, *Becoming Mexican American,* p. 105.

14. Although immigrant leaders were not interested in joining the mainstream, an

emergent group of Mexican Americans did seek integration into American society during the early years of the twentieth century. See, for instance, Carole E. Christian, "Joining the American Mainstream: Texas' Mexican Americans during World War I," *Southwestern Historical Quarterly* 93 (Apr., 1989): 559–96.

15. A few key leaders, however, sought fundamental transformations of the society. One of the most important "revolutionary" leaders in the Southwest was the anarchist Ricardo Flores Magon. For more information on him see Juan Gómez-Quiñones, *Sembradores: Ricardo Flores Magon y El Partido Liberal Mexicano: A Eulogy and Critique* (Los Angeles: UCLA Chicano Studies Research Center Publications, 1973). See also Rosales, *Chicano,* pp. 64–66.

16. Zamora, *World of the Mexican Worker.*

17. For an overview of the use of different tactics by a diverse group of activists involved in the workplace, community, and electoral arena during the early decades of the twentieth century see Gómez-Quiñones, *Roots of Chicano Politics,* pp. 295–402. On the role of the Mexican consul see Francisco Balderrama, *In Defense of La Raza: The Los Angeles Mexican Consulate the Mexican Community, 1929–1936* (Tucson: University of Arizona Press, 1982) and Gilbert G. González, *Mexican Consuls and Labor Organizing* (Austin: University of Texas Press, 1999).

18. De León, *Ethnicity in the Sunbelt,* p. 39.

19. Gómez-Quiñones, *Roots of Chicano Politics,* pp. 311–12.

20. One example of this was Club Cultural Recreativo México Bello, founded in 1924. See "50th Anniversary Program," HMRC; Club México Bello Collection, "Estatutos Club Cultural Recreativo México Bello," HMRC. See also *Houston Chronicle,* Jan. 21, 1979, p. 8D. For an overview of the growth of social organizations in the Houston barrios see chapter 1.

21. These types of community organizations began to appear in the Southwest as early as the 1860s. See Gómez-Quiñones, *Roots of Chicano Politics,* p. 312.

22. De León notes that at least nine mutual aid organizations and seven cultural/recreational clubs were organized to meet these needs during these years. See De León, *Ethnicity in the Sunbelt,* pp. 13–69.

23. See Zamora, *World of the Mexican Worker,* pp. 55–109.

24. For an overview of this conference see José E. Limón, "El Primer Congreso Mexicanista de 1911: A Precursor to Contemporary Chicanismo," *Aztlan* 1 (spring/fall, 1974): 85–118.

25. Limón, "El Primer Congreso," pp. 95–96; De León, *Ethnicity in the Sunbelt,* p. 13.

26. Limón, "El Primer Congreso," pp. 89–104. See also Emilio Zamora, "Las Escuelitas: A Texas-Mexican Search for Educational Excellence," unpub. MS., n.d. (in author's possession).

27. On Mercado's role in the Cortéz case see Americano Paredes, *With His Pistol in His Hand* (Austin: University of Texas Press, 1957), p. 100. On the latter two issues see, respectively, Rodolfo Rocha, "The Influence of the Mexican Revolution on the Mexico-Texas Border, 1910–1916" (Ph.D. diss., Texas Tech University, 1981), pp. 287, 291, 324, 344–45; and Juan Gómez-Quiñones, "Piedras Contra La Luna, Mexico en Aztlan y Aztlan in Mexico: Chicano Mexican Relations and the Mexican Consulates, 1900–1920," in James W. Wilkie et al., *Contemporary Mexico:*

Papers of the IV International Congress of Mexican History (Berkeley: University of California Press, 1976), pp. 516–17.

28. *Houston Chronicle,* Feb. 23, 1930, p. 14; Feb. 22, 1930, p. 3 (Mexican clubs use Rusk Auditorium to present plays).

29. Acta 21, No. 45, Felix Morales Collection (Unión Fraternal), HMRC. (Mexican consul used Rusk school to address the community and to hold fund-raisers).

30. For a history of the process of increasing Mexican political activity from 1940 to the early 1960s in the Southwest see Gómez-Quiñones, *Chicano Politics,* pp. 31–100.

31. Although this identity emerged in the late 1930s, it did not become dominant until the post–World War II era. Even after it became dominant a residual Mexicanist identity could still be found in the barrio. Mexican organizations and community agencies such as Spanish-language newspapers, businesses, and theaters continued to promote "lo mexicano" in the barrios. These organizations celebrated familiar cultural, religious, and secular holidays and traditions; spoke their native tongue in the community; and promoted Spanish-language films and radio and sponsored Mexican actors, musicians, and artists. Mexican immigration to Houston as well as limited opportunities and segregation likewise reinforced and allowed "lo mexicano" to exist in the barrio and to coexist with "lo americano." See De León, *Ethnicity in the Sunbelt,* pp. 113–14.

32. For further elaboration of the ideology of the Mexican American Generation see M. García, *Mexican Americans;* and San Miguel, Jr., *Let All Take Heed.*

33. Alvarez, for instance, says the following about this generation: "Because of his psychic identification with the superordinate Anglo, he abandoned his own language and culture and considered himself personally superior to the economically subordinate Migrant Generation." Chávez writes: "Trying to escape the discrimination aimed at their group, these Mexican-Americans disassociated themselves from anything Mexican, at times even boasting of their inability to speak Spanish." See Rodolfo Alvarez, "The Psycho-Historical and Socioeconomic Development of the Chicano Community in the United States," *Social Science Quarterly* (Mar., 1973): 920–42 (quote from p. 936); and John Chávez, *The Lost Land: The Chicano Image of the Southwest* (Albuquerque: University of New Mexico Press, 1984), p. 109.

34. Richard Griswold del Castillo and Arnoldo De León, *North to Aztlan: A History of Mexican Americans in the United States* (New York: Twayne, 1996), p. 92.

35. R. Garcia, *The Rise of the Middle Class;* Richard Garcia, "The Mexican American Mind: A Product of the 1930s," in *History, Culture and Society: Chicano Studies in the 1980s,* edited by Mario T. García et al. (Ypsilanti, Mich.: Bilingual Review Press, 1983), pp. 67–92. See also De León, *Ethnicity in the Sunbelt,* pp. 60–144.

36. See, for instance, Mario T. García, "Mexican Americans and the Politics of Citizenship: The Case of El Paso, 1936," *New Mexico Historical Review* 59, no. 2 (1984): 187–204.

37. M. García, *Mexican Americans;* see also Cynthia E. Orozco, "Beyond Machismo, La Familia, and Ladies Auxiliaries: A Historiography of Mexican-Origin Women's Participation in Voluntary Associations and Politics in the United States, 1870–1990," in *Perspectives in Mexican American Studies,* vol. 5, ed. Juan R. García (Tuc-

son: Mexican American Studies and Research Center, 1992), pp. 37–77. Sánchez notes that in Los Angeles the Mexican American activists came primarily from working-class rather than middle-class backgrounds. See Sánchez, *Becoming Mexican American,* pp. 209–270.

38. Gómez-Quiñones, *Chicano Politics.*

39. On the Mexican American Generation see M. García, *Mexican Americans.*

40. Regional organizations and unions such as the Spanish Speaking Congress; the International Union of Mine, Mill and Smelter Workers; and the Asociación Nacional México Americana were militant and progressive but not revolutionary in their ideology, in keeping with the reformist ideals of the middle-class members of the Mexican American Generation. For an overview of leftist or radical working-class politics in the Mexican-origin community during the years from 1930 to 1960 see M. García, *Mexican Americans,* pp. 145–230.

41. Representative of this ideology was the League of United Latin American Citizens. For a recent study of this group and its ideology see Márquez, *LULAC.*

42. Constitution of LULAC, art. 2, section 18 (1931), Paul Taylor Collection, Bancroft Library, Berkeley, Calif. For the views of Council 60 see De León, *Ethnicity in the Sunbelt,* pp. 80–96, 126–43.

43. M. García, *Mexican Americans,* p. 18. A few examples of direct action can be found during the years from 1930 to the 1946. One such example occurred in the mid-1940s when LULAC engaged in a boycott of the Pearland public school system over the issue of desegregation. See San Miguel, Jr., *Let All Take Heed,* p. 118.

44. For an overview of this strategy as it pertains to desegregation in Texas see San Miguel, Jr., *Let All Take Heed,* pp. 117–38. For a list of cases in the area of jury discrimination indicating the trend toward classifying Mexican Americans as white but placing them in a distinct category from other whites see "Memorandum to Ed Idar, Jr., from Sharon Province and Richard Garza" (Mexican American Legal Defense and Education Fund [MALDEF] lawyers), May 25, 1973, Abe Ramírez Collection, Box 1, No. 22, HMRC.

45. Acuna argued that older types of organizations such as *mutualistas* ceased to be important means for struggling against discrimination in this period. See Rodolfo Acuna, *Occupied America: A History of Chicanos,* 3d ed. (New York: HarperCollins, 1988), p. 243.

46. De León further adds that these types of organizations represented a point in the development of the community's ethnic identity "during which threads of old intellectual and cultural tenets persisted but were undergoing transformation." Their presence pointed to "the continuous process of cultural change among Houston's Mexican American people" (De León, *Ethnicity in the Sunbelt,* p. 76).

47. The Club Femenino Chapultepec was organized in 1931 and lasted until 1943. For more information on this organization see Kreneck, "The Letter from Chapultepec," pp. 268–69.

48. The FSMLA was part of a larger county organization established in 1938 that, though it was an important organization, lasted only until around 1941. See De León, *Ethnicity in the Sunbelt,* pp. 71–73.

49. La Unión Fraternal was formed in 1941 by Felix and Angelina Morales and lasted until the 1950s when it became defunct. See De León, *Ethnicity in the Sunbelt*, pp. 60–79.

50. Council 60 was a males-only group founded in 1934. The LAC was a splinter group established in 1935 that merged with Council 60 by 1939. Council 22 was a woman's auxiliary group originally established in 1935 as Ladies LULAC Council 14. It became inactive during the war but was reorganized in 1948. For an overview of LULAC's origins in Houston see De León, *Ethnicity in the Sunbelt*, pp. 83–85. For information on Council 14's origins see Mrs. Angelina Morales, interview by Tom Kreneck, Feb. 5, 1979, Oral History Collection, #246, HMRC; also see *El Puerto* (Houston), Aug. 9, 1935, p. 2; Aug. 23, 1935, p. 2; Aug. 30, 1935, p. 2; Sept. 6, 1935, p. 1; Oct. 18, 1935, p. 1. There was also a Junior LULAC but it played an insignificant role in the campaign for civil rights. For a more detailed look at the activities of all these groups between 1930 and 1960 see De León, *Ethnicity in the Sunbelt*, pp. 60–117.

51. De León, *Ethnicity in the Sunbelt*, p. 82.

52. *Houston Chronicle*, Mar. 13, 1935, p. 12; Apr. 9, 1935, p. 25.

53. *Houston Chronicle*, Mar. 13, 1935, p. 3.

54. "Constitution of the Latin American Club," Juvencio Rodríguez Collection, HMRC.

55. No studies exist on labor activism by Mexican-origin individuals in Houston during the years from 1930 to 1960. Scattered evidence suggests that some labor groups were in existence and actively involved in the 1930s, but data is lacking to indicate the extent of this activity. The I.L.A. Compress Local 1309, for example, held regular meetings during the mid-1930s at its Union Hall at 76th Street and Avenue N. Some Mexican American women belonged to the International Ladies' Garment Workers' Union (ILGWU) and met during the same period. Further research in the area of labor activism in Houston needs to be conducted in order to get a better understanding of the community's involvement in this area. On the I.L.A. Compress Local 1309 see *El Puerto*, July 5, 1935, p. 1; July 12, 1935, p. 1; Aug. 2, 1935, p. 1; Nov. 8, 1935, p. 1. On the ILGWU see ILGWU Local 214, Houston Box, Texas Labor Archives, University of Texas at Arlington, Arlington, Tex., cited in De León, *Ethnicity in the Sunbelt*, p. 55.

56. One example of this occurred in January, 1938. In this year LAC was relatively successful in getting several thousand Mexican Americans to pay their poll taxes so that they could vote in the upcoming election (*El Puerto*, July 15, 1938, p. 3).

57. *Houston Chronicle*, Aug. 22, 1935, p. 10.

58. "Latin Sons of Texas Host Meeting of Anglo Politicians Running for Office," *El Puerto*, July 15, 1938, p. 3. According to Juvencio Rodríguez, this was the first endorsement ever by a Mexican American organization in the city. See *Houston Chronicle*, Aug. 10, 1940, p. 6B; Nov. 1, 1940, p. 15A; Nov. 24, 1940, p. 14D.

59. The Pan American Political Council was founded in 1940 for the purpose of informing its members of the platform and qualifications of those seeking elective

office and to "invite candidates for public office to its meetings so that they may express their aims and views. "The Constitution of the Pan American Political Council," LULAC Council #60 Collection, HMRC. See also *Houston Chronicle,* Oct. 18, 1940, p. 4A; July 14, 1940, p. 5B.

60. The incident arose from a request for payment of wages lost by thirty-seven Water Department employees, including seventeen Mexicans, for having taken off to celebrate San Jacinto Day on April 21, 1938. City Council commissioner S. A. Starkey retorted to this demand by stating: "What! Pay Mexicans for the day they were beaten [at the Battle of San Jacinto]?" Both LAC and Council 60 protested this remark and argued that it was derogatory. They also responded that Mexican-origin individuals fighting on the American side at San Jacinto laid the foundation for the birth of Texas independence. Council 60 in addition presented a petition with thirty-seven names in support of the lost wages. All of them were American citizens and possessed a poll tax. See *Houston Chronicle,* May 11, 1938, p. 1. For a brief overview of this incident see De León, *Ethnicity in the Sunbelt,* pp. 88–89.

61. *Houston Press,* May 12, 1938, p. 12; *Houston Chronicle,* May 11, 1938, p. 1; Juvencio Rodríguez Collection, HMRC.

62. Résumé of John J. Herrera, HMRC, John J. Herrera Collection, cited in De León, *Ethnicity in the Sunbelt,* p. 131.

63. De León, *Ethnicity in the Sunbelt,* pp. 87–89. On Club Chapultepec's criticism of "societal" mistreatment of Mexican-origin individuals see Kreneck, "The Letter from Chapultepec," pp. 268–69.

64. De León, *Ethnicity in the Sunbelt,* p. 87.

65. *Houston Chronicle,* Aug. 22, 1935, p. 10.

66. Judge Alfred J. Hernández, interview by Tom Kreneck, Jan. 15, 1979, #248, Oral History Collection, HMRC.

67. De León, *Ethnicity in the Sunbelt,* p. 74.

68. For a history of the campaign against educational inequality in Texas see San Miguel, Jr., *Let All Take Heed,* especially pp. 91–112.

69. For an overview of the work of these two organizations during the 1940s see De León, *Ethnicity in the Sunbelt,* pp. 69–76.

70. LULAC not only contributed to the civil rights struggle but also participated in patriotic rituals such as laying a wreath at the annual San Jacinto Day and getting the federal government to name several naval ships after prominent Mexican-origin individuals. For an overview of these activities see ibid., pp. 90–93.

71. Letter, "To Whom It May Concern," Jan. 15, 1944, Lulac Council #60 Collection, HMRC.

72. Moises Sandoval, *Our Legacy: The First Fifty Years* (Washington, D.C.: LULAC, 1979), pp. 34–36; San Miguel, Jr., *Let All Take Heed,* pp. 117–18.

73. San Miguel, Jr., *Let All Take Heed,* p. 118.

74. These efforts were led by a group called the "Good Citizens League," an integrated group of Anglo leaders and prominent figures of the Mexican community such as Félix Tijerina. See De León, *Ethnicity in the Sunbelt,* p. 109.

75. This effort was not simply limited to persuading youths to turn to sports and

education instead of crime. It also emphasized getting them to change their style of clothing and grooming habits so that they could become more respectable. See *Houston Chronicle,* Oct. 12, 1945, p. 15A; "Circular," Feb. 18, 1946, Federación de Sociedades México Latino Americanas, HMRC, LULAC Council #60 Collection.

76. Council 22 was reorganized and incorporated in October, 1948 (*LULAC News,* June, 1954, p. 15).

77. It also developed several other programs and contributed money to the March of Dimes, the Polio Drive, and several emergency relief committees. For examples of their extensive involvement see *Houston Chronicle,* Aug. 20, 1950, p. 19A; *LULAC News,* Jan., 1956, p. 5; Apr., 1954, p. 6; June, 1954, p. 15; May, 1955, p. 21. For a brief overview of these activities see Steven W. Prewitt, "Everything from Ditch Diggers to Doctors: LULAC Council 60, A Mexican American Civic Organization in Houston, Texas, 1945–1960" (M.A. thesis, University of Houston, 1995), pp. 60, 54–56.

78. Prewitt, "Everything from Ditch Diggers to Doctors," p. 60.

79. Ibid., pp. 49–53, 57–60.

80. "Minutes," Dec. 8, 1955, LULAC Collection, HMRC. See also Prewitt, "Everything from Ditch Diggers to Doctors," pp. 61–62.

81. "Minutes," Aug. 8, 1950; June 17, 1954, LULAC Collection, HMRC. See also Electra D. King to Sam Alderete, May 11, 1950, LULAC Collection, HMRC.

82. Felix Tijerina, "Message from the National President," *LULAC News,* Sept., 1955, p. 2, LULAC Collection, HMRC.

83. Prewitt, "Everything from Ditch Diggers to Doctors," p. 62.

84. Guadalupe C. Quintanilla, "The Little School of the 400 and Its Impact on Education for the Spanish Dominant Bilingual Children of Texas" (Ph.D. diss., University of Houston, 1976), p. 59.

85. Prewitt, "Everything from Ditch Diggers to Doctors," p. 62. For a history and evaluation of this program see San Miguel, Jr., *Let All Take Heed,* pp. 139–63. See also Quintanilla, "Little School of the 400."

86. For a history of the origins, evolution, controversies, and consequences of this preschool program see San Miguel, Jr., *Let All Take Heed,* pp. 113–87.

87. *Independent School District v Salvatierra,* 33 S.W.2d 790, Tex. Civ. App., San Antonio (1930), cert. denied, 284 U.S. 580 (1931).

88. Prewitt, "Everything from Ditch Diggers to Doctors," pp. 75, 77.

89. *Delgado et al. v Bastrop Independent School District et al.* (1948). A copy of this decision can be found in George I. Sánchez, *Concerning Segregation of Spanish-Speaking Children in the Public Schools,* Inter-American Education Occasional Papers No. 9 (Austin: University of Texas Press, 1951), pp. 72–73.

90. For instance, this ruling clarified the definition of segregation. The segregation of Mexican American children, when no clearly stated regulation or policy existed to that effect, was illegal. This was also the case even when the policy was the result of custom and practice. See *Delgado et al. v Bastrop Independent School District et al.* (1948), pp. 72–73.

91. According to the decision, school districts could establish segregated facilities, but

there were several stipulations: they could be established "on the same campus in the first grade only and solely for instructional purposes" for those pupils who "clearly demonstrate, as a result of scientific and standardized tests, equally given and applied to all pupils, that they do not possess a sufficient familiarity with the English language to understand classroom instruction" (See ibid., p. 73).

92. According to the decision, school officials could now be held responsible for condoning or aiding segregation. See ibid.

93. For a history of this campaign for educational equality during the years from 1946 to 1957 see San Miguel, Jr., *Let All Take Heed,* especially pp. 113–38.

94. Ibid.

95. In Houston the local LULACs did not seek legal redress of their educational grievances. Their approach was more political than legal. In addition to finding ways of eliminating segregation without going to court, they provided linguistic and social services to children and increased school enrollment through the development of back-to-school rallies. For a more detailed history of these efforts, especially the preschool English language efforts, see ibid., pp. 139–63.

96. Beginning as early as 1929 federal and state agencies began to change the classification of Mexican American from white to "nonwhite" or to assign them a nonwhite racial category where none existed. See Irving G. Hendrick, *Final Report: Public Policy toward the Education of Non-White Minority Group Children in California, 1849–1970* (Riverside: School of Education, University of California, Riverside, Mar., 1975); San Miguel, Jr., *Let All Take Heed;* Ricardo L. Garza, Memo to Ed Idar, Jr., on "Judicial Recognition of Chicanos as an Identifiable Class within the Caucasian Race," June 27, 1973, Abraham Ramírez Collection, HMRC.

97. For instance, prior to the 1930s the Texas Constitution read: "separate schools shall be provided for white and colored children and impartial provision shall be made for both" (art. 7, sec. 7). No reference was made to Mexican-origin individuals.

98. See Garza, Memo to Ed Idar, Jr.

99. Arnoldo De León, *In Re Ricardo Rodríguez: An Attempt at Chicano Disfranchisement in San Antonio, 1896–1897* (San Antonio: Caravel Press, 1979).

100. Cited in De León, *Ethnicity in the Sunbelt,* p. 88.

101. Congressman Eagle, in his response to the Social Security Board, "insisted" that Mexican Americans were members of the white race since they were descendants of the Spaniards. See ibid., p. 88.

102. For the response by Mexican Americans in San Angelo and El Paso, Tex., see, respectively, Arnold De León, *San Angelenos: Mexican Americans in San Angelo, Texas* (San Angelo, Tex.: Published for Fort Concho Museum Press by Mulberry Avenue Books, 1985), p. 52; and M. García, "Mexican Americans and the Politics of Citizenship," p. 191.

103. For a history of Mexico's quest for an identity and the emergence of indigenous thought in the 1920s see Henry C. Schmidt, *The Roots of Lo Mexicano: Self and Society in Mexican Thought, 1900–1934* (College Station: Texas A&M University Press, 1978), pp. 118–21.

104. Ibid., p. 120.

CHAPTER 4. THE COMMUNITY IS BEGINNING TO RUMBLE

1. De León, *Ethnicity in the Sunbelt,* pp. 163–70.
2. For a history of the Chicano movement's rise and decline in Houston see ibid., pp. 163–85.
3. *Houston Post,* July 27, 1961, sec. 8, n.pag.
4. Kreneck, *Del Pueblo,* pp. 151–52.
5. The CAC had been founded in 1958 to promote Mexican American involvement in the political process. Roy Elizondo, Alfonso Vásquez, E. P. Lean, and Dr. Alfredo Hernández played key roles in the evolution of this organization. See ibid., pp. 151–52.
6. Ibid., p. 153.
7. San Miguel, Jr., *Let All Take Heed,* p. 141.
8. This program expired in 1967. See ibid., pp. 156–60.
9. For data on the success of this program in improving school achievement see Texas Education Agency, *Report on the Preschool Instructional Program* (Austin: Texas Education Agency, 1962).
10. San Miguel, Jr., *Let All Take Heed,* pp. 158–59.
11. Kreneck has argued that the Little School of the 400 was the model for the federally sponsored Project Headstart program established under President Lyndon B. Johnson's administration, but I have been unable to find any evidence to substantiate this claim. See Kreneck, *Del Pueblo,* p. 121.
12. De León, *Ethnicity in the Sunbelt,* p. 164.
13. Kreneck, *Del Pueblo,* p. 155.
14. The city of Houston under the Welch administration in 1967 also developed a program similar to Jobs for Progress. Mayor Welch's program, entitled Houston City Job Fair, targeted Mexican American neighborhoods. It involved Mexican American volunteers who assisted residents, particularly youth, in finding summer employment and encouraged them to further their education. See ibid., p. 155.
15. The former view is held by Carlos Muñoz, Jr., in *Youth, Identity, Power;* and Mario Barrera, in *Beyond Aztlan: Ethnic Autonomy in Comparative Perspective* (New York: Praeger, 1988). The latter view is held by Juan Gómez-Quiñones, in *Chicano Politics;* and De León, *Mexican Americans in Texas,* 2d ed., p. 127.
16. One historian refers to this process as "a variegated burst of activity" (Gómez-Quiñones, *Chicano Politics,* p. 103). For different interpretations of the Chicano movement see Ignacio M. García, *Chicanismo: The Forging of a Militant Ethos among Mexican Americans* (Tucson: University of Arizona Press, 1997), pp. 3–18.
17. I. García, *Chicanismo,* pp. 3–12.
18. On the 1966 walkout see Joan W. Moore and Ralph Guzman, "The Mexican Americans: New Wind from the Southwest," *Nation* (May 30, 1966): 645–48. On the 1967 Cabinet meeting in El Paso see Philip Darraugh Ortego, "The Minority on the Border," *Nation* (Dec. 11, 1967): 624–27; and Armando Rendon, "La Raza: Today Not Manana," in *Mexican Americans in the United States: A Reader,* ed. John H. Burma (New York: Schenkurein, 1970), pp. 307–324.

19. Moore and Guzman, "Mexican Americans," pp. 645–48.
20. I. García, *Chicanismo,* pp. 19–42. For a recent study of Chávez see Richard Gris-
    wold del Castillo and Richard Garcia, *César Chávez: A Triumph of Spirit* (Norman:
    University of Oklahoma Press, 1995). See also episode 2 (César Chávez) of the
    four-part PBS special *Chicano! The Mexican American Civil Rights Movement,*
    1996.
21. On the Alianza see Peter Nabokov, *Tijerina and the Court House Raid* (Albuquer-
    que: University of New Mexico Press, 1969); and Richard Gardner, *Grito! Reies
    Tijerina and the New Mexico Land Grant War of 1967* (Indianapolis: Bobbs-Merrill,
    1970). Strangely enough, no current studies have been done on Reies Tijerina and
    the land grant movement.
22. On Corky see I. García, *Chicanismo,* pp. 34–36.
23. Ibid., pp. 40–42.
24. On MAYO see Armando Navarro, *Mexican American Youth Organization: Avant
    Garde of the Chicano Movement in Texas* (Austin: University of Texas Press, 1995).
    On La Raza Unida Party see Ignacio M. García, *United We Win: The Rise and Fall
    of La Raza Unida Party* (Tucson: Mexican American Studies Research Center, the
    University of Arizona, 1989). See also episode 4 of the four-part PBS special *Chi-
    cano! The Mexican American Civil Rights Movement,* 1996. Finally, see José Angel
    Gutiérrez, *The Making of a Chicano Militant: Lessons from Cristal* (Madison: Uni-
    versity of Wisconsin Press, 1998).
25. Navarro, *Mexican American Youth Organization,* chap. 2.
26. The members of the committee were: Mrs. Howard Barnstone, a school board
    member and chair; Mrs. Ruth Denny, supervisor of the basic skills project;
    Mrs. Ethel Sloan, director of the Focus on Achievement Program; and Dr. Alberta
    Baines, assistant superintendent for the elementary curriculum. See "Mexican
    American Education Problems Are Reviewed," Nov. 17, 1968, unidentified news-
    paper article, Gregory Salazar Collection, Blue Folder, HMRC.
27. Sometime in the fall of 1968 the board had asked the chair of an existing compen-
    satory education committee, Mrs. Barnstone, to determine what the Houston In-
    dependent School District (HISD) should do to assist Mexican Americans in the
    schools. She sent a questionnaire to teachers and principals in schools with large
    numbers of Mexican American students to obtain data on the problem and estab-
    lish a list of priorities on possible solutions. On the basis of this questionnaire four
    recommendations were made for improvement of Mexican American students'
    education:

    1. In-service training for teachers to broaden and develop their knowledge of and
       attitudes toward Mexican Americans;
    2. Special counseling for parents of these children;
    3. Creation of a bilingual program for elementary school children;
    4. Purchase of instructional materials that emphasize Mexican American culture.

    Although these were positive steps, the proposed solutions were based on a com-
    pensatory or remedial framework whose aim was to change the child or the

teacher rather than the structural aspects of educational inequality and under-achievement. The recommendations also did little to appease the increasingly growing frustration of Chicanos with the discriminatory character of public schools. See "Mexican American Education Problems Are Reviewed," Nov. 16, 1968, unidentified newspaper article, Gregory Salazar Collection, Blue Folder, HMRC.

28. This program was held at Strake Jesuit Prep during summer, 1969. Most students were headed into the seventh and eighth grades. Their reading level was deter-mined after they were given a battery of recognized achievement tests. See "Educa-tion of Latins Called Inferior," *Houston Chronicle,* Oct. 2, 1969, n.pag., Gregory Salazar Collection, Blue Folder, HMRC.

29. According to De León, UOIC was founded in 1966 or 1967 to "develop, promote, and encourage, by the preparation and distribution of literature, pamphlets, mag-azines, periodicals, tokens, and otherwise to act as a clearing house of informa-tion" (De León, *Ethnicity in the Sunbelt,* p. 181).

30. "Education of Latins Called Inferior," *Houston Chronicle,* Oct. 2, 1969, n.pag.

31. Youth and grassroots individuals were conspicuously absent from this hearing before the board's compensatory committee. It is unclear whether the students and more radical activists declined to participate or whether the board only in-vited select "leaders." For the role of youth and grassroots individuals see next section.

32. For one scholar's analysis of several court cases pertaining to testing issues in the Chicano community see Blandina Cardenas, "Defining Equal Access to Educa-tional Opportunity for Mexican American Children: A Study of Three Civil Rights Actions Affecting Mexican Americans Students" (Ph.D. diss., University of Massa-chusetts, 1974).

33. "Education of Latins Called Inferior," *Houston Chronicle,* Oct. 2, 1969, n.pag.

34. Ibid.

35. "Latin Dropouts, Low Achievement Talked," *Houston Post,* Oct. 14, 1969, p. 10.

36. Ibid.; "Mexican American Schooling Held Worse than Negroes," *El Sol,* Oct. 17, 1969, p. 1.

37. "Latin Dropouts, Low Achievement Talked," *Houston Post,* Oct. 14, 1969, p. 10.

38. Ibid.

39. Ken Sheets, "Latin Student Harassment in City Schools Denied," n.d., article found in Gregory Salazar Collection, unfoldered materials, HMRC.

40. Ibid.

41. Ibid.

42. Ibid.

43. De León, *Ethnicity in the Sunbelt,* p. 164.

44. One also ran for city council. His name was Dan Treviño, and he got over thirty-five thousand votes but did not get elected to office. See "Editorial," *El Sol,* Dec. 5, 1969, p. 2.

45. Raul Gutiérrez, Novarro, and Ramírez shared these beliefs. Only Coronado was opposed to direct action (Abraham Ramírez, interview by author, July 18, 1995, Houston, Tex.).

46. For a discussion of this march and Novarro's role see Marilyn Rhinehart and Thomas H. Kreneck, "Minimum Wage Walk of 1966," *Houston Review* 11 (1989): 27–44.

47. "School Board Race Becoming Heated," *El Sol,* Oct. 24, 1969, p. 1.

48. Out of the four candidates, Novarro was the most involved not only in school issues but in other civil rights concerns as well, especially the struggle by farm workers for union recognition and fair wages. For the role Novarro played in this latter struggle see Rhinehart and Kreneck, "Minimum Wage Walk of 1966."

49. "Editorial," *El Sol,* Nov. 7, 1969, p. 2.

50. Ibid.

51. "Editorial," *El Sol,* Dec. 5, 1969, p. 2.

52. LOMAS was influenced by Tatcho Mindiola, Ramón Villagómez, Al Pérez, Ninfa Zepeda, George Rangel, Susie Quintanilla, and others during its early years. See Kreneck, *Del Pueblo,* p. 157; Frank Alvarez, interview by author, Oct. 15, 1995, Houston, Tex.

53. More research needs to be done on the work of LOMAS. See Kreneck, *Del Pueblo,* p. 157.

54. LOMAS changed its name to MAYO in the spring of 1970. See Jaime de la Isla, interview by author, June 8, 1999, Houston, Tex.

55. For an example of a Raza Unida Conference held in Dallas in January, 1971, and attended by six hundred persons see "Conferencia de la Raza Unida," *MAYO Newsletter,* n.d., n.pag., Gregory Salazar Collection, Box 1, unfoldered materials, Houston Metropolitan Research Center, Houston, Tex.

56. For an overview of MAYO see Navarro, *Mexican American Youth Organization.*

57. Kreneck, *Del Pueblo,* p. 156.

58. De León, *Ethnicity in the Sunbelt,* p. 143.

59. Ibid., p. 152.

60. MALDEF, *Diez Años* (San Antonio: MALDEF, 1978); "Chicanos Boycott High School," *Compass* 2 (Dec., 1968): 1.

61. U.S. Commission on Civil Rights, *Hearings before the United States Commission on Civil Rights, San Antonio, Dec. 9–14, 1968* (Washington, D.C.: Government Printing Office, 1968).

62. *The Compass* began publication in April, 1967, as a newspaper of LULAC Council 406 but quickly adopted a more political posture. Its publishers were Felix and Lena Ramírez, two residents from the Northside barrio. Kreneck argues that the commencement of *The Compass* in many respects marked the beginning of Houston's Chicano movement as it coincided with the more strident activities of Houston Mexican Americans (see Kreneck, *Del Pueblo,* p. 156). *El Yáqui* began publishing in 1970 and was the newspaper for a grassroots organization by the name of Barrios Unidos and led by Raul Gutiérrez and Daniel Reséndez (see *El Yáqui* 2 [Feb., 1970], found in the Luís Cano Collection, Box C, unfoldered materials, HMRC). *Papel Chicano* began publication in the summer of 1970 through the efforts of a group of young people including Johnny Almendárez, Carlos Calbíllo, Leo Tanguma, Kris Vasquéz, Enrique Pérez, Al Durán, and others. From its office in Magnolia Park it reported grassroots activism taking place

in various barrios, including El Dorado, South Houston, Denver Harbor, the Northside, Magnolia Park, the Second Ward, and Manchester (see Kreneck, *Del Pueblo,* p. 157). A few copies of *The Compass,* one copy of *El Yáqui,* and all of the issues of *Papel Chicano* are located in the Houston Metropolitan Research Center.

63. Raul Gutiérrez, "Mexican Americans Boycott Elsa High School-Greater Houston-Uneasy?," *Compass* 2 (Dec., 1968): 2.

64. This picket at HISD to protest funding cuts was organized by Abel Álvarez, who argued that the need was for more, not less, funding of the free breakfast program as a way to improve school performance among Chicano children. See "An Example from Houston?," *Compass* 111 (Mar., 1969): 6.

65. Advocating Rights for Mexican American Students (ARMAS) handout, n.d., Gregory Salazar Collection, Blue Folder, HMRC.

66. Richard Atwater, "Chicano Students' Walkout," *Space City News,* Sept. 27–Oct. 11, 1969, in Gregory Salazar Collection, unfoldered materials, HMRC.

67. As early as December, 1968, community members and students had been discussing the need for "a revolution of walkouts, sit-ins, or stay out" as ways of pressuring school officials to improve the schools for Mexican Americans. See Gutiérrez, "Mexican Americans Boycott."

68. Atwater, "Chicano Students' Walkout."

69. Ibid.

70. "Latins Demonstrate at Schools To Mark Mexican Holiday," *Houston Post,* Sept. 17, 1969, sec. 1, p. 3.

71. Ibid.

72. David M. Yeager, principal at Marshall, said he did not lock the front or side entrance gates to the school or any doors to prevent a walkout as reported in the newspaper. He said that most decided not to participate. See ibid.

73. Atwater, "Chicano Students' Walkout."

74. ARMAS also distributed many leaflets and articles from their newspaper. These leaflets were passed out to gain student support and also to announce the demands made by ARMAS. See ibid.

75. Ibid. In another part of the article Atwater noted the biased and inadequate coverage of the walkout by the mainstream media. He said that it printed distorted versions of the walkout and omitted most of the facts. The *Houston Chronicle,* for instance, reported that only 32 students walked out at Jefferson Davis; yet according to one eyewitness there were at least 130.

76. See Muñoz, *Youth, Identity, Power,* pp. 66, 70–71.

77. John Staples Shockley, *Chicano Revolt in a Texas Town* (Notre Dame, Ind.: University of Notre Dame Press, 1974). For a more comprehensive analysis of political developments in Crystal City from the 1960s to the 1980s see Armando Navarro, *The Cristal Experiment: A Chicano Struggle for Community Control* (Madison: University of Wisconsin Press, 1998). On the development and impact of school reforms under La Raza Unida Party in that city see Armando Trujillo, *Chicano Empowerment and Bilingual Education: Movimiento Politics in Crystal City, Texas* (New York: Garland Publishing, 1998).

78. Poncho Ruíz, former MAYO member, interview by author, June 22, 1995, Houston, Tex.

79. Atwater, "Chicano Students' Walkout."

80. Some student leaders, especially those at San Jacinto, were expelled the day after the walkout, but by the end of the week all students were back in class. See ibid.

81. "Chicanos Too: Students Are Not All Black and Anglo," *El Yáqui* 2 (Feb., 1970): 5, in Luís Cano, Box C, unfoldered materials, HMRC.

82. Ibid.

83. Ibid.

84. Ibid.

CHAPTER 5. PAWNS, PUPPETS, AND SCAPEGOATS

1. This zoning plan also provided that the schools have a 66-34 white-Negro teacher ratio (*Houston Chronicle,* Sept. 16, 1970, p. 1). The equidistant school zoning plan involved the "drawing of zone lines equidistant between adjacent schools, with students required to attend school nearest their home at time of enrollment except for voluntary transfer of student whose race is a majority to another school in which his race is in the minority and transfer in case of transportation hardship or desire to attend vocational courses and under which every Negro child in high school and junior high level would receive his education in an integrated atmosphere" (*Ross v Eckels,* 317 F.Supp. 512 (1970).

2. By 1970 there were approximately 31,600 Mexican American children in the Houston Independent School District. They comprised 13 percent of the total school-age population. See Stan Redding, "Schools Consider Plea by Chicanos," *Houston Chronicle,* Aug. 16, 1970, sec. 1, p. 1.

3. In 1967, for instance, Congress passed the nation's first bilingual education act. In doing so, it recognized the language needs of Mexican Americans. On May 25, 1970, the Office for Civil Rights issued a memorandum identifying Mexican Americans as a national origin minority group. See *Bilingual Education Act, Public Law No. 90-247,* 81 Stat. 816, 20 U.S.C.A. sec 880(b) (1968); and J. Stanley Pottinger, *Memorandum of May 25, 1970* (Washington, D.C.: Office for Civil Rights, 1970).

4. For an overview of Mexican American activism in education prior to 1970 see Guadalupe San Miguel, Jr., "The Community Is Beginning To Rumble: The Origins of Chicano Educational Protest in Houston, 1965–1970," *Houston Review* 13, no. 3 (1991): 127–48.

5. For elaboration on these actions see De León, *Ethnicity in the Sunbelt,* pp. 178–80.

6. Abraham Ramírez, Jr., interview by author, July 18, 1995, Houston, Tex.

7. The fathers of the children were all members of the United Steel Workers of America in the Corpus Christi area. Due to the lack of resources they asked the union for financial aid. It agreed to pay the litigation expenses and attorney fees. See "Judge Seals Extends Integration to Latins," newspaper clipping in Gregory Salazar Collection, unfoldered materials, HMRC.

8. "Judge Seals Extends Integration to Latins", newspaper clipping in Gregory Salazar

Collection, unfoldered materials, HMRC. This is probably a *Caller-Times* article published in the summer of 1970.

9. For a brief overview of these legal strategies and their impact on the desegregation struggles of Mexican Americans see San Miguel, Jr., *Let All Take Heed*, pp. 177–81.

10. The United States Supreme Court did rule in a 1954 jury discrimination case that Mexican Americans were a separate class distinct from whites, but it only applied to one particular county in Texas. See *Hernández v State of Texas*, 74 S.Ct. 667 (1954).

11. Specifically, they asked the court to rule on the following questions:

1. Can Brown apply to Mexican Americans?
2. If it can, does it apply to the particular case in Corpus Christi?
3. Is there a dual or unitary school system for blacks and whites?
4. If there is segregation, is it de jure or de facto?
5. If there is segregation, how can the court disestablish the dual system and maintain a unitary one?

See *Cisneros v Corpus Christi Independent School Dist.*, 324 F. Supp. 604 (1970).

12. More specifically, Judge Seals ruled "that where Mexican Americans in school district were an identifiable ethnic minority group and for that reason had been segregated and discriminated against in the schools, they, as well as Negroes, were entitled to all the protection announced in United States Supreme Court decision holding unconstitutional segregation in the public schools" (*Cisneros v CCISD*, 324 F. Supp. 599 [1970]).

13. *Cisneros v CCISD*, 324 F. Supp. 616 (1970).

14. *Cisneros v CCISD*, 324 F. Supp. 599 (1970).

15. Abraham Ramírez, Jr., letter to Mario Obledo, June 20, 1970, A. Ramírez Collection, Box 1, No. 22, HMRC.

16. Alan Exelrod, letter to Abraham Ramírez, Jr., July 28, 1970, A. Ramírez Collection, Box 1, No. 22, HMRC.

17. On July 30, 1970, Ramírez wrote to Exelrod that the Court of Appeals in New Orleans was expected to make a decision on the Ross case sometime in the first week of August. "Therefore, it becomes imperative that your appeal to the Court of Appeals be on file Monday or Tuesday of next week at the latest" (A. Ramírez, letter to A. Exelrod, July 30, 1970, A. Ramírez Collection, Box 1, No. 22, HMRC).

18. This report was based on data from two primary sources: the Department of Health, Education, and Welfare annual enrollment figures for the 1969–70 school year; and the enrollment estimates of HISD for the 1970–71 school year. See A. Ramírez, letter to A. Exelrod, Aug. 2, 1970, A. Ramírez Collection, Box 1, No. 22, HMRC.

19. Ibid.

20. One of the high schools—Jacinto—showed a tremendous drop in total enrollment—from 2,385 to 604—because of its transformation from a comprehensive to a vocational training school. See ibid.

21. Ibid.

22. Ibid.

23. Ibid.

24. *Houston Chronicle,* Sept. 16, 1970, p. 1. The lawyers handling the case were Mario Obledo, Alan Exelrod, and Abraham Ramírez, Jr. See "Editorial," *Papel Chicano,* Aug. 22, 1970, p. 4.

25. "Editorial," *Papel Chicano,* Aug. 22, 1970, p. 4.

26. See Amicus Curiae Brief, *Ross v Eckels,* Aug. 11, 1970, Abe Ramírez Collection, Box 1, MALDEF Lawsuit Folder, HMRC. A summary of this suit can be found in *Houston Chronicle,* Sept. 16, 1970, p. 1.

27. Order and Decree, *Ross v Eckels,* Civil Action No. 10444, June 30, 1970, Abe Ramírez Collection, Box 1, No. 5, HMRC.

28. HISD, *Guidelines for Student Assignments* (Houston: HISD, Aug. 10, 1970), p. 1.

29. Ramírez argues that Mexican American parents who for many years have sent their children to Anglo schools are now caught in a "squeeze play" and are forbidden from taking this action as a result of the court's ruling and the school board's decree. See Abe Ramírez, letter to Alan Exelrod, Aug. 2, 1970, p. 3, in Abe Ramírez Collection, Box 1, No. 22, HMRC.

30. Ibid.

31. Ramírez had a large following in the community and had run for political office in November, 1969. See *El Sol,* Oct. 24, 1969, p. 1; Nov. 21, 1969, p. 1.

32. A. Ramírez, letter to A. Exelrod, Aug. 2, 1970, A. Ramírez Collection, Box 1, No. 22, HMRC.

33. Ibid. The confrontation Ramírez mentions is in reference to the 1970 killing of a black activist whose group the police considered revolutionary as well as to other incidents such as the 1967 confrontation between police and black students at Texas Southern University. See De León, *Ethnicity in the Sunbelt,* p. 149; Robert A. Calvert, "The Civil Rights Movement in Texas," in *The Texas Heritage,* ed. Ben Procter and Archie P. McDonald (Saint Louis: Forum Press, 1980), pp. 161–63.

34. Davis Senior High already had 298 African American students and slightly over 1,000 white students, including 834 Mexican Americans. Under the new plan it would receive an additional 246 African American students. See A. Ramírez, letter to A. Exelrod, Aug. 2, 1970, p. 2, A. Ramírez Collection, Box 1, No. 22, HMRC.

35. Pedro Vasquez and Lorenzo Díaz, "But We're Brown! Una Raza de Bronze," *Papel Chicano,* Aug. 27–Sept, 11, 1970, p. 4.

36. "MAYO on Boycott," undated and unnamed, Gregory Salazar Collection, Blue Folder, HMRC.

37. *Papel Chicano,* Aug. 27–Sept. 11, 1970, p. 10.

38. *Papel Chicano* was founded in Aug., 1970, and for two years publicized and wrote about the political, cultural, and social activities of the Houston barrios on the east side of town. It ceased all operations by the summer of 1972. All the copies of this important newspaper can be found in the *Papel Chicano* archives at the Houston Metropolitan Research Center.

39. "Editorial," *Papel Chicano,* Aug. 27–Sept. 11, 1970, p. 4.

40. The group began to meet on Monday nights at Saint Patrick's Church. See Vasquez and Díaz, "But We're Brown!," p. 4.
41. As early as July 30, 1970, he was asked for advice by "cross representatives of the Mexican American community" in Houston on how to proceed. By August 2, 1970, Ramírez was providing the following advice to Mexican Americans who called him:

    1. Follow the equidistant plan to the letter and change the integration plan in the courts;
    2. Disobey the equidistant plan and send the children (if they can get away with it) to the school they prefer;
    3. Keep the children at home, in which case be ready to go to jail;
    4. Move their residences before August 30, 1970, in the school zone where they wish their children to enroll.

    See Ramírez, letter to Alan Exelrod, Aug. 2, 1970, A. Ramírez, Box 1, No. 22, HMRC. See also A. Ramírez, letter to Alan Exelrod, July 30, 1970, A. Ramírez, Box 1, No. 22, HMRC.
42. Vasquez and Díaz, "But We're Brown!," p. 4.
43. "Shutdown on Ryan," *Papel Chicano,* Sept. 5, 1970, p. 5.
44. *Ross v Eckels,* 434 F. 2d 1140 (1970).
45. The Court of Appeals directed HISD to achieve a higher degree of desegregation by rezoning secondary schools, pairing elementary schools, and broadening student transfer policies. See ibid.
46. Even one of the dissenting judges in the court's ruling, Judge Clark, argued that pairing blacks and Mexican Americans was unjust. "I say it is mock justice," he said, "when we 'force' the numbers by pairing disadvantaged Negro students into schools with members of this equally disadvantaged ethnic group." See *Ross v Eckels,* 434 F.2d 1150 (1970).
47. The Cabinet Committee on Opportunity for the Spanish Speaking was a federal organization that helped develop programs for Spanish speaking individuals in the areas of economic and manpower development, housing and community development, legislative and legal affairs, communications and research, and limited government placement services. Mr. Castillo was the director of this office. He came to Houston to meet with HISD and Mexican American Education Council (MAEC) officials over the federal integration order. See "Martin Castillo Helps Raza," *Papel Chicano,* Sept. 26, 1970, p. 4.
48. "Raza . . . ," *Papel Chicano,* Sept. 5–25, 1970, p. 3.
49. "MAYO on Boycott," n.d., newspaper clipping in Gregory Salazar Collection, unfoldered materials, HMRC.
50. "Raza . . . ," *Papel Chicano,* Sept. 5–25, 1970, p. 3.
51. *Houston Chronicle,* Sept. 28, 1970, p. 2.
52. He urged federal assistance in the matter. More specifically he urged direct intervention by the Department of Justice in the appeal of the court order by the HISD and the technical assistance of the Department of Health, Education, and Wel-

fare to improve the educational techniques for the Mexican American children. "Martin Castillo Helps Raza," *Papel Chicano,* Sept. 26, 1970, p. 4.

53. Lucy Moreno and Ralph Moreno, interviews by author, June 1, 1999, Houston, Tex.

54. These names are obtained from a list that was passed around that Thursday night. This list has only twenty names on it. That there were two activists who were present at that meeting but whose names do not appear on my list suggests either that many individuals in attendance did not sign the list or that I have an incomplete list. For a copy of this list see "List of Those Attending Meeting," Abraham Ramírez Collection, Box 1, No. 16, HMRC. The activists mentioned above are Lucy and Ralph Moreno. See Lucy Moreno interview, June 1, 1999, and Ralph Moreno interview.

55. Its first Board of Directors was officially listed as Leonel Castillo, Ben Reyes, and Mario Quiñones (MAEC Articles of Incorporation, n.d., Abe Ramírez Collection, Box 1, unassorted clippings, HMRC.

56. Jaime de la Isla, representing UH-MAYO, was not on the list of those who signed in that Thursday evening. However, he was present at a Saturday press conference. "List of Those Attending Meeting," Abraham Ramírez Collection, Box 1, No. 16, HMRC.

57. John Castillo, a member of the Political Association of Spanish Speaking Organizations (PASSO), for instance, was part of MAEC, but he represented the barrio he lived in and not the PASSO organization to which he belonged. According to the roster of September 25, 1970, John Castillo became the treasurer for the group. See "Roster of Barrio Representatives as of 9-25-70," Mexican American Education Council, Abraham Ramírez Collection, Box 1, No. 2, HMRC.

58. Abraham Ramírez, Jr., interview.

59. Press release, Aug. 29, 1970, Abe Ramírez Collection, Box 1, unassorted clippings, HMRC.

60. The *Houston Post* reported two hundred picketers, while *Papel Chicano* reported three hundred. See Frank Davis, "Chicano Boycott Pushed," *Houston Post,* Aug. 29, 1970, sec. 1, p. 2; "Rallies and Pickets," *Papel Chicano,* Sept. 5, 1970, p. 4.

61. "Rallies and Pickets," *Papel Chicano,* Sept. 5, 1970, p. 4; "Chicano Group Asks Boycott To Protest Pairing," *Houston Chronicle,* Aug. 28, 1970, sec. 1, p. 1.

62. The newspapers reported a Mrs. Lorenzo Díaz and a Mrs. Mario Quiñones. I have substituted their actual names based on the official roster of MAEC. See Davis, "Chicano Boycott Pushed"; "Raza . . . ," *Papel Chicano,* Sept. 5–25, 1970, p. 3.

63. "Raza. . .," *Papel Chicano,* Sept. 5–25, 1970, p. 3.

64. Ibid.

65. These comments are attributed to Bill Gutiérrez and Leonel Castillo. See ibid.

66. "Chicanos on Strike," *Space City,* n.d., n.pag., Gregory Salazar Collection, unfoldered materials, HMRC.

67. Davis, "Chicano Boycott Pushed."

68. This number was based on the number of students enrolled during the 1969–70 school year in the fourteen minority schools to be paired. See ibid.

69. Ibid.

70. "Raza. . .," *Papel Chicano,* Sept. 5–25, 1970, p. 3.

71. "Chicano Group Asks Boycott To Protest Pairing," *Houston Chronicle,* Aug. 28, 1970, sec. 1, p. 1. For a similar quote from Ramírez see also Davis, "Chicano Boycott Pushed."

72. An article in the *Houston Post* originally stated that the boycott rally would take place at the El Dorado Community Center on 9700 Wallisville Road. However, according to an article in *Papel Chicano,* it actually took place at Saint Philip of Jesus Catholic Church grounds located at 9700 Villita Street, off Wallisville Road. See Davis, "Chicano Boycott Pushed"; "Rallies and Pickets," *Papel Chicano,* Sept. 5, 1970, p. 4.

73. Lucy Moreno interview, June 1, 1999.

74. Leonel Castillo, interview by author, July 17, 1995, Houston, Tex.

75. Leonel Castillo, interview by Tom Kreneck, 1975, Leonel J. Castillo Collection, HMRC. See also Leonel Castillo, interview by author.

76. The church is located at 9700 Villita. Two different sources reported different numbers. *Papel Chicano* reported four thousand, whereas the *Houston Post* reported over one thousand. See Jeff Scott, "Chicanos Form School Boycott Plans," *Houston Post,* Aug. 31, 1970, sec. 1, p. 19; and "Rallies and Pickets," *Papel Chicano,* Sept. 5, 1970, p. 4. *Papel Chicano* refers to this as El Dorado Park, but there is no such park by that name.

77. Scott, "Chicanos Form School Boycott Plans."

78. Leonel Castillo, interview, 1975, Leonel Castillo Collection, HMRC. See also Leonel Castillo, interview by author.

79. "Rallies and Pickets," *Papel Chicano,* Sept. 5, 1970, p. 4.

80. Ibid.

81. MAEC also set up a Board of Directors for the Huelga schools and the boycott. See "Huelga Schools," an undated leaflet announcing the establishment of Huelga schools and the boycott rally at El Dorado to be held on Sunday, August 30, 1970, found in Gregory Salazar Collection, Box 1, unfoldered materials, HMRC. According to a *Papel Chicano* article Tina Reyes, a local educator, was selected to head the Huelga schools ("Rallies and Pickets," *Papel Chicano,* Sept. 5, 1970, p. 4).

82. "Rallies and Pickets," *Papel Chicano,* Sept. 5, 1970, p. 4.

83. Ibid.

84. Ibid.

85. These names are obtained from a list that was passed around that Thursday night. It is possible that others were present but did not sign the list. For a copy of this list see "List of Those Attending Meeting," Abraham Ramírez Collection, Box 1, No. 16, HMRC.

CHAPTER 6. RAIN OF FURY

1. Various names were given to these schools, including Huelga escuelas, freedom schools, and huelga schools. For consistency purposes, I have decided to use the term "huelga schools." See "Freedom Schools Will Open during Boycott," *Houston*

Chronicle, Aug. 30, 1970, sec. 1, p. 1; "Huelga Schools Have 2000 Students," *Houston Chronicle,* Sept. 3, 1970, sec. 1, p. 1.

2. "Huelga Schools Have 2000 Students," *Houston Chronicle,* Sept. 3, 1970, sec. 1, p. 1. There were other officials in charge of various aspects of Huelga school development. These positions and the individuals appointed to them, most likely by Leonel Castillo, were as follows: director of Huelga Schools—Leonel Castillo; director of Administrative Services—David Ortiz; Management and Planning—John E. Castillo and Paul Telles; Public Information officer—Raymond Rodríguez; Logistics—David Shoup (MAEC leaflet on Huelga Schools, Sept. 9, 1970, Gregory Salazar Collection, Box 1, unfoldered materials, HMRC).

3. Leonel Castillo, interview by author. See also "Huelga Schools Have 2000 Students," *Houston Chronicle,* Sept. 3, 1970, sec. 1, p. 1; MAEC leaflet on Huelga Schools, Sept. 9, 1970, Gregory Salazar Collection, Box 1, unfoldered materials, HMRC.

4. "Huelga Schools Have 2000 Students," *Houston Chronicle,* Sept. 3, 1970, sec. 1, p. 1; MAEC leaflet on Huelga Schools.

5. For an overview of this dispute see Pete Wittenberg, "Chicanos Expect HCCAA Support," *Houston Post* clipping, Gregory Salazar Collection, Box 1, Blue Folder, HMRC; Pete Wittenberg, "OEO Refuses Facilities to Boycotting Chicanos," *Houston Post,* Sept. 2, 1970, p. 2A. Questions were also raised about the role that the Catholic Church was playing in this effort to "circumvent" desegregation mandates. See Zarko Franks, "Catholic Aid in Latin Strike is 'Unofficial,'" *Houston Chronicle,* Sept. 4, 1970, sec. 1, pp. 1, 6.

6. This school was located at the Magnolia Park Branch YWCA at 7206 Navigation. See "Church's Aid Is 'Unofficial,'" *Houston Chronicle,* Sept. 4, 1970, sec. 1, p. 6.

7. "Latin Boycott Is Felt on First Day of School," *Houston Chronicle,* Sept. 1, 1970, sec. 4, p. 4.

8. These schools and their locations were:

   1. School #1, 6323 Force;
   2. School #2, 1146 Gazin;
   3. Port Houston HCCAA,1821 Daughert;
   4. San Felipe Church. 9800 Wallisville Rd.;
   5. Juan Marcos Presbyterian Church, 3600 Fulton;
   6. Northside People Center, 1501 Brooks;
   7. Saint Joseph's Church, 1505 Kane;
   8. Our Lady of Saint John, 7500 Hirsch Rd.;
   9. Magnolia Park Branch YWCA, 7305 Navigation.

   See "Chicanos Sign 3,000," *Houston Post,* Sept. 3, 1970, p. 13A. The original six school locations were slightly different from the ones that were opened on Tuesday. These schools and their locations were:

   1. Northside People Center, 1501 Brooks;
   2. Saint Joseph's Church, 1505 Kane;

3. Saint Stephen's Church, 1901 Center;

4. Our Lady of Saint John, 7500 Hirsch Rd.;

5. Magnolia Park Branch YWCA, 7305 Navigation;

6. Fifth–sixth Ward Community Center, 1503 State.

See "Freedom Schools Will Open during Boycott," *Houston Chronicle*, Aug. 30, 1970, sec. 1, p. 1; Wittenberg, "Chicanos Expect HCCAA support."

9. "Freedom Schools Will Open during Boycott," *Houston Chronicle*, Aug. 30, 1970, sec. 1, p. 1; "Chicanos Sign 3,000."

10. "Chicanos Sign 3,000."

11. "Latin Boycott Hit Secondary Schools," *Houston Chronicle*, Sept. 5, 1970, sec. 1, p. 2.

12. The new schools and their addresses were:

1. Resurrection Hall, 915 Zoe (grades 2–8);

2. Unnamed facility, 6312 Alderson St. (k–1);

3. McAshan Memorial Methodist Church, 102 Sampson (k–8);

4. Saint Patrick's Chapel, 3717 Robertson (k–8);

5. Dance Hall, Norvick and McCarty (5–8);

6. Resurrection Mission, ? Munn (k–4);

7. Saint Paul Baptist Church, 4513 Salinas (k–8);

8. Holy Name School, 915 Cochran.

Mimi Crossley, "Chicano Boycott Growing, 7 New Strike Schools Open," *Houston Chronicle*, Sept. 8, 1970, sec. 1, pp. 1, 4.

13. "Chicano Leaders Call for Every Student To Boycott," *Houston Chronicle*, Sept 9, 1970, sec. 1, p. 16.

14. Ibid.

15. Crossley, "Chicano Boycott Growing."

16. Ibid.

17. This senior high school was originally located in Saint Joseph's Church, but on Friday it was transferred to the newer, well-equipped Holy Name School, 1913 Cochran. The principal of the school was Eliseo Cisneros, age thirty-one. Classes were held at night. See Crossley, "Chicano Boycott Growing."

18. Cam Duncan, "La Raza vs. School Board," *Papel Chicano*, Sept. 26–Oct. 9, 1970, p. 20.

19. Mimi Crossley, "Boycotting Latins Given Warning," *Houston Chronicel*, Sept. 9, 1970, sec. 1, p. 16.

20. Ibid.

21. Ibid.

22. Gregory Salazar said that MAYO would cover this aspect of the instruction. See comments in "Freedom Schools Will Open during Boycott," *Houston Chronicle*, Aug. 30, 1970, sec. 1, p. 22.

23. "Why I'm Boycotting," *Papel Chicano*, Sept. 26–Oct. 9, 1970, p. 3.

24. "Why We're on Boycott," *Papel Chicano*, Sept. 26–Oct. 9, 1970, p. 3.

25. Duncan, "La Raza vs. School Board." Samples of statements are on the front page of the newspaper.

26. An unnamed VISTA lawyer taught the course. See "Huelga Schools," undated newspaper clipping, Gregory Salazar Collection, Box 1, Blue Folder, HMRC.

27. See ibid.

28. Crossley, "Chicano Boycott Growing."

29. Ibid.

30. She asked one class of fifth graders to write a paragraph on why they were boycotting the schools and how the huelga school was different from the public one they had attended. The students answered that they went to the huelga schools because there was not as much homework, they had better teachers, they had free lunch and air-conditioning, and there were no "colored people" in them. See Duncan, "La Raza vs. School Board."

31. Ibid.

32. While a few students and instructors disagreed with these statements, they were not effectively dealt with in the huelga schools. One ninth-grade student, for instance, stated the following: "Many people say we're just fighting because we chicanos don't want to get mixed with the blacks, but its not true. We've been living with them all our lives." For this citation and examples of other racist sentiments see Duncan, "La Raza vs. School Board."

33. Ibid.

34. Ibid.

35. It is important to note here that the court-ordered pairing of the schools was not in effect for the 1970–71 school year. The existing desegregation order was based on the court's May 30 ruling calling for what was known as the equidistant zoning plan. This plan failed to consider Mexican Americans as an identifiable minority group and integrated schools in the north and east sides of town attended by two minority groups. For a summary of these court rulings see "Pockets of Dissent Mark School Start," *Houston Chronicle,* Aug. 31, 1970, sec. 1, p. 1.

36. Sister Gloria Guallardo, "Another First in Houston," *Papel Chicano,* Sept. 26–Oct. 9, 1970, p. 3.

37. "Moody (Park) Hosts Raza," *Papel Chicano,* Sept. 5–25, 1970, p. 6.

38. The total student population at Ryan was about nine hundred. See "Pockets of Dissent Mark School Start," *Houston Chronicle,* Aug. 31, 1970, sec. 1, p. 1.

39. Ibid.

40. Ibid.

41. The children enrolled in this school, located at 1616 Hebert Street, had been attending a predominantly Mexican American school in the East End, J. R. Harris Elementary. See Frank Davis, "Schools Open Calmly; 3,500 Latins Absent," *Houston Post,* Sept. 1, 1970, sec. 1, p. 9.

42. J. R. Harris Elementary was located at 811 Broadway. See ibid.; "Pockets of Dissent Mark School Start," *Houston Chronicle,* Aug. 31, 1970, sec. 1, p. 1.

43. "Pockets of Dissent Mark School Start," *Houston Chronicle,* Aug. 31, 1970, sec. 1,

p. 1. The protests at the school district office appeared daily during the boycott. See Crossley, "Chicano Boycott Growing."

44. "Pockets of Dissent Mark School Start," *Houston Chronicle*, Aug. 31, 1970, sec. 1, p. 1.
45. Ibid.
46. "Moody (Park) Hosts Raza," *Papel Chicano*, Sept. 5–25, 1970, p. 6.
47. Ibid.
48. Ibid.
49. Ibid.
50. Cam Duncan, "La Raza vs. School Board," newspaper clipping found in Gregory Salazar Collection, Box 1, Blue Folder, HMRC.
51. Leonel Castillo, interview by author; Abraham Ramírez, Jr., interview.
52. Poncho Ruíz, interview by author, June 22, 1995, Houston, Tex.
53. These comments are based on Mr. Ramírez's recollections of the rally and the invited guests. See Abraham Ramírez interview.
54. "Moody (Park) Hosts Raza," *Papel Chicano*, Sept. 5–25, 1970, p. 6.
55. "Latin Boycott Is Felt on First Day of School," *Houston Chronicle*, Sept. 1, 1970, sec. 4, p. 4.
56. "Head of Schools Invites Chicano Chiefs To Meet," *Houston Chronicle*, Sept. 10, 1970, sec. 1, p. 1.
57. Mr. Mario Peña also accompanied this group of *mujeres*. See Eugene Mendoza, "Wet Protest," *Papel Chicano*, Sept. 5–25, 1970, p. 7.
58. Ibid.
59. Ibid.
60. The group of picketers varied and included *madres* and *niños* from the Second Ward; Andy Guerrero, spokesperson for Familias Unidas; and other members of MAEC and MAYO. A Mrs. Hernández and Rosemary Galvan were present at Jackson on this day. Mrs. Galvan said, "Estoy aquí porque quiero ayudar a mi Raza ganar Freedom of Choice." See "Jackson Blows," *Papel Chicano*, Sept. 5–25, 1970, p. 14.
61. "Jackson Blows," *Papel Chicano*, Sept. 5–25, 1970, p. 14.
62. Mexican Americans were not the only group members protesting the integration order. Two other groups of different political persuasions—the conservative Committee for Sound American Education and the South Harris Citizens Alliance—were also conducting protest activities on Friday. Ken Kridner, chair of the conservative group, praised the Mexican Americans' boycott of the elementary schools and urged them to continue. See "Mothers Block Move of School Building, Integration Protests Continuing," *Houston Chronicle*, Sept. 5, 1970, sec. 1, p. 1.
63. Poncho Ruíz, interviews by author, June 22, 29, 1995, Houston, Tex.; "Latin Boycott Hits Secondary Schools," *Houston Chronicle*, Sept. 5, 1970, sec. 1, p. 1; "Mothers Block Move of School Building, Integration Protests Continuing," *Houston Chronicle*, Sept. 5, 1970, sec. 1, p. 1.
64. "4 Arrested So Far," *Papel Chicano*, Sept. 5–25, 1970, p. 14. In the next week at least three additional Mexican Americans were to be arrested for boycott activities. A

picketer, Joe Navarro, was arrested for "failure to move on" in front of Reagan Senior High School on September 8. Another striker, Valentine Flores, was arrested after a scuffle with a policeman at Washington Junior High on September 9. A Mrs. Gutiérrez was arrested while picketing Jackson High on September 10. *La Raza vs. The School Board,* a four-page newsletter, appears to be an MAEC publication and probably was published on September 17, 1970. Information on the arrests comes from page 3. See Gregory Salazar Collection, Blue Folder, HMRC.

65. "700 Crowd St. Joseph's," *Papel Chicano,* Sept. 5–25, 1970, p. 7.

66. "Boycott Support Urged," *Houston Post,* Sept. 7, 1970, p. 14A, part of newspaper clipping found in Gregory Salazar Collection, Blue Folder, HMRC; "Chicanos Meet on Boycott," *Houston Post,* Sept. 7, 1970, p. 14A.

67. "Boycott Support Urged," *Houston Post,* Sept. 7, 1970, 14A.

68. Whether this was his own proposal or one developed in conjunction with MAEC is unclear at this point.

69. "Boycott Support Urged," *Houston Post,* Sept. 7, 1970, 14A.

70. Ibid.

71. Little information is available on the tactics of the boycott or on its impact on individual schools. Most of the information found focuses on the politics of negotiation rather than of protest.

72. Leonel Castillo; Abraham Ramírez, Jr.; Mrs. Carmen Beltran; Abel Alvarez; and Gregory Salazar were the MAEC representatives. Salazar and Alvarez also represented MAYO and Barrios Unidos, respectively. See Frank Davis, "Ethnic Status of Mexican Americans Up to Courts, School Leader Contends," unnamed newspaper clipping, Sept. 9, 1970, sec. 1, p. 1, found in Gregory Salazar Collection, Blue Folder, HMRC.

73. "Chicano Leaders Call for Every Student to Boycott," *Houston Chronicle,* Sept. 9, 1970, sec. 1, p. 16.

74. Davis, "Ethnic Status of Mexican Americans Up to Courts."

75. Ibid.

76. Ibid., sec. 1, p. 1.

77. "Chicano Leaders Call for Every Student to Boycott," *Houston Chronicle,* Sept. 9, 1970, sec. 1, p. 16.

78. Mario Obledo, general counsel for MALDEF, said the following day that the motion did not "include any 20 steps or any other definite rezoning plan." It was only a motion asking that MALDEF be included as an intervenor in the integration suit before U.S. Dist. Judge Ben C. Connally. See "Garver's Public Invitation," *Houston Chronicle,* Sept. 11, 1970, p. 1.

79. Ibid., p. 6.

80. "Chicanos Plan Houston Integration Suit," *Houston Chronicle,* Sept. 10, 1970, p. 1.

81. Ramírez also called for additional teachers for the huelga schools, especially the overcrowded high school being held at the Holy Name Catholic School. See "Chicanos Plan Houston Integration Suit," *Houston Chronicle,* Sept. 10, 1970, p. 1.

82. Statement issued by Dr. George G. Carver, superintendent of schools, Houston Independent School District, Sept. 10, 1970.

83. At least one member of the board, Rev. Leon Everett II, supported the commu-

nity's effort toward ethnic identification. However, he had "grave misgivings and serious reservations" about the boycott and called for the children to attend the public schools. See "Garver's Public Invitation," *Houston Chronicle,* Sept. 11, 1970, p. 1.

84. "Chicano Leaders Have Plan for School Board," *Houston Chronicle,* Sept. 11, 1970, p. 1.

85. "Parts of Latin Plan Workable—Garver," *Houston Chronicle,* Sept. 12, 1970, p. 1.

86. Cruz reissued this call. See "Chicano Leaders Have Plan for School Board," *Houston Chronicle,* Sept. 11, 1970, p. 6.

87. "Latins Given Minority Status," undated newspaper article, Gregory Salazar Collection, Blue Folder, HMRC. This is the second page to a two-page article on the superintendent's statement.

88. No evidence has been found indicating that he or his group showed up at the board meeting or played any other significant role in community politics. See "Chicano Leaders Have Plan for School Board," *Houston Chronicle,* Sept. 11, 1970, p. 6.

89. The only group to support the boycott officially was the Mexican American Clergymen Association of Houston, a group of seven religious leaders from the Houston area, who said, "We believe the Boycott is justified through natural rights of men, Christian conscience and the rights guaranteed under the Constitution of the United States of America. We are further convinced, in light of the apathetically slowness of 'due process' in achieving social change, that the exercise of this right will expedite the final acceptance of our people as an ethnic minority." The statement was signed by the following: Rev. Arturo M. Fernández, Methodist, director of Casa de Amigos; Rev. Ruben M. Armendáriz, pastor, Juan Marcos Presbyterian; Rev. Noe Montéz, pastor, El Mesías Methodist; Rev. Antonio J. Marañon, associate pastor, Holy Name Catholic Church; Rev. Guillermo Chávez, pastor, El Buen Pastor Methodist; Rev. Doroteo Alaníz, pastor, Discípulos de Cristo Church; and Rev. Ismael Maldonado, associate pastor, Juan Marcos Presbyterian. See "To the Houston City Council and the Houston Independent School District Board from the Mexican American Clergymen Association of Houston," Sept. 21, 1970, Houston, Tex., Abe Ramírez Collection, Box 1, No. 20, HMRC.

90. Lucy Moreno interview, June 1, 1999, and Ralph Moreno interview.

91. Although no list is available on who attended, some activists, outside of those already involved, have argued that they were part of these negotiations. Lucy Moreno, Ralph Moreno, and Jaime de la Isla, representing UH-MAYO, were among the twenty participants involved in this particular session. See Lucy Moreno interview, June 1, 1999, and Ralph Moreno interview; Jaime de la Isla, telephone interview by author, June 7, 1999.

92. Gregory Salazar Collection, Box 1, unfoldered materials, HMRC.

93. Henry Holcomb, "Mexican Americans Drop Part of Boycott," *Houston Post,* Sept. 13, 1970, p. 12B.

94. "Parts of Latin Plan Workable-Garver," *Houston Chronicle,* Sept. 12, 1970, p. 1.

95. Ibid.; "Latins Sue To Intervene in School Case," *Houston Chronicle,* Sept. 11, 1970, pp. 1, 6.

96. He also urged school officials to go "one step further" and join a federal lawsuit filed Friday by fourteen Mexican American pupils and their parents. The lawsuit sought recognition of the Mexican American population as a separate minority. See Holcomb, "Mexican Americans Drop Part of Boycott."

97. "Latins May End School Walkout," *Houston Chronicle,* Sept. 13, 1970, p. 1.

98. Leonel Castillo, interview by author.

99. Other groups besides MAEC were also protesting the integration plan. One such group, led by a conservative north Houston community leader, for instance, conducted a one-day boycott of the schools on that day to protest the integration order. Over three thousand students boycotted the schools. Unlike MAEC, the group conducting the boycott opposed the integration order because of its mandatory attendance zone changes and favored freedom of choice. Elmer Bertelsen, "Violence Erupts at School Meeting," *Houston Chronicle,* Sept. 15, 1970, sec. 1, p. 12.

100. See the next chapter for details of the "mini-riot."

101. Abraham Ramírez, Jr., interview.

102. Castillo noted that the council and the school district failed to agree on the three following demands: declaring September 16 and May 5 official school holidays, announcement by the district of its preference for district as opposed to at-large elections, and approval of extra pay for bilingual teachers who use Spanish as part of their daily work. See statement by Leonel J. Castillo, Sept. 17, 1970, p. 3, Abe Ramírez Collection, Box 1, No. 20, HMRC.

103. Elmer Bertelsen, "Chicanos Plan To End Boycott Here Monday," *Houston Chronicle,* Sept. 17, 1970, sec. 1, p. 1; "Boycott Ends," *Papel Chicano,* Sept. 5–25, 1970, p. 3.

104. Valdes was a staff member to George Haynes, associate superintendent in charge of human relations for the district. The other two individuals appointed were Hayes, an African American, and Dr. Charles R. Nelson, deputy superintendent in charge of elementary schools. Dr. Nelson was an Anglo. See Bertelsen, "Chicanos Plan To End Boycott," p. 10.

105. The statement was drafted on September 14, 1970, and had five provisions:

1. Any students who have been absent from school because their parents have kept them out because of a matter of conscience may return to school by bringing a note from their parents indicating that they have been absent because of their parents' wishes.

2. All students who return to school shall be allowed to resume their normal activities as regular students in the HISD. There should be no penalties nor other punishment of any sort merited out to these students.

3. These students shall be allowed to make up their work under the same provisions that exist when students have been ill.

4. While the school district believes the boycott was inappropriate, school officials should refrain from any dialogue which casts any type of judgment concerning these students' absence.

5. Students who do not return to school with a note from their parents shall be admitted to school on the first day with the provision that they secure a note for

the second day. Failure to supply a note shall be treated in the same fashion as regular unexcused absences.

See *Memorandum* to Mr. H. W. Elrod, Dr. Charles R. Nelson, and Dr. Woodrow Watts, from George G. Garver, Sept. 14, 1970, available from the General Superintendent, HISD.

CHAPTER 7. ALL HELL BROKE LOOSE

1. Leonel Castillo, "Confusion at HISD," *Papel Chicano,* Sept. 26–Oct. 9, 1970, p. 3.
2. This was a misleading comment since it was part of school board business to allow public input at the end of each meeting. See Frank Davis, "Militant Latins Disrupt Meeting of School Board," *Houston Post,* no date, probably Sept. 15, 1970, p. 7A, in Gregory Salazar Collection, Blue Folder, HMRC.
3. L. Castillo, "Confusion at HISD," pp. 3–4.
4. Ibid., p. 4. Mrs. Cullen's comment was made after the mini-riot but it illustrated her support of MAEC's right to be heard, especially since they "sent in their requests." See Davis, "Militant Latins Disrupt Meeting."
5. L. Castillo, "Confusion at HISD," p. 4.
6. Ibid.
7. Ibid.
8. Ibid., p. 4; Lorenzo Díaz, "Struggle Never Ends," *Papel Chicano,* Sept. 26–Oct. 9, 1970, p. 5.
9. Barrio-MAYO was organized in April, 1969, but it was not fully chartered as a branch of the statewide MAYO group until May 10, 1969. See "MAYO Platform," undated MS., p. 1, in Luís Cano Collection, Box 1, unfoldered materials, HMRC. On the establishment of UH-MAYO see "LOMAS Becomes MAYO; Chicano Conference Ends," *Daily Cougar,* Mar. 10, 1970, p. 8.
10. See "MAYO Platform," undated MS., pp. 1–2, in Luís Cano Collection, Box 1, unfoldered materials, HMRC.
11. See ibid.
12. " 'Gringos' May Be Killed To Force Changes, Hints MAYO Leader," *Houston Chronicle,* Apr. 11, 1969, sec. 1, p. 6.
13. For an elaboration of Barrio-MAYO's views in the early 1970s see "MAYO Positions," undated MS., pp. 1–3, in Gregory Salazar Collection, Box 1, Barrio Program Folder, HMRC.
14. Jaime de la Isla, interview by author, June, 1999, Houston, Tex.
15. Pete Wittenberg, "MAYO at U of H Endorses Revolution, Rejects Violence," *Houston Post,* Mar. 8, 1971, newspaper clipping found in Gregory Salazar Collection, Box 1, MAYO Clippings Folder, HMRC.
16. For media reporting on these events see the following newspaper articles: *Houston Chronicle,* Feb. 16, 1970, sec. 1, p. 1; Feb. 17, 1970, sec. 1, p. 7; Feb. 19, 1970, sec. 3, p. 4; Feb. 20, 1970, p. 1; Feb. 26, 1970, p. 1; Feb. 27, 1970, pp. 1, 2. For a brief overview of these events see De León, *Ethnicity in the Sunbelt,* pp. 178–79; and Kreneck, *Del Pueblo,* pp. 158–59.

17. The First Presbyterian Church filed a suit against MAYO after some of its members disrupted church services in the first week of April. Named defendants were Gregory Salazar, Yolanda Garza Birdwell, Pedro Vásquez, Poncho Ruíz, and Bonito [sic] Maldonado. See "Church Works against MAYO," *Daily Cougar,* Apr. 8, 1970, p. 4.

18. "MAYO Criticizes Ideas Conference," *Daily Cougar,* Apr. 23, 1970, p. 1; Jim Rice, "Latins Disrupt Banquet, Insult Sen. Tower, Officials," *Houston Chronicle,* undated newspaper clipping, in Gregory Salazar Collection, unfoldered materials, HMRC.

19. For media reporting on these events see the following newspaper articles: *Houston Chronicle,* Apr. 6, 1970, sec. 1, p. 7; Apr. 7, 1970, sec. 1, p. 5; Apr. 11, 1970, sec. 1, p. 11; Apr. 28, 1970, sec. 1, p. 5; and June 8, 1970, sec. 1, p. 24. See also Kreneck, *Del Pueblo,* pp. 158–59; and Elmer Bertelsen, "Violence Erupts," pp. 1, 12.

20. UH-MAYO, for instance, held workshops on campus on the proposed antiwar moratorium and protested at the University of Houston law school. See J. M. Contreras, "Chicano Workshop Plans August 29 Moratorium," *Dailey Cougar,* July 9, 1970, p. 3; "MAYO To Hold Chicano Rally," *Summer Cougar,* July 23, 1970, p. 8; "MAYO Criticizes Ideas Conference," *Daily Cougar,* Apr. 23, 1970, p. 1.

21. Salazar, for instance, held informal discussions with students in the senior high huelga school on what they should be learning and doing to improve the education of Chicanos. Most likely these discussions led to the organization of the Chicano Student Committee. See "Huelga Schools," undated newspaper clipping, Gregory Salazar Collection, Box 1, Blue Folder, HMRC.

22. For a list of a few of the Chicano Student Committee's (CSC) demands see "MAYO's Busted at School Board," in *La Raza vs. School Board,* a four-page newsletter that appears to be a MAEC publication and probably was published on Sept. 17, 1970, in Gregory Salazar Collection, Blue Folder, HMRC. I have been unable to locate all the demands prepared by CSC.

23. Mexican Americans were not the only ones present to protest the integration plan. Conservative Anglos also showed up to oppose the mandated integration plan and to support a freedom of choice plan. Board members J. W. McCullough, Jr., and Dr. Ed Franklin were supporters of this alternative. See Bertelsen, "Violence Erupts," p. 12.

24. L. Castillo, "Confusion at HISD," p. 4.

25. Pedro Vasquez, "Brown Power," *Papel Chicano,* Sept. 26–Oct. 9, 1970, p. 2.

26. Díaz, "Struggle Never Ends," p. 5.

27. One source said that two MAYO members, Yolanda Garza Birdwell and Gregory Salazar, rushed forward as board president Dr. Leonard R. Robbins began to get up and leave the meeting. See "MAYO's Busted at School Board," in *La Raza vs. School Board,* Gregory Salazar Collection, Blue Folder, HMRC; Bertelsen, "Violence Erupts," p. 1.

28. One other source reported Salazar as saying, "You're going to have a mess if you don't sit down and listen." See Davis, "Militant Latins Disrupt Meeting." Salazar was upset not simply because MAEC's and CSC's demands were not going to be heard but also because he was planning to condemn the presence of the military

on secondary school campuses. The abrupt cancellation of the meeting deprived him of this opportunity. See Bertelsen, "Violence Erupts," p. 1.

29. Díaz, "Struggle Never Ends," p. 5.

30. Vásquez, "Brown Power," p. 2.

31. Josie Pérez also saw the police hit Edgar. See ibid.

32. L. Castillo, "Confusion at HISD," p. 7.

33. "MAYO's Busted at School Board," in *La Raza vs. School Board*, Gregory Salazar Collection, Blue Folder, HMRC; Bertelsen, "Violence Erupts," p. 1.

34. Bertelsen, "Violence Erupts," pp. 1, 12.

35. Luís Cano recalls that he was outside the school board meeting on that night because it was packed inside. Once the "mini-riot" began he joined the other MAYO members and helped overturn chairs and tables. Once the arrests began he left through a side door. See Luís Cano, interview by author, Houston, Tex., Mar., 1991.

36. Bertelsen, "Violence Erupts," p. 12.

37. The other five individuals were: Carlos Carrizal Calbillo, age twenty-one, a community organizer; José Francisco Campos, age seventeen, unemployed; Anthony Merced López, age seventeen, a student; Hector Almendárez, age nineteen, a laborer; and Santos Hernández, age thirty, a draftsman. See Bertelsen, "Violence Erupts," p. 12.

38. John Castillo, "14 Arrested at HISD," *Papel Chicano*, Sept. 26–Oct. 9, 1970, p. 7.

39. Ironically, before the disturbance the board voted to appeal to the U.S. Supreme Court one of MAEC's main objections to the district's desegregation plan. See Bertelsen, "Violence Erupts," p. 1.

40. Ibid., p. 12.

41. Frank Davis, "Misunderstood, Latin Says," *Houston Post*, no date found, in Gregory Salazar Collection, Blue Folder, HMRC.

42. Both Castillo and Ramírez felt that it could negatively impact MAEC's negotiations with the board. See Leonel Castillo, interview by author; Abraham Ramírez, Jr., interview.

43. See Frank Davis, "Misunderstood, Latin Says."

44. School officials responded negatively to this action. Robbins, for instance, called the disturbance tragic, and Reverend Everett, who had expressed some support for MAEC the week before, now said that he did not feel like supporting the group in "any of its demands." See Bertelsen, "Violence Erupts," p. 12.

45. This was in response to the mistaken belief that MAYO engaged in disruption at the school board meeting in support of freedom-of-choice, a position taken by conservative groups in the city opposed to integration. See Frank Davis, "Boycotters Given Rules for Returning," *Houston Post*, Sept. 17, 1970, p. 20A.

46. The mainstream media reported that other unnamed witnesses reported police used restraint until they were struck by the demonstrators and after the young militants began smashing furniture and damaging the sliding wall in the board room. For the different accounts of what occurred at the school board meeting see Davis, "Boycotters Given Rules," p. 20A; Bertelsen, "Violence Erupts," p. 12.

47. Vásquez, "Brown Power," p. 2

48. Díaz, "Struggle Never Ends," p. 5.

49. Dolores Castillo, "Chicano Power," *Papel Chicano*, Dec. 12–Jan. 15, 1971, p. 9.

50. Bertelsen, "Chicanos Plan To End Boycott," p. 1; "Boycott Ends," *Papal Chicano*, Sept. 5–25, 1970, p. 3.

51. J. Castillo, "14 Arrested at HISD," p. 8.

52. Steve Singer, "Behind School Boycott: New Image of Chicano," *Houston Chronicle*, Sept. 6, 1970, sec. 1, p. 1.

53. Ibid., p. 19.

54. William Ashworth, "Boycotts, Hallmark of Rights Era," *Houston Post*, undated, newspaper clipping, Gregory Salazar Collection, unfoldered materials, HMRC.

55. Lucy Moreno interview, June 1, 1999, and Ralph Moreno interview.

56. Singer, "Behind School Boycott," p. 19.

57. Ashworth, "Boycotts, Hallmark of Rights Era."

58. Singer, "Behind School Boycott," p. 19.

59. I. García, *Chicanismo*.

60. J. Castillo, "14 Arrested at HISD," p. 8.

61. L. Castillo, "Confusion at HISD," p. 4.

62. Ibid.

63. Ibid.

64. Ibid.

65. Ibid.

66. In addition to assuring compliance with the demands in particular and to promoting additional school changes, MAEC's future role also became one of increased educational activities, especially in developing alternative or parallel community educational services and institutions. This renewed interest in community education emerged out of its participation in the huelga schools. See L. Castillo, "Confusion at HISD," p. 4.

CHAPTER 8. SIMPLE JUSTICE

1. The decision to ask for a stay in the Fifth Circuit Court's order, made on November 9, 1970, was prompted specifically by that court's recent decision granting a stay order to the Fort Lauderdale, Florida, public schools. Prior to this decision, the Circuit Court had not granted stay orders in cases of desegregation rulings. See "Regular Meeting of Nov. 9, 1970," *School Board Reporter*, HISD, p. 1.

2. "5th Circuit Court Denies HISD Plea To Delay Pairing," *Houston Chronicle*, Dec. 12, 1970, sec. 1, pp. 1, 3.

3. "Board To Appeal Pairing Order to District Court," *Houston Chronicle*, Dec. 13, 1970, p. 17F; Elmer Bertelsen, "Board's Proposal To Alter Pairing Given to Judge," *Houston Chronicle*, Dec. 14, 1970, sec. 1, pp. 1, 4.

4. Bertelsen, "Board's Proposal," pp. 1, 4.

5. For a review of Garver's comments on the drafting of this plan see "Board Adopts Plan To Be Submitted to Judge Connally for Pairing Elementary schools," *Regular Board Meeting*, Dec. 16, 1970, HISD, p. 4. For MAEC's views see Leonel Castillo,

letter to Leonard Robbins, Jan. 8, 1971, Abe Ramírez Collection, Box 1, No. 20, HMRC.

6. Barry Lawes, "Chicanos Are Considering Second School Boycott," *Houston Chronicle,* Dec. 17, 1970, p. 1A.

7. Mel Freeland, "21 School Pairing Proposal Would Transfer 2043," *Houston Chronicle,* Dec. 16, 1970, sec. 1, p. 1. The final number reported by the board was not 2,043 but 1,876. See "Board Adopts Plan," *Regular Board Meeting,* Dec. 16, 1970, HISD, p. 3.

8. "Board Adopts Plan," *Regular Board Meeting,* Dec. 16, 1970, HISD, pp. 3–4. Likewise, the new pairing plan fell short of achieving the 10 percent integration ratio required by Judge Connally's guidelines. According to Judge Connally's guidelines, a school in which at least 10 percent of the pupils were of a minority race was considered integrated.

9. The superintendent, speaking on behalf of all those involved in the formulation of the new plan, believed that "perhaps we could accomplish a pairing concept and not have as much disruption as that plan might create" (Freeland, "21 School Pairing Proposal," p. l).

10. "Board Adopts Plan," *Regular Board Meeting,* Dec. 16, 1970, HISD, p. 4.

11. Barry Lawes, "Latins Talk Second School Boycott," *Houston Chronicle,* Dec. 17, 1970, sec. 1, pp. 1, 18; Frank Davis, "Pairing Plan Omits 2 Boycott Schools," *Houston Post,* Dec. 18, 1970, p. 3A.

12. Lawes, "Latins Talk Second School Boycott," pp. 1, 18.

13. Lawes, "Chicanos Are Considering," p. 1.

14. Lawes, "Latins Talk Second School Boycott," pp. 1, 18; Davis, "Pairing Plan," p. 3A.

15. For additional responses by the Mexican American community to the pairing plan see Maggie Landron, "Hell No, No Vamos," *Papel Chicano,* Feb. 3, 1971, pp. 1, 14.

16. MAEC honored four persons who were instrumental in organizing the fall boycott: Mrs. Carmen Beltran, community activist; Sister Gloria Gallardo, coordinator of the huelga schools; Abraham Ramírez, Jr., legal adviser; and Leonel Castillo, chair. See "MAEC Honors 4 Leaders in Boycott of Schools," *Houston Post,* Dec. 16, 1970, p. 18A.

17. Lawes, "Chicanos Are Considering," p. 13.

18. Davis, "Pairing Plan," p. 3A.

19. Ibid.

20. Integration, Barrio-MAYO leaders argued, was a " 'white liberal handout' to hide the fact that the minds of American children are being destroyed by the lack of relevance and meaning of what is taught." See "MAYO on the Issue of Integration," *Papel Chicano,* Jan. 16–29, [1971], p. 12.

21. See ibid., p. 12. MAYO also proposed that HISD should be divided into smaller school districts, each with its own school board. See Davis, "Pairing Plan," p. 3A.

22. *El Plan Espiritual de Aztlan,* Mar. 29, 1969, Gregory Salazar Collection, Crusade for Justice Folder, HMRC. For the list of workshops and activities at the 1970 National Chicano Youth Liberation Conference, see *National Chicano Youth Liberation Conference of Aztlan* (program), Mar. 25–29, 1969, Gregory Salazar Collection, Crusade for Justice Folder, HMRC.

23. For a fascinating history of this peaceful revolution see Navarro, *The Cristal Experiment.*

24. This new emphasis is apparent in a letter Castillo wrote to Dr. Robbins, president of the school board, on January 8. See Leonel Castillo, letter to Leonard Robbins, Jan. 8, 1971, Abe Ramírez Collection, Box 1, No. 20, HMRC.

25. See Landron, "Hell No," p. 14.

26. Leonel Castillo, letter to Leonard Robbins, Jan. 8, 1971, Abe Ramírez Collection, Box 1, No. 20, HMRC.

27. Ibid.

28. John Wheat, letter to Leonel J. Castillo, Jan. 7, 1971, Abe Ramírez Collection, Box 1, No. 20, HMRC. Note that this letter makes reference to Castillo's January 5 letter, but I have not been able to find it.

29. Louis Tellez, second vice chair, would present on the Northside barrio; Romualdo M. Castillo, first vice chair, would report on Port Houston and Denver Harbor; Ben Reyes, treasurer, on the Second Ward; and Sister Gloria Gallardo, assistant secretary, on Magnolia. See Outline of Presentation, Jan. 19, 1971, Abe Ramírez Collection, Box 1, No. 6, HMRC.

30. I have been unable to find the actual statements or minutes of this hearing. The only source I have found is Castillo's presentation and an interview with him. See Leonel J. Castillo, interview by author.

31. Leonel J. Castillo's Remarks Before Bi-Racial Committee, Jan. 19, 1971, Abe Ramírez Collection, Box 1, No. 6, HMRC.

32. Ibid.

33. One source reports that on December 31, 1970, HISD officials filed with the district court a motion to amend the pairing order. But it is unclear whether this was in reference to the plan that had been approved on December 16 or to a new one incorporating the ideas of Mexican Americans as members of an identifiable minority ethnic group. See Jerris Leonard, assistant attorney general, Office for Civil Rights, letter to Ben C. Connally, Mar. 17, 1971, p. 3, Abe Ramírez Collection, Box 1, No. 21, HMRC.

34. "MAEC To Meet: School Pairing To Start Soon," *Denver Harbor News,* Jan. 28, 1971, p. 1.

35. The school board did make special provision for families with children of different ages. According to the board, if more than one child in a family attended an elementary school, all of them would attend the same school. See "MAEC To Meet," *Denver Harbor News,* Jan. 28, 1971, p. 1.

36. See Landron, "Hell No," p. 14.

37. Tomás García, "Justice: A Struggle But How Long La Raza?," *Papel Chicano,* July 29, 1971, pp. 8–9.

38. "Noncooperation in Pairing Urged," *Houston Chronicle,* Jan. 29, 1971, sec. 1, p. 1; Richard Vera, "Chicanos Balk at Pairing Order," *Houston Post,* Jan. 29, 1971, p. 1A.

39. Castillo stated that one major huelga school and some neighborhood ones could be established in three days. See Bill Furlow, "Parents Threaten To Set Up Schools," *Houston Post,* Feb. 9, 1971, p. 6A.

40. Landron, "Hell No," p. 14.
41. Although huelga schools were promised, few were established. Sister Gloria, a MAEC member, stated that a huelga school would be opening up with a teaching staff for up to six hundred students. No concrete evidence, however, has been found of this or any other school. Sister Gloria, the huelga school coordinator, left the religious order several years after the boycott. For her comments about the huelga school see "One Student Stabbed, 12 Hurt in Sam Houston Clash," *Houston Chronicle,* Feb. 5, 1971, sec. 1, pp. 1, 6. Castillo did not recall this or any other schools, nor did he know where Sister Gloria might be residing. See Leonel Castillo, interview by author.
42. "Noncooperation in Pairing Urged," *Houston Chronicle,* Jan. 29, 1971, sec. 1, p. 1; Vera, "Chicanos Balk," p. 1A.
43. "Pairings Begin without Incident," *Houston Chronicle,* Jan. 29, 1971, sec. 1, p. 1.
44. Landron, "Hell No," p. 1.
45. Only 75 out of 150 children, most of them Anglos, boarded the bus going to Dobson. See Pedro Vásquez, "Adelante MAEC," *Papel Chicano* (1971): 4.
46. Ibid.
47. Vasquez notes that the counselor at Port Houston later took five more individuals to Pleasantville. In total only seven of the eighty children enrolled in the paired school (see ibid.). The mainstream newspaper reported that only seventy-five pickets were at Port Houston (see "Parents Picket Two Paired Schools Here," *Houston Chronicle,* Feb. 3, 1971, sec. 1, p. 20).
48. Vásquez, "Adelante MAEC," p. 4.
49. "One Student Stabbed," *Houston Chronicle,* Feb. 5, 1971, sec. 1, pp. 1, 6.
50. Vásquez, "Adelante MAEC," p. 4.
51. Ibid.
52. Ibid.
53. See, for instance, the low estimates of individuals out of school and picketing the schools as reported in the mainstream newspaper ("Parents Picket," *Houston Chronicle,* Feb. 3, 1971, sec. 1, p. 20).
54. Vásquez, "Adelante MAEC," p. 4.
55. Maggie Landron, "Pairing Brings Picketers," *Papel Chicano,* Feb. 20, 1971, pp. 1, 4.
56. Ibid., p. 4.
57. Ibid.
58. Ibid.
59. Three additional actions also were mentioned:

    1. Why MAEC supported separate school districts with "communities of common interests (and) with equal per capita income distribution";
    2. Why MAEC criticized all groups opposed to busing and in support of "neighborhood schools";
    3. Why MAEC opposed "minority with minority" integration and assimilation.

    See "Conservatives, Liberals, All the Same," *Papel Chicano,* Feb. 20, 1971, p. 7.

60. Ibid.
61. Ibid.
62. Ibid.
63. Ibid.

CHAPTER 9. CONTINUING THE STRUGGLE

1. Abraham Ramírez, Jr., letter to Leonel Castillo, Catholic Council on Community Relations, May 20, 1971, Abraham Ramírez Collection, Box 1, No. 20, HMRC.
2. Memorandum: On Motions To Amend Decree and To Intervene, May 24, 1971, *Ross v Eckels,* Civil Action No. 10444, p. 1.
3. The court also ruled that the HISD's modified plan for pairing elementary schools to achieve racial desegregation was unacceptable. See Memorandum: On Motions To Amend Decree and To Intervene, May 24, 1971, *Ross v Eckels,* Civil Action No. 10444, p. 2.
4. For the response by NAACP and the school district see "Judge Raps Chicanos Over Pairing Protest," *Houston Chronicle,* May 26, 1971, sec. 1, p. 11; "Houston Pairing Plan Is Ruled Unacceptable," *Houston Chronicle,* May 25, 1971, sec. 1, p. 1.
5. "Judge Raps Chicanos Over Pairing Protest," *Houston Chronicle,* May 26, 1971, p. 11.
6. De León reports the following approximate figures for the period from 1950 to 1970:

Year	Total Population	Mexican American	% of Total
1950	600,000	40,000	.06
1960	938,000	75,000	7.90
1970	1,200,000	144,000	12.00

See De León, *Ethnicity in the Sunbelt,* p. 98, 147.
7. *Public Law 90-247* [The Bilingual Education Act], 81 Stat. 816, 20 U.S.C.A. 880(b) (Jan. 2, 1968).
8. Under this provision the executive branch of the federal government was mandated to establish an enforcement mechanism aimed at ensuring that no person in the United States would "on the ground of race, color, or national origin, be excluded from participation in, be denied the benefits of, or be subjected to discrimination under any program or activity receiving Federal financial assistance." The ultimate sanction available under the enforcement mechanism was the termination of the eligibility of a school district to receive federal assistance. See *Civil Rights Act of 1964,* Sec. 601, 78 Stat. 252, 42 U.S.C. 2000d.
9. See, for instance, U.S. Department of Health, Education, and Welfare, Office for Civil Rights, "Identification of Discrimination and Denial of Services on the Basis of National Origin," *Federal Register* 35, no. 139 (1970): 11595–96.

10. See, for instance, *Cisneros v Corpus Christi Independent School District,* 324 F. Supp. 599 (S.D. Tex 1970).

11. He was making reference to a national survey of the educational opportunities of Mexican Americans conducted by the Office of Civil Rights. These reports were published between 1969 and 1974. The one on segregation was officially published in 1972, but its findings were reported in 1970. See U.S. Commission on Civil Rights, *The Excluded Student,* Report III: Mexican American Study (Washington D.C.: Government Printing Office, 1972).

12. Frank Davis, "Attorney Urges Appeal of Court School Rulings," *Houston Post,* May 26, 1971, pp. 1A, 2A.

13. The article was in Spanish, and this is my translation of López's comments. See Eduardo N. López, "Carta Abierta Al Juez Federal Ben C. Connally," *Papel Chicano,* June 12, 1971, p. 2.

14. Felix Ramírez, "The Supreme Duty," *Papel Chicano,* June 12, 1971, p. 3.

15. Davis, "Attorney Urges Appeal," pp. 1A, 2A.

16. "8 Schools Here Becoming Neighborhood Centers," *Houston Chronicle,* Mar. 21, 1971, sec. 4, p. 6.

17. No evidence has been found yet to suggest that MAEC met with her office or that there was any follow-up on this request for a meeting. See Leonel J. Castillo, letter to Beatrice M. Smith, director, Title I/Model Cities Planning and Coordination Department, HISD. Apr. 2, 1971, Abraham Ramírez Collection, Box 1, No. 20, HMRC.

18. I have been unable to find the names of the original biracial committee, but one of the Mexican American individuals apparently appointed was Frank Piñedo, a local attorney. The board nominated Piñedo in early September. See "Five Nominated to Bi-Racial School Panel," *Houston Chronicle,* Sept. 8, 1970, sec. 1, p. 1. In mid-December the Department of Health, Education, and Welfare (HEW) suggested expanding the biracial committee to include five members to represent Mexican Americans and the poor. No action was taken at this time, although John Wheat, acting chair of the committee, stated that he would welcome additions. See Elmer Bertelsen, "HEW Suggests Chicanos Be Added to School Panel," *Houston Chronicle,* Dec. 18, 1970, sec. 1, p. 1.

19. Garza was the first Mexican American to be hired in a high administrative position. In February, 1971, he was hired as one of six area superintendents. See Tom Curtis, "Area Supt. Garza Recalls: Someone Took an Interest," *Houston Chronicle,* Sept. 15, 1971, sec. 4, pp. 1, 9.

20. The list of names, he argued, was submitted to the Justice Department in Houston prior to the formation of the committee. "I doubt the names were presented," noted Ramírez. See Abraham Ramírez, Jr., letter to Gonzalo Garza, Area 5, assistant superintendent, May 20, 1971, Abe Ramírez Collection, Box 1, No. 6, HMRC.

21. Maggie Landron, "Franklin Parents Confront School," *Papel Chicano,* 1, no. 15 (1971): 2.

22. Ibid.

23. Ibid.

24. Ibid.

25. "Cinco de Mayo Student Walkout," *Papel Chicano* 1, no. 16 (May 21, 1971): 7. Although it is unclear how many other schools in Houston participated, some evidence suggests that at least two other cities — Corpus Christi and San Marcos — were involved in walkouts. See above as well as "School Boycott Set on Mexican Holiday," *El Sol,* May 7, 1971, p. 1.

26. "Raza Pushed Around at Burnet Elementary," *Papel Chicano* 1, no. 16 (May 21, 1971): 3.

27. The trophy was called the "Lamp for Learning." See "Houston School Board Cited for Best Achievement in U.S.," *Houston Chronicle,* May 11, 1971, sec. 1, p. 1.

28. "Chicanos Protest Award for Board," *Houston Chronicle,* May 20, 1971, sec. 1, p. 20.

29. The exchange program met from 8:30 to 10:30 A.M. Tuesday through Thursday. The project coordinator was Gene Lozano. See "Students Protest Conditions in Jeff Davis," *Papel Chicano* 1 (July, 1971): 5.

30. "HISD-Band-Aid of the Year Award," *Papel Chicano,* Aug. 12, 1971, p. 14.

31. Irene S. Sanley and Jerry P. McGee, "Area Citizens Propose New East End School District," *Houstoneer,* June 9, 1971, p. 1.

32. Quiñones's proposal was made on June 9, 1971, two weeks after Anglos in the wealthy Westheimer area proposed the creation of a new school district that would serve the middle-class white students residing in the western part of the HISD. See Elmer Bertelsen, "Group Is Moving To Carve Out New School District," *Houston Chronicle,* May 28, 1971, sec. 1, p. 1.

33. Sanley and McGee, "Area Citizens," p. 1.

34. Mr. Quiñones dropped this idea once the local school board members eliminated the school his child was attending from the desegregation plan. See Mario Quiñones, interview by author, June 23, 1995, Houston, Tex.

35. Leonel J. Castillo, letter to Richard Holgin, executive director, Magnolia Business Center, Inc., Jan. 20, 1971, Abraham Ramírez Collection, Box 1, No. 20, HMRC.

36. After the September, 1970, boycott MAEC transformed some of the huelga schools into extensive tutoring or college counseling programs. Castillo and others also developed plans for a Mexican American college. Most of the funding for these activities came from these community-based fund-raisers. See Leonel J. Castillo, letter to Richard Holgin, executive director, Magnolia Business Center, Inc., Jan. 20, 1971, Abraham Ramírez Collection, Box 1, No. 20, HMRC.

37. Before it could incorporate as MAEC, the organization had to have the permission of another similarly named group in Waco. This hurdle was resolved by the second week in January. See Abraham Ramírez, Jr., letter to Martin Dies, Jr., secretary of state, Jan. 4, 1971, Abraham Ramírez Collection, Box 1, No. 7, HMRC; and Abraham Ramírez, Jr., letter to Sam Gómez, Mexican American Educational Foundation, Jan. 7, 1971, Abraham Ramírez Collection, Box 1, No. 7, HMRC.

38. The Mexican American Education Council's purpose was to "study, plan, coordinate, encourage, promote and execute the members' wishes in securing an equitable education for the Mexican American." The Council also provided "leadership, direction and resources for the educational objectives of its people." See Constitution of the Mexican American Education Council, n.d., in Abe Ramírez

Collection, Box 1, No. 7, HMRC. For the official incorporation papers see Office of the Secretary of State, Certificate of Incorporation of Mexican American Education Council, Incorporated, Charter No. 285645, Jan. 22, 1971, in Abe Ramírez Collection, Box 1, No. 7, HMRC.

39. MAEC's incorporation afforded the organization some form of stability to conduct its activities, but there was a failure of attention to taxes; on September 8, 1972, the organization's charter was revoked due to nonpayment of franchise taxes. By 1973 the organization had changed its name to the Educational Advancement for Mexican Americans. See Abraham Ramírez, Jr., letter to Mexican American Education Council, Sept. 29, 1972, in Abe Ramírez Collection, Box 1, No. 20, HMRC, which informs the membership of the forfeiture of the charter effective September 8. He also asks that his name be deleted as "registered agent" for the organization. In 1973 Raul De Anda was "director" of the organization. For a brief history of MAEC see Richard Vara, "A New Educational Era Dawned," *M.A.E.C.-E.S.A.A. Newsletter* 1 (Oct.–Nov., 1973): n.pag. This apparently was an article that originally appeared in the *Houston Post*, Oct. 28, 1973.

40. Enrique Pérez, "MAEC Funded for $65,000," *Papel Chicano*, Apr. 1, [1971], p. 3.

41. Leonel J. Castillo, letter to MAEC officers, Mar. 19, 1971, Abe Ramírez Collection, Box 1, No. 20, HMRC.

42. Pérez, "MAEC Funded," p. 3.

43. Leonel J. Castillo, letter to Henry Ramírez, U.S. Commission on Civil Rights, June 2, 1971, Abe Ramírez Collection, Box 1, No. 20, HMRC.

CHAPTER 10. THE MOST RACIST PLAN YET

1. Brief for the Appellees, *Ross v Eckels*, No. 71-2347, Aug. 13, 1971, p. 8. This document lists the types of actions taken by the school board during the past two years in order to meet the special needs of Mexican American students.

2. Ibid., p. 9.

3. Curtis, "Area Supt. Garza Recalls," pp. 1, 9.

4. In late July the HISD school board received legal sanction from the Fifth Circuit Court. This court called for some modifications but approved the plan as submitted (Brief for the Appellees, *Ross v Eckels*, No. 71-2347, Aug. 13, 1971, p. 9).

5. HISD school administration also asked for funds to cover other costs associated with the implementation of the court order (ibid.).

6. Mel Freeland, "Triethnic Panel To Review 41 Aid Applications," *Houston Chronicle*, Aug. 7, 1971, sec. 1, p. 1.

7. The Mexican Americans appointed were: Dramartina (Tina) Reyes, Joe Ramos, Mrs. Carmen Flores, Armando Martínez, and Adam Treviño. Reyes had been one of the huelga coordinators during the boycott activities of September, 1970. See "HISD Names Triethnic Panel To Get Funds," *Houston Chronicle*, Aug. 6, 1971, sec. 1, p. 2.

8. The total proposal included five other components in addition to transportation: preschool bilingual TV series, $1.6 million; High School of Performing and Visual

Arts, $361,000; Mexican American community programs, $298,000; and 3-4-5 Club, $317,000. See Freeland, "Triethnic Panel," pp. 1, 2.

9. "Triethnic Panel OKs Aid Requests," *Houston Chronicle,* Aug. 12, 1971, sec. 1, p. 5.

10. Tom Curtis, "Involves Pairing in 22 Units," *Houston Chronicle,* Aug. 7, 1971, sec. 1, p. 1.

11. Under the proposal for the paired schools there were four alternatives: bus all children at the paired schools; bus all children who live more than one mile from the schools to which they are assigned; bus all children who live more than two miles from their schools; or bus nobody. He also suggested staggered bus schedules as a possibility so that fewer buses would be required. See ibid.

12. Conservative member J. W. McCullough, Jr., opposed any busing unless all the children in the district who had to take "hazardous routes" were also provided this service. The board agreed to postpone the decision until information indicating how many children took "hazardous routes" could be determined. See "Board Defers Action on Busing Children to Paired Schools," *Houston Chronicle,* July 13, 1971, sec. 1, p. 10.

13. During the week of August 8–15, the school board was embroiled in a controversy over the firing of Dr. Garver as superintendent of the schools. His firing was due to dissatisfactions on the part of several conservative school board members. Leon Everett, the only African American on the board, provided the decisive vote to oust Garver. Mexican Americans were not active participants in this internal power struggle. For a positive evaluation of Garver prior to his dismissal see "Garver Rating by Trustees above Par," *Houston Chronicle,* Aug. 24, 1971, sec. 1, pp. 1, 8. For Garver's response to this firing, see Elmer Bertelsen, "Garver Fired, Plans Quick Appeal," *Houston Chronicle,* Aug. 24, 1971, sec. 1, pp. 1, 8; Tom Curtis, "Save Schools from Politics, Garver Says," *Houston Chronicle,* Aug. 25, 1971, sec. 1, pp. 1, 8; Elmer Bertelsen, "Garver Calls Firing Illegal and Political," *Houston Chronicle,* Aug. 24, 1971, sec. 1, pp. 1, 8.

14. Out of the twenty-two paired schools three of them had a bilingual education program: Looscan, Anson Jones, and Sherman. According to the writer, one of the results of the pairing would be that the bilingual programs "will be completely destroyed now." See "HISD Announces Racist Pairing Plan Again," *Papel Chicano,* July 15, 1971, p. 2.

15. Ibid.

16. Abel Álvarez, "Letters to the Editor," *Papel Chicano,* July 15, 1971, p. 13.

17. Tomás García, "MAEC—What's It All About," *Papel Chicano,* July 15, 1971, p. 2.

18. An election for MAEC officers was held in late June. Romualdo Castillo replaced Leonel Castillo in June, 1971; Leonel Castillo had been chair since June, 1970. Although they had the same last name, they were not related. See "MAEC Elects Officers," *Papel Chicano* 1 (July, 1971): 6; Tom Curtis, "Massive Chicano Boycott of HISD School Brewing," *Houston Chronicle,* Aug. 1, 1971, sec. 1, p. 1.

19. "Latin Group To Fight HISD Pairing Plan," *Houston Chronicle,* July 4, 1971, sec. 4, p. 2. The latter quote comes from "HISD Announces Racist Pairing Plan Again," *Papel Chicano,* July 15, 1971, p. 2.

20. Carolyn Raeke, "MAYOs Here Fold: New Group Foreseen," *Houston Post,* Mar. 2,

1971, n.pag., newspaper clipping, in Gregory Salazar Collection, Box 1, MAYO Clippings Folder, HMRC.

21. "Chicano Youth Council," *Papel Chicano* 1 ([Jan.?], 1971): 7.

22. Richard Vara, "These Chicanos Came Back," *Houston Post,* n.d., n.pag., newspaper clipping, in Luís Cano Collection, Box B, unfoldered materials, HMRC.

23. This house was located at 102 Sampson ("AAMA Sponsors Rally at Settegast Park," *Papel Chicano,* July 29, 1971, p. 8). For information on the origins of AAMA see Luís Cano, interview by author, Mar., 1991, Houston, Tex. Some information on its history can be gleaned from several documents, including *Programs and Services of AAMA,* Nov. 18, 1974, pp. 1–3, Luís Cano Collection, Box I, Capability State-ment Folder, HMRC; and *Programs and Services of AAMA,* undated (probably 1975), pp. 1–3, Luís Cano Collection, Box D, unfoldered materials, HMRC.

24. "AAMA Sponsors Rally," *Papel Chicano,* July 29, 1971, p. 8.

25. They were not allowed to speak until after four hours of regular board business. See "HISD Board Meeting Dedicated 'Just-us,'" *Papel Chicano,* July 29, 1971, p. 9.

26. "MAEC Declares Boycott Against HISD," *Papel Chicano* 2, no. 1 (Aug. 12, 1971): 1. Many in the Mexican American community supported MAEC. Representative of this support was Tomás García's comments in an article he wrote in early July in support of MAEC's efforts to seek justice in the schools. To get justice, he argued, more work needed to be done "by each one of us and together with groups such as MAEC." See Tomás García, "Justice," pp. 8–9.

27. See "Boycott the Hell Out of Them: Editorial," *Papel Chicano,* Aug. 12, 1971, p. 6.

28. Curtis, "Massive Chicano Boycott," p. 1.

29. Ibid.

30. In addition to a triethnic desegregation plan and the recognition of Mexican Americans as a separate ethnic group, MAEC also sought instruction in Chicano studies in the school curriculum and more Mexican American teachers and ad-ministrators. See ibid.

31. Ibid.

32. "Latin Group To Fight HISD Pairing Plan," *Houston Chronicle,* July 4, 1971, sec. 4, p. 2; Ricardo L. Garza, Attorney, Memorandum to Ed Idar, Jr., prominent civil rights lawyer, June 27, 1973, Abe Ramírez Collection, Box 1, No. 22, HMRC. The latter document "lists cases and cites various comments in which Americans of Mexican descent or Chicanos have been referred to as a group, or as a race, na-tionality or a class." It covers the period from 1931 to 1973.

33. "MAEC Preparing for Possible Boycott of Houston Schools," *Texas Catholic Her-ald,* Aug. 6, 1971, p. 1.

34. Scroggins had been paired with Eliot and Atherton Elementary according to the district's integration plan. Atherton had first and second grades, Eliot had third and fourth grades, and Scroggins had fifth and sixth grades. According to the plan all the schools would have a kindergarten. See "School Problems: Will There Be a Boycott?," *Houston Post,* Aug. 6, 1971, pp. 1, 4B.

35. Although she supported integration, she was an advocate for "neighborhood schools" and believed that the former could be achieved without eliminating the latter. See ibid., p. 4B.

36. Ibid., pp. 1, 4B.

37. Tom Curtis, "Group To Ask Total Chicano Boycott of Houston Schools," *Houston Chronicle,* Aug. 15, 1971, sec. 1, p. 2.

38. Ibid.

39. Tom Curtis, "Romualdo Castillo: The Times Have Changed—Yet It's the Same," *Houston Chronicle,* Aug. 8, 1971, sec. 2, p. 9.

40. Ibid.

41. "School Problems," *Houston Post,* Aug. 6, 1971, pp. 1, 4B.

42. Community control of schools, the police, and other institutions in the barrio were expressed in several of Barrio-MAYO's statements. See, for instance, *MAYO,* undated, p. 1, Luís Cano Collection, Box E, unfoldered materials, HMRC; and *MAYO Positions,* undated, pp. 1, 3, Gregory Salazar Collection, Box 1, Barrio Program Folder, HMRC.

43. Curtis, "Group To Ask," p. 2.

44. Curtis, "Romualdo Castillo," p. 9.

45. Curtis, "Group To Ask," p. 2.

46. Early expectations of five thousand to six thousand individuals did not materialize. The rally lasted from 2:00 to 6:00 P.M. See "At Moody Park: MAEC Calls for Boycott Support," *Papel Chicano,* Sept. 2, 1971, p. 1.

47. Printed copies of the speeches at this rally have not been found. I have used *Papel Chicano* and the mainstream media as sources for reconstructing Castillo's comments. An interview with him also did not shed any new light. See Tom Curtis, "NAACP Head Would Back Firing of Garver," *Houston Chronicle,* Aug. 16, 1971, sec. 1, p. 16.; "At Moody Park," *Papel Chicano,* Sept. 2, 1971, p. 1; Leonel Castillo, interview by author.

48. Curtis, "NAACP Head," p. 16.

49. For a sample of documents indicating early communication between these federal officials and MAEC leaders such as Castillo, see Leonel Castillo, letter to Armando Rodríguez, Sept. 28, 1970, Abraham Ramírez Collection, Box 1, HMRC; Statement from Martin G. Castillo, Chairman of the Presidents' Cabinet Committee on Opportunity for the Spanish Speaking, Washington, D.C., Sept. 21, 1970, in Abraham Ramírez Collection, Box 1, HMRC. Also see "MAEC Preparing," *Texas Catholic Herald,* Aug. 6, 1971, p. 1.

50. Bill Lee, "LULAC To Fight Integration Plan," *Houston Chronicle,* Oct. 11, 1970, sec. 2, p. 3; Abraham Ramírez, Jr., president, #60, letter to Paul Garza, national president, Sept. 26, 1970, Abraham Ramírez, Jr., Collection, Box 1, No. 11, HMRC (letter requesting immediate action by LULAC national office).

51. Ramírez, Jr., noted that it was difficult to gain the support of LULAC members for MAEC's efforts. Many were interested in participating as individuals but not as an organization. LULAC was still committed to the ideology and tactics of the Mexican American Generation and did not believe in the politics of protest. See Abraham Ramírez, Jr., interview; Lucy Moreno interview, June 1, 1999, and Ralph Moreno interview.

52. Lee, "LULAC To Fight," p. 3; Abraham Ramírez, Jr., president, #60, letter to Paul Garza, national president, Sept. 26, 1970, Abraham Ramírez, Jr., Collection, Box 1,

No. 11, HMRC (letter requesting immediate action by LULAC national office); Abraham Ramírez, Jr., interview; "MAEC Preparing," *Texas Catholic Herald,* Aug. 6, 1971, p. 1.

53. Officially, this was known as the "Triple T" Program. Up until this time the one-year summer program had been concerned with blacks only. The federal government applied pressure on this program to include Mexican Americans in its sessions. See "Browns and Blacks Meet To Discuss Education," *Papel Chicano,* July 29, 1971, p. 2.

54. Sister Gloria's last name is cited as Guarjardo in this and several other articles. According to MAEC documents, however, Sister Gloria's last name was Gallardo. See ibid.

55. Ibid.

56. Curtis, "NAACP Head," p. 16.

57. Curtis, "Romualdo Castillo," p. 9.

58. Curtis, "NAACP Head," p. 16.

59. It is unclear if the two groups ever met with the district. However, at the next regular board meeting, held on Monday, August 23, the school board was too preoccupied with its own internal matters to meet with any groups. That day the board fired Superintendent Garver and created a storm of controversy that would last for the next several weeks. On the Chicano's perspective of his firing see "George Garver Fired, Por Terco," *Papel Chicano,* Sept. 12, 1971, p. 2. For articles explaining the politics of his firing see note 13.

60. NAACP threatened to join the boycott based on the outcome of the proposed meeting with the board. No such meeting took place. See Steve Singer, "Chicanos, NAACP Will Seek Meeting on School Boycott," *Houston Chronicle,* Aug. 22, 1971, sec. 2, p. 7.

61. Leon Everett, the only African American on the school board and one of the most influential African American leaders in Houston, believed, like many other black leaders, that an underlying motivation for the boycott was racism. One of the MAEC leaders acknowledged that many Mexican Americans were boycotting for racist reasons. See, for instance, "Moody [Park] Hosts Raza," *Papel Chicano,* Sept. 5–25, 1970, p. 6.

CHAPTER 11. A RACIST BUNCH OF ANGLOS

1. Dr. Boney became acting general superintendent of the Houston school after the firing of Dr. Garver. Although his tenure as superintendent was brief, he was the first African American to serve as chief administrative officer in the Houston school district. See "Acting School Chief Boney Urges Unity," *Houston Chronicle,* Aug. 24, 1971, sec. 1, p. 1.

2. "Latin School Boycott Fails to Develop," *Houston Chronicle,* Aug. 26, 1971, sec. 1, pp. 1, 6; "199,664 in Public Schools on First Day," *Houston Chronicle,* Aug. 27, 1971, sec. 1, p. 1; "HISD Becomes 'Lost But No Find' Dept.," *Papel Chicano,* Oct. 14, 1971, p. 11.

3. *Papel Chicano* reported that HISD had lost between four thousand and seven

thousand students. See "HISD Becomes 'Lost But No Find' Dept.," *Papel Chicano*, Oct. 14, 1971, p. 11.

4. "Latin School Boycott Fails to Develop," *Houston Chronicle*, Aug. 26, 1971, sec. 1, pp. 1, 6; "199,664 in Public Schools on First Day," *Houston Chronicle*, Aug. 27, 1971, sec. 1, p. 1; "HSD [*sic*] Enrollment Up to 218,316," *El Sol*, Sept. 3, 1971, p. 2.

5. "HSD [*sic*] Enrollment," *El Sol*, Sept. 3, 1971, p. 2; "HISD Becomes 'Lost But No Find' Dept.," *Papel Chicano*, Oct. 14, 1971, p. 11.

6. Charles Guerrero, "Chicanos Slowly Losing 'Cool,'" *Papel Chicano*, Nov. 9, 1971, p. 14; Eduardo López, "Despierten Ya Mejicanos," *Papel Chicano*, Sept. 16, 1971, p. 14; Houston Council on Human Relations, *The Black/Mexican American Project Report*, (Houston: Houston Council on Human Relations, 1972), p. 27.

7. No further information on the leaders or followers or on the goals of the group was provided. See Mel Freeland, "Parents Charge Busing Making 'Instant Drop-outs,'" *Houston Chronicle*, Sept. 3, 1971, sec. 1., p. 1.

8. Freeland, "Parents Charge," p. 1.

9. Ibid.

10. Ibid.

11. The newspaper also argued that racism had impacted the oppression of two other racial groups as well, American Indians and black Americans. See "Racism: The White Supremacy Complex," *Papel Chicano*, 2, no. 2 (Sept. 2, 1971): 5.

12. Guerrero, "Chicanos Slowly Losing 'Cool,'" p. 14.

13. William D. Broyles, Jr., "Letter to the Editor," *Papel Chicano*, Sept. 16, 1971, p. 2.

14. "Papel Editor Responds to Broyles," *Papel Chicano*, Sept. 16, 1971, p. 2.

15. Gómez-Quiñones, *Chicano Politics*.

16. *MAYO*, undated, set of beliefs found in Luís Cano Collection, Box E, unfoldered materials, HMRC.

17. De León, *Ethnicity in the Sunbelt*, pp. 176–78.

18. San Miguel, Jr., *Let All Take Heed*.

19. According to Castillo, the Mexican American community in Houston was whole-heartedly "united in purpose" in the struggle for equity and justice in the fall of 1970. He further argued that the notion of disunity usually attributed to Chicanos was merely a myth used by those in power to keep the people "in their place" and confused. See Leonel J. Castillo, "Mexican American Unity Myth," *Papel Chicano*, Nov. 21–Dec. 11, 1970, p. 3.

20. This is my translation of the author's statement. The actual wording is "Despierten ya MEJICANOS. . . . No permitan que por causa de la decidia y la pereza, los grin-gos se vayan a reír de nosotros. Hay que gritar, hay que marchar, hay que aser tanto escándalo que los sutoriades [*sic*] y las cortes comprendan que nosotros los mejicanos no soportamos ya más injusticias." See López, "Despierten Ya Meji-canos," p. 14.

21. López had complained about "apathy" among the Mexican American community as early as May, 1971. He had argued then that some of the community organiza-tions had become "nothing more than social or service clubs" or that they were merely taking advantage of the community. See Eduardo López, "Four Hundred Years, Six Months of Sorrow," *Papel Chicano*, May 21, [1971], p. 4.

22. This is my translation of the author's statement. See López, "Despierten Ya Mejicanos," p. 14.

23. "Editorial," *Papel Chicano*, Feb. 29, 1972, p. 11. Also quoted in De León, *Ethnicity in the Sunbelt*, p. 177.

24. "Raza Marches from Hidalgo to Eastwood Park for Justice in Education," *Papel Chicano*, Oct. 14, 1971, p. 1.

25. López, "Despierten Ya Mejicanos," p. 14.

26. "Martin-No Habla-HACE," *Papel Chicano*, Nov. 18, 1971, p. 3.

27. The local LULACs were not targeted for criticism, probably because the president and several members of chapter 60 were active supporters of the boycott. See "LULACs Where Are You?," *Papel Chicano*, Nov. 9, 1971, p. 11.

28. Ibid.

29. "Coconut" is in reference to assimilated Mexican Americans who are brown on the outside and white on the inside. See Eduardo López, "La Voz del Barrio," *Papel Chicano*, Feb. 29, 1972, p. 11.

30. *El Sol*, Oct. 24, 1989, pp. 1, 3; Nov. 21, 1969, p. 1; quoted in De León, *Ethnicity in the Sunbelt*, p. 191.

31. "Papel Chicano Interviews the School Board Candidates," *Papel Chicano*, Oct. 28, 1971, pp. 4–7.

32. Gloria Guardiola, "Papel Becomes Right-Wing-Letter to the Editor," *Papel Chicano*, Nov. 18, 1971, p. 2.

33. "Papel Chicano Interviews," *Papel Chicano*, Oct. 28, 1971, pp. 4–7.

34. Ibid.; "Campaigning for Position 6: Abel Álvarez Confident of Victory," *Papel Chicano*, Nov. 18, 1971, p. 6.

35. One positive result of this political activity was the election not only of López to the board but also of Leonel Castillo, the former chair of MAEC, to the city controller position and the following year of Ben Reyes to the state legislature. For a brief review of these activities see De León, *Ethnicity in the Sunbelt*, pp. 193–94.

36. "Despierten Mejicanos Despierten," *Papel Chicano*, July 1, 1971, p. 3.

37. "MAEC-ESAP at Odds with Community," *Papel Chicano*, Feb. 29, 1972, p. 12.

38. "MAEC Sponsors Successful Fiesta," *Papel Chicano*, Oct. 14, 1971, p. 11; "MAEC Halloween Carnival," *Papel Chicano*, Oct. 28, 1971, p. 14; "MAEC Presents Boxing Show," *Papel Chicano*, Nov. 9, 1971, p. 13; Eduardo López, "MAEC in Action," *Papel Chicano*, Jan. 13, 1972, p. 3.

39. "Pedro Vásquez No Longer with Papel," *Papel Chicano*, June 1, 1971, p. 15.

40. Other organizations continued to be active in the schools. Parents at Marshall Junior High, for instance, demanded and got a larger voice in school affairs after they organized a PTA. Rachel Lucas, social work coordinator at Wesley House, relates the story of the parents' several years of struggle in "Progress Seen for La Raza at Marshall Jr. High," *Papel Chicano*, Nov. 9, 1971, p. 6. As in many of the newspaper's articles, few details are provided on the individuals involved.

41. De León, *Ethnicity in the Sunbelt*, p. 189.

42. Letter, May 25, 1972, Huelga Schools Collection, HMRC.

43. López was elected to the board in November, 1971. Castillo won in a run-off election in December, 1971. See *El Sol*, Nov. 26, 1971, p. 1; "Will Success Spoil Leonel

Castillo?," *Texas Monthly,* Aug., 1976, pp. 134–36; "Bio-Data-Leonel Castillo," Leonel Castillo Collection, HMRC; De León, *Ethnicity in the Sunbelt,* pp. 192–93.

44. MALDEF initially filed a "friend-of-the-court" suit in mid-August, 1970. The Fifth Circuit Court rejected MALDEF's request on August 25, 1970, and ordered the pairing of twenty-five elementary schools. Sixteen of them were predominantly black schools, and nine were predominantly Mexican American. See "Motion for Leave To File Brief Amicus Curiae," *Ross v Eckels,* No. 30,080 (Sept. 21, 1970), Abraham Ramírez Collection, Box 1, No. 22, HMRC; *Ross v Eckels,* 434 F.2d 1140 (1970).

45. The lead attorney for this intervention suit was Abraham Ramírez, Jr. Several MALDEF lawyers, including Mario Obledo, John Serna, Alan Exelrod, and Jim Heidelberg, assisted him. The plaintiffs-intervenors were fourteen individual children and their parents. The children listed were: Narciso Rodríguez, Jr., Rachel Godinez, Roy and Linda Díaz, Minerva Anastasia Rivera, Tammy and Joel Reyes, Elias Soria, Daniel and Eloisa Meza, Sylvia Guzmán, Andy González, Oscar Saldana, and Moises Mansillas, Jr. See "Complaint in Intervention," *Ross v Eckels,* C.A. No. 10, 144 (Sept., 1970), Abraham Ramírez Collection, Box A, N. Rodríguez File, HMRC; and "Memorandum of Law," *Ross v Eckels,* C.A. No. 10,144 (Sept., 1970), Abraham Ramírez Collection, Box A, N. Rodríguez File, HMRC.

46. The court also ruled that HISD's plan for pairing elementary schools to achieve racial desegregation was unacceptable. See "On Motions To Amend Decree and To Intervene," *Ross v Eckels,* May 24, 1971, rpt. by the Houston Independent School District. See also "Houston Pairing Plan Is Ruled Unacceptable," *Houston Chronicle,* May 25, 1971, sec. 1, pp. 1, 11; "Judge Raps Chicanos over Pairing Protest," *Houston Chronicle,* May 26, 1971, sec. 1, pp. 1, 11.

47. "Houston Attorney Urges Appeal of Connally's School Ruling," *Houston Post,* May 26, 1971, pp. 1A, 2A.

48. *Ross v Eckels,* 468 F.2d 649 (1972), p. 650.

49. *United States v Texas Education Agency (Austin Independent School District),* 467 F.2d 848 (Fifth Cir. en banc, 1972); *Cisneros v Corpus Christi Independent School District,* 459 F.2d 13 (Fifth Cir. en banc, 1972).

50. "Appeals from the United States District Court of the Southern District of Texas," *Ross v Eckels,* No. 71-2926 (Sept. 6, 1972), pp. 2–3.

51. HISD officials did not immediately comment on this decision. Dr. George G. Garver, general superintendent, had no comment on the decision. Harry Patterson, the board's attorney, said: "We will have to wait and see how it will affect our desegregation plan." See Frank Davis, "HSD [*sic*] Unsure of Mexican-American Minority Ruling Impact," *Houston Post,* Sept. 8, 1972, p. 3A.

52. Abraham Ramírez, Jr., letter to Mrs. James A. Tinsley, president, HISD Board of Education, Sept. 8, 1972, Abraham Ramírez, Jr., Collection, Box 1, No. 11, HMRC; "Chicanos Guaranteed Full Rights in School Desegregation," *MALDEF Newsletter* 3 (Sept., 1972): 1.

53. Tom Curtis, "Garver To Ask OK for Chicano Transfer Plan," *Houston Chronicle,* Sept. 8, 1972, p. 1.

54. The HISD school board also directed its attorneys to ask Judge Connally to amend the desegregation order. See Davis, "HSD [*sic*] Unsure," p. 3A.
55. *Tri-Ethnic Policy,* Sept., 1972 (Houston: HISD, 1972), in Abraham Ramírez Collection, Box 1, No. 11, HMRC.
56. Curtis, "Garver To Ask OK," p. 1.
57. See *Keyes v School District No. 1,* 380 F. Supp. 673 (D. Colo, 1973), 521 F.2d 465 (Tenth Cir., 1975).
58. Richard Vara, "A New Educational Era Dawned," *Houston Post,* Oct. 28, 1973, p. 3DD.
59. Cano, "Illegal Discrimination."
60. MAEC, Sam Saenz told De Anda, was not even supposed to be working at Edison. See "Charge of Bias against Chicanos To Be Probed," *Houston Chronicle,* Feb. 18, 1974, sec. 1, p. 2.
61. In March, in a response to MALDEF, De Anda reported that the investigation of OCR as well as the organization of the Black-Brown Coalition was proceeded at a slow pace. See Ricardo De Anda, letter to Peter Roos, MALDEF, Mar. 18, 1974, Ramírez Collection, Box 1, No. 4, HMRC.
62. In the early fall of 1974 a few Mexican American parents involved with an organization called Committee of Concerned Parents criticized the lack of adequate facilities at Marshall Junior High and Jefferson Davis, but none actively protested these conditions. See Susan Bischoff, "Parents Claim Old School Building as One Proof of Discrimination," *Houston Chronicle,* Aug. 27, 1974, sec. 1, pp. 1, 8.
63. Abraham Ramírez, Jr., resident attorney for MALDEF, letter to Harry W. Patterson, HISD attorney, Sept. 14, 1972, A. Ramírez Collection, Box 1, No. 11, HMRC.
64. Memo from Guadalupe Salinas to file, RE: *Ross v Eckels,* July 17, 1973, Ramírez Collection, Box 1, No. 8, HMRC.
65. Ibid.
66. Guadalupe Salinas, MALDEF staff attorney, letter to Abraham Ramírez, Jr., Nov. 26, 1973, A. Ramírez Collection, Box 1, No. 22, HMRC.
67. Carol Faye Bruchac, "Minority Parents Demand End to Elementary School Pairings," *Houston Chronicle,* Feb. 26, 1974, p. 1A.
68. Garylyn McGee, "Suit Charges School Pairing System Excludes White Areas," *Houston Post,* Feb. 22, 1975, p. 3A.
69. For an excellent history of these developments, especially the eight-year struggle from 1971 to 1978 to halt the creation of the breakaway Westheimer Independent School District, see William Henry Kellar, *Make Haste Slowly: Moderates, Conservatives, and School Desegregation in Houston* (College Station: Texas A&M University Press, 1999), pp. 151–78.
70. Ibid., p. 165.
71. On February 14, 1973, for instance, Ramírez specifically requested data on HISD's recruitment of Mexican American teachers. On January 14, 1974, Ramírez requested that HISD eliminate the pairing plan and the court-ordered Bi-Racial Committee. He argued that in its place the board should establish a Tri-Ethnic Committee to advise the board. He also asked the board for formal recognition of

Mexican Americans as a separate ethnic minority group and to review the bilingual education plan in light of desegregation concerns. These requests were done
after meeting with López. In January, MALDEF informed Ramírez that he should
not deal with the trustees until MALDEF got official permission to intervene. See
Guadalupe Salinas, MALDEF staff attorney, letter to A. Ramírez, Jan. 21, 1974,
A. Ramírez Collection, Box 1, No. 22, HMRC.

72. The report with twenty-five recommendations was accepted on February 25, 1974.
See John Self, "Integration Report Accepted," *Houston Post,* Feb. 25, 1974, p. 10A.

73. De Anda, in response to an inquiry from MALDEF, reported that as of Mar. 18,
1974, the OCR investigation was "continuing in a positive direction." See Raul
De Anda, MAEC director of MAEC-Emergency School Aid Act Project, letter to
Guadalupe Salinas, MALDEF lawyer, Mar. 18, 1974, Ramírez Collection, Box 1,
No. 4, HMRC.

74. On October 11, 1974, for instance, Ramírez sent MALDEF a packet of information
listing community objections to existing desegregation plans. Eleven days later,
however, MALDEF responded by saying that the community objections were not
clearly stated. MALDEF asked Ramírez to send clearer objections for presentation
to the court hearing on MALDEF's intervention lawsuit to be held soon thereafter.
See Carlos M. Alcala, interim director, Education Litigation, letter to A. Ramírez,
Oct. 22, 1974, A. Ramírez Collection, Box 1, No. 22, HMRC.

75. Gonzalo Garza again was appointed chair of the Task Force, which was composed
of thirteen citizens and nine staff. Six of the members were Mexican Americans.

76. Jim Craig, "Desegregation Panel Taking Stances," *Houston Post,* Dec. 7, 1974, p. 1D;
Susan Bischaff, "Magnet Schools as Integration Aid Would Affect Few Students,"
Houston Post, Feb. 21, 1975, sec. 1, p. 15.

77. One newspaper source inaccurately states that the Mexican American Service Organization filed its intervention lawsuit in district court on Thursday, May 15, 1975.
The lawsuit is officially known as *José I. Torres et al. v HISD,* Civil Action 75H327.
According to this source, the lawsuit calls for an end to pairing, the establishment
of bilingual/bicultural education, and affirmative action to hire more Mexican
American teachers. See "Latins Ask To Join Suit on Integration," *Houston Chronicle,* May 16, 1975, sec. 1, p. 3.

78. McGee, "Suit Charges," p. 3A.

79. Prior to the magnet school plan adoption, David López unsuccessfully proposed
extensive district-wide desegregation instead of the district's magnet school plan.
See Jim Craig, "HISD Adopts Plan To End School Pairing," *Houston Post,* Mar. 11,
1975, p. 1.

80. That same year López lost his position on the school board. For the remainder of
the 1970s Mexican Americans therefore had no official representation on the
school board.

81. The other Chicanos who supported the Majority Report were Dorothy Carám,
Abe Ramírez, Dr. Juan Flores, Mrs. Suzanne Gómez, and Gonzalo Garza. Carám
and Ramírez were community activists; the others were school staff members. It is
unclear why these two community activists signed the document while the other
three did not. Both, however, had been known as being more in the politically

moderate camp of Chicano/a community politics than in the militant camp. For a summary of the report see *Task Force for Quality Integrated Education Report Received,* Regular Board Meeting, Feb. 24, 1975, pp. 42–55, HISD School Board Minutes, vol. 155. For a copy of the minority report see *Minority Report: Making HISD Educational Policies and Programs More Responsive and Responsible to Needs of Educationally Deprived Students,* Feb. 24, 1975 (in author's possession).

82. Note that most of these comments on Mexican American activism came from a draft of a manuscript found in the Luís Cano manuscript collection and entitled "Illegal Discrimination and Segregation of Chicano Students in the Houston Independent School District." This was written by Dr. Cano but never finished (n.pag. noted, but the comments come from the last two pages of this manuscript).

83. This ruling was based on Mr. Berry's testimony. A month earlier, on January 29, 1976, Mr. Weldon H. Berry, HISD's attorney, appeared before and at the request of the new district judge James Noel to discuss the composition of the Bi-Racial Committee. He agreed that its makeup should change from five black and five white members to four black, four Anglo, and two Mexican American members. See F. Tarrant Findley, Jr., chairman, Bi-Racial Committee, letter to Judge Finis E. Cowan, U.S. Distr. judge, Aug. 5, 1977, pp. 1–2, in Ramírez Collection, Box 1, No. 27, HMRC.

84. U.S. District Judge Finis E. Cowan, *Order of December 22, 1977 Relating to Tri-Ethnic Committee,* Dec. 22, 1977, A. Ramírez Collection, Box 1, No. 24, unfoldered materials, HMRC.

85. Ramírez argued that while Judge Cowan did not invite MALDEF, "we must insist on being heard, on the issue of what it would take for the Houston Independent School District to be a unitary school district." See A. Ramírez, letter to Peter D. Roos, MALDEF, Apr. 14, 1978, A. Ramírez Collection, Box 1, No. 26, unfoldered clippings, HMRC.

86. Kellar, *Make Haste Slowly,* pp. 151–78.

87. Vara, "New Educational Era," p. 3DD.

CONCLUSION. REFLECTIONS ON IDENTITY, SCHOOL REFORM, AND THE CHICANO MOVEMENT

1. For a general history of LULAC see Sandoval, *Our Legacy;* and Márquez, *LULAC.* For a history of the American G.I. Forum see Carl Allsup, *The American G.I. Forum: Origins and Evolution* (Austin: Center for Mexican Americans Studies, University of Texas, 1982).

2. On the relatively exclusive nature of Chicano movement organizations see Vicki L. Ruíz, *From Out of the Shadows: Mexican Women in Twentieth-Century America* (New York: Oxford University Press, 1998), pp. 99–126; and Ramón A. Gutiérrez, "Community, Patriarchy, and Individualism: The Politics of Chicano History and the Dream of Equality," *American Quarterly* 45 (Mar., 1993): 44–72.

3. On the relatively inclusive nature of La Raza Unida Party in Texas see I. García, *Chicanismo,* especially pp. 86–116. Armando Navarro, in *The Cristal Experiment,* pp. 360–64, however, notes that the La Raza Unida Party in Crystal City changed

over time. Although it initially was committed to community empowerment, over time power in La Raza Unida Party became concentrated in the hands of the elite who obstructed the empowerment of the masses and social change. On the relatively inclusive nature of Centro de Acción Autonoma-Hermandad General de Trabajadores (CASA) and on Chicana feminism in general see Ruíz, *From Out of the Shadows,* especially, pp. 99–126.

4. On opposition to MAYO and to La Raza Unida Party see, respectively, I. García, *Chicanismo;* and Navarro, *The Cristal Experiment.*

5. See Leonel Castillo, "Status," 1972, Leonel Castillo Collection, HMRC.

6. For the next decade former members of what used to be MAEC, in alliance with David López, a school board member, pressured the school board to appoint Mexican Americans to a variety of district committees, to develop a triethnic desegregation plan, and to increase the number of Mexican Americans in administration and in the instructional force. Community activists continued to criticize the changes in desegregation plans and the slow progress made by the district in dealing with the educational problems of Mexican American students. For the actions taken by community activists from 1970 to 1976 see Cano, "Illegal Discrimination." For a general overview of educational developments from 1975 to the 1980s see De León, *Ethnicity in the Sunbelt,* pp. 185–219.

7. Navarro, *The Cristal Experiment,* pp. 317–33.

8. As late as June 19, 1996, a modest gathering of the Houston political leadership and activist community met at the Magnolia Multi-service Center to discuss the status of Mexican Americans in Houston and issues that needed to be addressed. Most participants agreed that education should be one of the areas to concentrate their political energies because of the high degree of unity that this issue inspires. See Public Meeting Scheduled to Discuss Hispanic Leadership Issues, June 19, 1996, Magnolia Multi-Service Center, Houston, Tex. (meeting attended by author).

9. M. García, *Mexican Americans,* pp. 1–22.

10. The Chicano Movement was not limited to the participation solely of working-class individuals with working-class aspirations as stated by Gómez-Quiñones in *Chicano Politics,* p. 105.

11. For an excellent history of this generation see M. García, *Mexican Americans.*

12. The liberal agenda primarily meant the ideals of cultural pluralism, the moderate pace of reform, and the traditional means for achieving social change. See I. García, *Chicanismo,* p. 20.

13. Carlos Muñoz, Jr., for instance, argues that students in 1969 made a dramatic break with the politics of assimilation and accommodation of the Mexican American Generation. See Muñoz, Jr., *Youth, Identity, Power,* p. 80.

14. Acuna, *Occupied America,* 3d ed., p. 324.

15. Vicki L. Ruíz argues that the imagery and language of cultural nationalism empowered primarily males. Chicanas criticized these gendered notions of cultural nationalism in the 1970s and began to develop what one scholar referred to as Chicano feminist reinventions of indigenismo in the 1980s. For a critique of the imagery of cultural nationalist thought see Ruíz, *From Out of the Shadows,* pp. 99–126.

On the development of a feminist-based cultural nationalism see Alesia García, "Aztec Nation: History, Inscription, and Indigenista Feminism in Chicana Literature and Political Discourse" (Ph.D. diss., University of Arizona, 1998).

16. Carlos Castañeda, for instance, argued that the Texas-Mexican legacy complemented rather than competed with the Anglo-American. According to him, the Mexican population in Texas shared many characteristics with the Anglos, including their white European and Christian heritage and their efforts to "civilize" Indians and colonize the New World. On Castañeda's writings see M. García, *Mexican Americans*, pp. 231–51.

17. Ignacio García refers to these ideals as the reaffirmation of race and class. See I. García, *Chicanismo*, pp. 68–85.

18. For an elaboration of some of these intellectual strains of the Chicano identity see I. García, *Chicanismo*; and Richard A. Garcia, "The Origins of Chicano Cultural Thought: Visions and Paradigms—Romano's Culturalism, Alurista's Aesthetics, and Acuna's Communalism," *California History* 74 (fall, 1995): 290–305.

19. I. García, *Chicanismo*.

20. For the earliest statement (1964) arguing for revolution or the fundamental restructuring of American society see Luís Valdez and Roberto Rubalcava, "Vencerémos!: Mexican American Statement on Travel to Cuba," in *Aztlán: An Anthology of Mexican American Literature*, ed. Luís Valdez and Stan Steiner (New York: Vintage Books, 1972), pp. 214–17.

21. For a history of La Raza Unida Party see I. García, *United We Win*.

22. This task of defining the character of the brown identity was left, in many ways, to the artists, poets, and essayists of the Chicano movement. Some argued that Mexican Americans were mestizos, that is, a mixture of Spanish and Mexican Indian. Others argued that they were primarily indigenous and nonwhite in origin. In later years increased efforts were made to refine the definition of this identity and to incorporate class, gender, and sexuality notions. The idea of multiple identities soon emerged. For an excellent overview of the redefinition of identity through poetry during the Chicano movement years see Tomás Ybarra-Frausto, "The Chicano Movement and the Emergence of a Chicano Poetic Consciousness," in *New Directions in Chicano Scholarship*, ed. Romo and Paredes, pp. 81–110. For an example of continuing efforts to define the "Chicano" identity see Gloria Anzaldúa, *Borderlands: La Frontera: The New Mestiza* (San Francisco: Aunt Lute Books, 1987).

23. See, for instance, *Cisneros v Corpus Christi Independent School District*, 324 F. supp. 599 (S.D. Tex., 1970).

24. See, for instance, *Bilingual Education Act of 1968*, Pub. L. No. 90-247, 81 Stat. 816, 20 U.S.C.A. sec. 880(b) (1968); and Pottinger, *Memorandum of May 25, 1970*.

25. Lucy Moreno, interview by author, May 1, 1999.

26. Luís Valdez, "The Tale of La Raza," *Bronze*, Nov. 25, 1968, p. 1.

27. According to El Plan, Chicanos "conscious of their proud historical heritage and aware of the 'brutal Gringo invasion' of the Southwest, were reclaiming the land that belonged to them." "Aztlan," it further noted, "belongs to those who plant the seeds, water the fields, and gather the crops, and not to the foreign Europeans"

("El Plan Espiritual de Aztlán," *El Grito del Norte* 2 [July 6, 1969]: preamble). It is published in its entirety in Luís Valdez and Stan Steiner, eds., *Aztlán: An Anthology of Mexican American Literature* (New York: Alfred A. Knopf, 1972), pp. 403–406.

28. The preamble was followed by demands in several major areas of community life. These demands were linked to a specific geographic homeland—Atzlán—and to the rights of workers. Juan Gómez-Quiñones says that these demands were linked to the rights of Indian heritage, but no specific mention is made of this in El Plan. See Gómez-Quiñones, *Chicano Politics,* p. 123.

29. "The cultural values of our people," El Plan noted, "strengthen our identity and the moral backbone of the movement." This culture also served as a powerful weapon "to defeat the gringo dollar value system and encourage the process of love and brotherhood." See "El Plan Espiritual de Aztlan," preamble and Punto Segundo (point, or goal, number two).

30. Poncho Ruíz, interview by author, June 22, 1995, Houston, Tex.

31. Demands of the Mexican American Education Council to the Houston Independent School District, Sept., 1970, Gregory Salazar Collection, Box 1, unfoldered materials, HMRC.

32. Rufus P. Browning, Dale Rogers Marshall, and David H. Tabb, *Protest Is Not Enough: The Struggle of Blacks and Hispanics for Equality in Urban Politics* (Berkeley: University of California Press, 1984).

33. De León, *Ethnicity in the Sunbelt,* pp. 45–144.

34. For an overview of Chicana participation in organizations see Cynthia E. Orozco, "Beyond Machismo, La Familia, and Ladies Auxiliaries," pp. 1–34.

35. They also contributed to the establishment of community educational services and alternative institutions. See Dr. Luís Cano, interview by author, July 15, 1993, Houston, Tex.

36. Mrs. Celine Ramírez, wife of Abraham Ramírez, specifically noted that "we, the older folks, were involved in leadership roles." The youths, mostly MAYO members, were involved, but "the school board would probably not have met with them unless they (the older folks) were involved." See Celine Ramírez, interview by author, Houston, Tex., July 18, 1995.

37. The officers for 1971–72 were: chair, Romualdo M. Castillo; first vice chair, Otto Landron; second vice chair, Lucy Moreno; secretary, Sister Gloria Gallardo; and treasurer, Leonel J. Castillo (Huelga Schools Collection, File 1, Box 1, Community Support-Rally, HMRC).

38. Celine Ramírez interview.

39. The double standard had two dimensions. One of these pertained to sexual activity. The other pertained to politics and was present when women were expected to assume visible public leadership roles and bear the brunt of "women's work" in planning fund-raisers, selling tickets, and preparing food. See Ruíz, *From Out of the Shadows,* p. 118.

40. Ibid., pp. 108–110.

41. Mario Quiñones, interview by author, July 19, 1995, Houston, Tex.; Abraham Ramírez interview.

42. Mrs. Vera Quiñones also expressed a similar statement. See Vera Quiñones, interview by author, July 19, 1995, Houston, Tex.

43. This phenomenon also occurred in the African American community. See Charles Payne, "Men Led, But Women Organized: Movement Participation of Women in the Mississippi Delta," in *Women in the Civil Rights Movement: Trailblazers and Torchbearers, 1941–1965*, ed. Vicki L. Crawford, Jacqueline Anne Rouse, and Barbara Woods (Bloomington: Indiana University Press, 1990), pp. 1–13.

44. Ruíz, *From Out of the Shadows*, p. 111.

45. Yolanda Birdwell, interview by author, June 16, 1996, Houston, Tex.

46. "Browns and Blacks Meet To Discuss Education," *Papel Chicano*, July 29, 1971, p. 2.

47. Blacks had briefly enjoyed political and social rights in the 1860s, but between 1872 and the 1920s they were denied the right to participate in mainstream institutions. Beginning in the 1920s they initiated challenges to political disfranchisement, educational discrimination, and police brutality but did not begin to see major changes until the 1960s. Not until 1966, for instance, was one of their own elected to the state legislature. In 1971 Judson Robinson was the first African American to get elected to the city council in one hundred years. The demand for recognition by Mexican Americans thus came at the time of increasing civil rights gains and threatened to short-circuit them. See Cary D. Wintz, "Blacks," in *The Ethnic Groups of Houston*, ed. von der Mehden, pp. 9–40.

48. Mexican Americans and blacks, for instance, both settled in the Second and Fourth Wards (ibid., pp. 9–40). On Houston see De León, *Ethnicity in the Sunbelt*, especially pp. 3–40.

49. For a similar view of black and Hispanic relations in Miami see Raymond A. Mohl, "On the Edge: Blacks and Hispanics in Metropolitan Miami Since 1959," *Florida Historical Quarterly* 69 (1990): 37–63.

50. A recent article has suggested that the "reign" of this generation of political leaders was coming to an end in 1996 as a result of an FBI sting investigating corruption in city hall. See Lori Rodríguez, "Fear of Backlash," *Houston Chronicle*, July 30, 1996, pp. 1A, 21A.

51. For an overview of the successes and failures of this group of political leaders during the 1970s and 1980s see De León, *Ethnicity in the Sunbelt*, especially pp. 185–232.

52. For a brief history of the conflict between Mexican Americans and HISD over the selection of a new superintendent in the early 1990s see Kellar, *Make Haste Slowly*, pp. 168–70; and Alfredo Rodríguez Santos, comp., *Houston Independent School District: When the Board of Trustees Tries to "Sneak in" a New Superintendent* (Houston: Privately published, 1994). For a description and chronology of the controversies over the selection of Mexican Americans to fill unexpired terms of school board members see Guadalupe San Miguel, Jr., "Summary Account of the Controversies over the Appointments of Latinos To Fill Unexpired Terms on the School Board, 1990–2000," unpub. MS., Jan. 10, 2000, in author's possession.

Index

ISBN 1-58544-115-5

90000